THE EARLIEST PRINTED LAWS OF NEW JERSEY 1703 - 1722

THE COLONY LAWS OF NORTH AMERICA SERIES

General Editor: JOHN D. CUSHING

THE EARLIEST PRINTED LAWS OF NEW JERSEY 1703 - 1722

With an Editorial Note
by
JOHN D. CUSHING

Michael Glazier, Inc.
Wilmington, Delaware

This edition published in 1978 by:

MICHAEL GLAZIER, INC., 1210A King Street,
Wilmington, Delaware 19801

Copyright© Introduction 1978 by John D. Cushing

Library of Congress Catalog Card Number   78-55500

International Standard Book Number   0-89453-091-7

Publisher's Note

Every effort has been made to produce exact
facsimiles of the original editions. Some
pages have faded with the passing of the
centuries, but we have decided to reproduce
them as they stand as the meaning of the text
is quite clear.

Printed in the United States of America

TABLE OF CONTENTS

*Pages 79 to 91, unnumbered in the original, are added
in this edition for the sake of continuity.
**To distinguish between two page 123's which appear in
the original, this page has been designated 123[a].

Editorial Note

THE POLITICAL HISTORY of what is now the state of New Jersey is probably as complicated as that of any other North American colony. For present purposes it will suffice to note in brief that the area was populated by the Dutch as early as 1623, was invaded by the Swedes in 1635, and came again under Dutch rule in 1655. Nine years later the area became part of the Duke of York's vast American dominions, and for the next forty years experienced a series of divisions, sub-grants and leases that were further complicated in 1676 when the area was divided into East and West Jersey. Neither the subsequent proprietary government nor the annexation of the Jerseys to the Dominion of New England in 1686 did anything to help the establishment of a uniform and regular government, and it was not until 1702, when all jurisdictional rights reverted to the crown, that a single united province of New Jersey was created. Even then, the rights to the soil remained vested in proprietors and until 1738 the governor of New York was also the governor of New Jersey.

Given those conditions it is not surprising that no regular body of law was developed during the early years of the settlement. The early Dutch and Swedish communities were essentially mercantile expeditions organized along more or less military lines, and the law of the area was usually the orders of the commanders or governors. As the individual communities began to develop, most of them were ruled at the municipal level by self generated customs and local ordinances. After 1655, Peter Stuyvesant and his council, sitting at New York, enacted most of the major legislation, just as they did for the Delaware counties. After 1664, when the Jerseys passed to the Duke of York, the area was subject, along with New York, Pennsylvania and the Delaware counties, to "The Duke of York's Laws," a rudimentary system devised by Richard Nicholls with an eye to creating some uniformity of government throughout the Duke's North American holdings. The law applied was generally English in its derivation, tempered by local needs and customs. After the division of 1676, the legislation enacted by the Quaker majority in West Jersey tended to be more liberal in nature than anything known in England, comporting more with the dictates of the Quaker conscience than with English precedent or practice. Needless to say, no body of laws for the first seventy years of New Jersey's history was ever drawn up or printed.

Beginning in 1703, the assembly of the newly created and united province began to sit on a regular basis, and printed session laws were issued a few pages each year. Thus the first printed laws of New Jersey consisted of four pages, printed at New York by William Bradford in 1703, recording the legislation of the assembly sitting at Perth Amboy in November of that year (Evans 1136). That and subsequent issues of session laws are listed in Charles Evans *American Bibliography* and Grace E. Macdonald. *Check-List of Session Laws*. (New York, 1936). Inasmuch as the substance of those issues was repeated in subsequent collective issues, they have not been used in this facsimile edition.

The present volume begins with a 58 page imprint published at New York by William Bradford in 1717 (Evans 1915). Containing legislation of the years 1703-1717, it was the first printed volume of New Jersey's collected laws. It contains no pages numbered 23 or 44. The second item, also printed in 1717 by Bradford (Evans 1916), consists of pages 61-78. Paged consecutively with the title given above, but beginning with signature B, it presumably once had, or was intended to have, a title page. The third item, printed by Bradford in 1718, contains the text of but a single act and consists of thirteen unnumbered pages (Evans 1986). The fourth issue, a Bradford imprint of 1719 (Evans 2058), contains pages 95-123. If it too once boasted a title page, then the several issues listed above would have been paged in a single sequence. The final item, published by Bradford in 1722 (Evans 2365), contains pages 123-145 and completes the first volume of New Jersey collected laws.

It should perhaps also be noted in passing that in 1720 Bradford printed an issue containing pages 79-115 (Evans-Bristol 39728), but it was nothing more than another printing of the fourth title listed above. The text contains substantial variations, including the printing of some acts by title only, and the inclusion of some 1720 legislation. No purpose could be served by including it in the present compilation.

Through the kindness of Dr. James E. Mooney, Director of the Historical Society of Pennsylvania, this facsimile edition has been made from the copy in the Society's Charlemagne Tower Collection of American Colonial Laws.

THE
LAWS,
AND
𝕬𝖈𝖙𝖘 of the 𝕲𝖊𝖓𝖊𝖗𝖆𝖑 𝕬𝖘𝖘𝖊𝖒𝖇𝖑𝖞

Of His Majesties Province of *Nova Cæsarea* or

New-Jersey,

As they were Enacted by the Governour, Council and General
Assembly, for the Time being, in divers Sessions, the first of
which began in *November,* 1703.

G   R

DIEV · ET · MON · DROIT

J. BLUNT.

Printed and Sold by *William Bradford*, Printer to the Kings Most Excellent
Majesty for the Province of *New-Jersey,* 1717.

An Act paſſed by the General Aſſembly of the Province of *New-Jerſey*, in *November*, *Annoq; Dom.* 1 7 0 3. being the ſecond Year of Her Majeſties Reign.

CHAP. I.

An Act for Regulating the Purchaſing of Land from the *Indians.*

WHereas ſeveral ill diſpoſed Perſons within this Province have formerly preſumed to enter into Treaties with the *Indians*, or Natives thereof, and have purchaſed Lands from them, ſuch Perſon or Perſons deriving no Title to any part of the Soil thereof under the Crown of *England*, or any Perſon or Perſons claiming by, from or under the ſame, endeavouring thereby to ſubvert her Majeſties Dominion in this Country. *Be it therefore Enacted by the Governour, Council and General Aſſembly, now met and aſſembled, and by the Authority, of the ſame*, That no Perſon or Perſons whatſoever forever hereafter ſhall preſume to buy, take a Gift of Purchaſe in Fee, take a Mortguage or Leaſe for Life or number of Years, from any of the *Indians* or Natives for any Tract or Tracts of Lands within this Province, after the firſt Day of *December*, 1 7 0 3. without firſt obtaining a Certificate, under the Hand of the Proprietors Recorder, for the time being, certifying ſuch Perſon hath a Right, and ſtands entituled to a Propriety or ſhare in a Propriety, ſuch Perſon or Perſons ſhall produce ſuch Certificate to the Governour for the time being, in order to obtain a Liſence to purchaſe ſuch Quantities of Land or Number of Acres from the *Indians* or Natives aforeſaid, as ſuch Certificate mentions.

And be it further Enacted by the Authority aforeſaid, That if any Perſon or Perſons ſhall preſume to buy, purchaſe, take Gift or Mortgage or Leaſe of any Land contrary to this preſent Act, he or they ſo offending ſhall forfeit *Forty Shillings*, Money of this Province, for each Acre of Land ſo obtained, to be recovered by any Perſon or Perſons who ſhall proſecute the ſame to effect, by Action of Debt, in any Court of Record within this Province, one half to the uſe of her Majeſty, her Heirs and Succeſſors, toward the ſupport of the Government, and the other to the Proſecutor. *Provided always*, That ſuch Purchaſors, their Heirs and Aſſigns ſhall forever hereafter be incapable to hold Plea for the ſaid Land in any Court of Common Law or Equity.

And be it further Enacted by the Authority aforeſaid, That all and every Perſon and Perſons whatſoever, that have bought, taken Gift of, or have purchaſed Land in Fee, or taken Mortgages or Leaſes, for Life or Number of Years, of the *Indians* or Natives, who is, and are not entituled to ſuch Tract or Tracts of Land, by virtue of a Right or Title to the ſame, derived from the Crown of *England*, or from any

A   Perſon

Person or Persons claiming by, from or under the same, such Gifts, Purchase, Mortgage, Lease or Leases, is and are hereby declared, and forever hereafter shall be taken, deemed and esteemed Illegal, Null and Void; and such Person or Persons, their Heirs and Assigns shall not be capable to hold Plea for the same in any Court of Common Law or Equity, at any time hereafter, unless such Person or Persons claiming under such *Indian* Gift, Purchase, Mortgage or Lease, shall within the space of six Moneths after the Publication of this Act, take out a Grant or Grants from the present Proprietors for the several Tracts of Land so claimed by them respectively, on such Conditions as shall be agreed upon with the said Proprietors.

Acts passed by the General Assembly of the Province of *New-Jersey*, in *May*, *Anno Dom.* 1704.

CHAP. II.

An Act for Suppressing of Immorality.

WHereas Prophaneness and Immorality have too much abounded within this Province, to the shame of Christianity, and the great grief of all good and sober Men; For the Suppressing whereof for the future, *Be it Enacted by the Governour, Council and Assembly now met and assembled, and by the Authority of the same,* That all and every Person and Persons whatsoever within this Province, who shall be convicted of *Drunkenness, Cursing, Swearing* or *breaking the Lords Day*, by doing any ordinary Work or Labour thereon (excepting works of Necessity or Mercy) by the information of every Constable within their respective Precincts, or of any other Person whatsoever, before any one of her Majesties Justices of the Peace of the County where such Fact is committed, by the Confession of the Offender, or the Oath or Attestation of one Witness (which every Justice of the Peace is hereby authorized to administer) every Person so convicted shall be fined by the said Justice of the Peace, for *Drunkenness* or *breaking the Lords Day*, in the Sum of *six Shillings*, Money of the said Province, for each Offence, besides Costs. And for *Cursing* or *Swearing*, in the Sum of *three Shillings*, Money aforesaid, beside Costs, for each Offence; all which Fines to be immediately levyed upon the Offenders Goods and Chattels by the Constables aforesaid, by Warrant from the said Justice of the Peace; and for want of effects to make such Distress, the said Constable, by Warrant from the said Justice of the Peace, shall commit the Offender to the Stocks for the space of *Four Hours*, for *Drunkenness*, or *for breaking the Lords Day*, and *Two Hours* for *Cursing* or *Swearing*; and each Distress so made, as above-said, to be by the said Constables sold at a publick Out-cry (unless redeemed by paying the said Fine and Costs, within three days and after full payment of the said Fine and Costs, the overplus (if any be) shall be returned to the owner. And all such Fines to

be

be by the Conſtables aforeſaid immediately paid to the Overſeers of the Poor of the Town where ſuch Fact is committed, for the uſe of the Poor of that Town; For all which Fines the Overſeers of the Poor ſhall be accountable yearly to the Juſtices in their General Quarter-Seſſions of the Peace.

And be it further Enacted by the Authority aforeſaid, That no Publick Houſe-keeper within this Province ſhall ſuffer any perſon or perſons to Tipple and drink in his Houſe on the Lords Day, eſpecially in the time of divine Worſhip (excepting for neceſſary Refreſhment) under the Penalty of *Six Shillings,* Money aforeſaid, for every ſuch Offence, to be proſecuted, ſued, recovered, levyed and diſpoſed of, as aforeſaid. *Provided,* That all or any the above-ſaid Offences be proſecuted within one Moneth after the ſame were committed.

And be it further Enacted by the the Authority aforeſaid, That all and every Perſon and Perſons within this Province, who ſhall be lawfully convicted of *Fornication* or *Adultery,* upon Preſentment, Indictment or Information in the Supream Court, or the Court of General Quarter-Seſſions of the Peace of the County where ſuch Fact ſhall be committed, every ſuch Offence ſhall be by the ſaid Court puniſhed in manner following, *viz.* Every *Woman* convict of *Fornication,* as aforeſaid, ſhall be fined by the ſaid Court, for every ſuch Fact, in the Sum of *Five Pounds,* Money aforeſaid, beſide Coſts; and if unable or unwilling to pay the ſame, ſhall receive *thirty Laſhes* or *Stripes* on the bare back : And every Man that ſhall by the ſaid Court be adjudged the reputed Father of every ſuch Baſtard, ſhall alſo be fined in the Sum of *Five Pounds,* Money aforeſaid, and give Security to ſave the Town or Precinct harmleſs from the Charge of ſuch Baſtard Child. And every Man convicted of *Adultery,* as aforeſaid, ſhall be Whipt at three ſeveral Courts, and each time ſhall receive *thirty Laſhes* or *Stripes* on the bare Back, or pay the Sum of *thirty Pounds,* Money aforeſaid. And every Woman ſo convicted of *Adultery,* as aforeſaid, ſhall be Whipt at three ſeveral Courts, and each time ſhall receive *thirty Laſhes* or *Stripes* on the bare Back, or pay the Sum of *thirty Pounds,* Money aforeſaid. The ſaid Sums and Penalties to be diſpoſed of in the like manner as is directed for the other Penalties herein before mentioned.

CHAP. III.

An Act for Uniting and Quieting the Minds of all Her Majeſties Subjects within this Province.

WHereas ſome unhappy Differences and Animoſities have ariſen amongſt many of her Majeſties good Subjects within this Province, occaſioned by ſeveral Diſorders, Irregularities and Miſdemeanours, acted and committed by ſeveral Perſons within both the Eaſtern and Weſtern Diviſion thereof, preceding the 13*th* Day of *Auguſt,* in the ſecond
Year

Year of her Majesties Reign, which have been fomented, promoted and continued by some ill affected and evil disposed Persons; And this Assembly seriously considering that nothing can tend more to the honour of our most Gracious Sovereign Lady the Queen, the good and quiet of the Country, than Unity, Love and Concord amongst all her Majesties Subjects. For the attaining of which great and good ends, and for the preventing all future Fears and Jealousies, and quieting the minds of all her Majesties loving Subjects within this Province, *Be it therefore Enacted by the Governour, Council and Assembly now met and Assembled, and by the Authority of the same*, That all and every of her said Majesties Subjects inhabiting within this Province, shall be and are hereby acquitted, pardoned, released and discharged against her Majesty, her Heirs and Successors, and every of them, of and from all manner of Fellonies (*High Treason, Petty Treason* and *Murther*, and *Accessaries* thereunto, *Pyracy* and *Robbery* on the High Seas, and *Accessaries* to the same, Wilful and Corrupt *Forgery* and *Perjury*, and *Subordination* thereof, and *Rapes*, only excepted) Riots, Routs Offences, Wrongs, Misdemeanours, Imprisonments, Escapes, Contempts, seditious and unlawful Meetings, Treasonable or Seditious Words or Libels, Batteries, Assaults, Trespasses and Quarrels before the said 13*th* Day of *August*, which was in the Year of our Lord One Thousand Seven Hundred and Three, wherein no Judgment hath been already given and Execution thereupon Executed.

And whereas several Assaults, Batteries and Imprisonments have been committed, Rescues and Escapes suffered, and Defamatory Words spoken and written in Disputes, which happened formerly in this Province, in relation to the Government of the same, or some part thereof; all which 'tis highly reasonable should be now forgiven and forgotten, *Be it therefore Enacted by the Authority aforesaid*, That no Person or Persons shall bring, commence or prosecute any Suit or Action for any such Assault, Battery, Rescues, Escapes or Imprisonments, done or committed within this Province, or for any Defamatory Words so spoken before the 13*th* Day of *August* in the Year of our Lord One Thousand Seven Hundred and Three. But that all such Suits, Actions and Prosecutions, for such Offences, so as aforesaid committed, shall be and are hereby Pardoned and Discharged.

And be it further Enacted by the Authority aforesaid, That all and every her Majestys Subjects, by him or themselves, his or their Attorney or Attorneys may plead this present Act, (or give in Evidence the General Issue) or true Copy thereof signed by the Secretary of the Province, in Bar and Discharge of any Action, Suit, Bill, plaint or Information of or for any matter, cause or thing above recited, or of or for any other matter, cause or thing whatsoever relating to the Government at any time or preceding the said 13*th* Day of *August* in the Year of our Lord One Thousand Seven Hundred and Three.

There was also passed at the same time these following Acts, Viz.

Chap. IV. An Act for Raising a Revenue of 200 *l.* per *annum* for the Support of her Majesties Government of *New-Jersey*, for Two Years.   Chap.

Acts passed by the General Assembly of the Province of *New-Jersey,* in *March* and *April, Annoq; Dom.* 1709. being the Seventh Year of Her Majesties Reign.

CHAP. XI.

An Act Regulating the Qualification of Representatives to serve in General Assembly in this Province of *New-Jersey.*

WHeras the present Constitution granted and allowed by our Soveraign Lady the Queen to the Free-holders, Inhabitants of this Province, concerning the Qualification of Representatives to serve in General Assembly, is found to be inconvenient, For the Remedying whereof, *Be it Enacted by the Governour, Council and Representatives in General Assembly met, and by the Authority of the same,* That after the Dissolution of this present Assembly, the Representatives to serve in the said General Assembly thereafter, shall be chosen by the Majority of Voices or Votes of the Free-holders of each County, every Free-holder having one Hundred Acres of Land in his own Right, or be worth Fifty Pounds current Money of this Province, in Real and Personal Estate; And the Persons elected to serve as Representatives in the said General Assembly shall have One Thousand Acres of Land in his own Right, or be worth 500 *l.* current Money of this Province, in real and personal Estate, in manner following, *viz.*

In the *Eastern Division,* For the City or Town of *Perth-Amboy,* Two. For the County of *Bergin,* Two. For the County of *Essex,* Two. For the County of *Middlesex,* Two. For the County of *Sommerset,* Two. For the County of *Monmouth,* Two.

In the *Western-Division,* For the City or Town of *Burlington,* Two. For the County of *Burlington,* Two. For the County of *Gloucester,* Two. For the County of *Salem,* Two. For the Town of Salem, Two. For the County of *Cape-May,* Two.

And be it further Enacted by the Authority aforesaid, That all or every Person or persons elected and chosen Representatives for the Counties aforesaid, shall be Free-holders in that Division for which he or they

B shall

shall be chofen to ferve in General Affembly, as aforefaid ; and that no perfon, who is not a Free-holder, as aforefaid, fhall be capable of electing, or being elected, nor of fitting in General Affembly ; and that the Houfe of Reprefentatives, elected and chofen as aforefaid, when met in General Affembly, are and fhall be Judges of the Qualifications of their own Members.

And be it further Enacted by the Authority aforefaid, That if any Sheriff or other Officer within this Province, do, or fhall prefume to make any Return contrary to this prefent Act, he fhall incur the fame Penalty and Forfeiture as in fuch cafes of undue Returns, provided and enacted by the Laws of *England,* and to be fued, recovered and difpofed, as in the faid Laws are directed. *See Chap.* 25.

CHAP. XII.

An Act for the Explaining of Grants and Patents for Land made and executed by *Phillip Carteret* and Council in the *Eaftern Divifion* of this Province, according to the true intent and meaning of Grantor and Grantee.

WHereas feveral of her Majefties Subjects in the firft fettlement of this Province, formerly known by the Name of *Eaft-New-Jerfey,* repaired hither with defigns of fettling Land for the fupport and maintenance of their Families, and applying themfelves to the Proprietors and their Governors for the time being, obtained Grants or Patents for the fame, which by the intent and good meaning of Grantor and Grantee, were to affure and fettle an Eftate of Inheritance, in Fee-fimple, to the feveral perfons to whom the faid Grants were made, referving certain Quit-Rents therein expreffed. And as the Law of this Province was then deemed and taken to be, the faid Grants were worded in purfuance of the faid end, and fo paft for feveral years ; on which affurance many of her Majefties Subjects have fpent their whole Lives and Subftance, and undergone extream Hardfhips and Difficulties in fubduing a Wildernefs, fupported only by this encouragement, That their Pofterity would reap the benefit of their labours. And finding that thro' the Ignorance of thofe Infant Times, the Particle [OR] in the *Habendum* of their feveral Deeds, was ufed in the ftead of [AND] Wherefore, for the quieting of Mens Minds, and for the further Affurance, and the firm and fure making of the faid Tenure, according to what was the true and real intent of the faid Grants, Charters, Patents, Deeds or Conveyances, Be *it Enacted by the Governour, Council and Affembly now met and affembled, and by the Authority of the fame,* That all Grants, Charters or Patents for Land within this Province, made and executed by *Phillip Carteret,* deceafed, formerly Governour of this Province, and his Council, in which the Particle (OR) is
                                                                        named

named or ufed in the *Habendum* of the faid Deeds, Grants, Charters or
Patents, fhall be taken, deemed and efteemed as effectual in the Law,
to all intents, conftructions and purpofes whatfoever, to the benefit of
each and every Party and Grantee therein named, as if the fame had
been granted in thefe words, *To Have and to Hold to him the faid* A. B.
his Heirs And Affigns forever.

CHAP. XIII.

An Act for the Relief of the Poor.

WHereas it is neceffary that the poor fhould be relieved by the
publick, where they cannot relieve themfelves, nor are not
able to work for their Support, *Be it therefore Enacted by the
Governour, Council and Reprefentatives met in General Affembly, and it is
Enacted by the Authority of the fame,* That from and after the publication hereof, it fhall and may be lawful for every Townfhip or Precinct
within this Province, by a Warrant from any one Juftice of the peace
within the faid County, to meet at fome convenient time and place
within their feveral and refpective Townfhips or precincts to chufe
Overfeers and Affeffors, which faid Affeffors are hereby impowered and
required to affefs the Inhabitants of each refpective Townfhip for fuch
Sum or Sums of Money as is neceffary, and in fuch manner as to the
faid Townfhips, at their Meetings, feems proper ; Which faid Overfeers,
fo chofen, as aforefaid, are hereby required to collect and gather all fuch
Sum or Sums of Money affift, as aforefaid, in every their refpective
Townfhips or Precincts, and to apply the fame to the ufe aforefaid. And
which faid Overfeers are alfo hereby required to take care to put forth
fuch Poor Children as have no Parents, and fuch as their Parents are
not able to maintain, with the affiftance of one or more Juftices of the
County ; and alfo to take care that all the Poor be fupplyed with
neceffary Maintenance in every of the refpective Townfhips and Precincts
where they dwell, and not fuffered to go from Town to Town for Relief.

And be it further Enacted by the Authority aforefaid, That the Affeffors of
every refpective Townfhip or Precinct are hereby impowered and
required to affefs their Towns or Precincts, feverally and refpectively,
for fuch Sum or Sums of Money as will be neceffary for fupplying the
Charge of making and maintaining Pounds for ftray Cattle and Horfes,
and pounding fuch as are Trefpaffers. Which faid Sums fo affeffed,
fhall alfo be collected and gathered by the Over-feers aforefaid in every
Town or Precinct, and be imployed by fuch Perfon as faid Towns, at
their faid Meetings, fhall elect and appoint by majority of Votes. And
if any perfon fhall refufe to pay their refpective Rates, as taxed, to the
Over-feers appointed to receive the fame, as aforefaid, that the faid Overfeers fhall make Complaint thereof to any one Juftice within faid
County wherein he refides, who is hereby required forth-with to iffue
out his Warrant to the Conftable of every Town or Precinct where
fuch Default is made, to make diftrefs upon the Offenders Goods and
Chattels,

Chattels; who shall immediately make Sale thereof, for paying the said Assessment and charges of Distress, and return the Over-plus (if any be) to the Owner. Which said Over-seers severally and respectively, shall keep fair Accounts of their collecting and Disbursements, and make Return thereof to the Over-seers who shall be elected in their several Towns and Precincts to serve in said Office for the next ensuing year.

And be it further Enacted by the Authority aforesaid, That if any person shall refuse to serve in said Offices when elected, or make default in performing their Duty, as herein is before exprest, shall forfeit the Sum of five Pounds for every such Offence, to be levyed upon the Goods and Chattels of the person or persons so offending, by Warrant of Distress from any one or more Justices of the Peace in said County where such default is made, to be applyed to the use of the Poor aforesaid.

CHAP. XIV.

An Act for preventing of Swine running at large. *vid. Chap.* 29.

WHereas it is found by experience that Swine runing at large hath been very prejudicial to the Inhabitants of this province. For the prevention of which, *Be it Enacted by the Governour, Council and Representatives now met and assembled in General Assembly, and by the Authority of the same,* That no person or persons whatsoever shall or may keep any Swine from and after the first Day of *January* next coming, but what he or they shall keep within his or their own Land.

And be it further Enacted by the authority aforesaid, That any person or persons that shall find any Swine trespassing upon his or their Land, may forth-with kill such Swine, and keep them to his or their own proper use, without any account to be given thereof. And that if any person or persons shall be sued or impleaded for the killing of any such Hogs or Swine so going at large, he shall plead the general Issue, and give this Act, or an authentick Copy thereof, signed by the Secretary, in evidence, and shall thereupon, if found for him, recover full Costs of Suti.

CHAP XV

An Act for destroying of Wolves, Panthers, Crows and Black-birds.

WHereas the neglect of killing of Wolves, Panthers, and other Vermin, hath proved very prejudicial to the Inhabitants of this Province. For the prevention of which, *Be it Enacted by the Governour, Council and Representatives now met in General Assembly, and by the Authority of the same,* That from and after the publication hereof, every White Man that shall kill or destroy any Wolf or Panther

of

of prey within this Province, ſhall have for his Reward Fifteen Shillings for each Wolf or Panther, and for killing or deſtroying Wolves or Panthers Whelps, half the Sum of Fifteen Shillings aforeſaid. And every *Indian* for killing and deſtroying any Wolf or Panther of prey, as aforeſaid, the Sum of eight Shillings; and for every Wolf or Panthers Whelp, not able to prey, the Sum of Four Shillings, all current Money of this Province. And for every Crow, Hawk and Wood-pecker that any one ſhall kill, three Pence; and for every Dozen of Black-birds, *Three Pence.*

And for the more effectual performing hereof, *Be it further Enacted by the Authority aforeſaid,* That the Juſtices of the Peace in their Seſſions, with the concurrence of the Grand Jury, in each reſpective County within this Province, are hereby impowered and required to pay ſuch Sum or Sums of Money for the defraying of the ſaid Charges, as ſhall be needful; who are likewiſe hereby impowered to nominate and appoint Aſſeſſors and Collectors in every reſpective County, to aſſeſs, collect and pay the ſame, for the uſe above-ſaid. And every Perſon or Perſons that ſhall kill any Wolf, Panther, Crows or Black-birds, as aforeſaid, are hereby required to bring the Heads of them to any one Juſtice of the Peace within the County, who ſhall give him or them a Certificate to the ſaid Collector, who is, upon ſight hereof, to pay him according as is herein before expreſt. And all ſuch Aſſeſſors and Collectors are hereby required to make up their Accounts to the Juſtices and Grand Jury of each reſpective County, when thereunto required. And if any of the ſaid Aſſeſſors or Collectors ſhall refuſe to officiate, as they are hereby required, ſhall for every ſuch Refuſal forfeit the Sum of *Forty Shillings,* current Money of ſaid Province, which ſhall be levyed by Diſtreſs on the Goods and Chattels of ſuch as ſhall ſo refuſe, by virtue of a Warrant from ſaid Court, to the Conſtable; and after the Sum of *Forty Shillings,* aforeſaid, with Coſts, ſhall be paid, the Over-plus ſhall be returned to the Owner, if any be; and the ſame to be applyed towards the defraying of the Charges aforeſaid. And the Aſſeſſors are hereby allowed to have and receive the Sum of *Four Pence per Pound* for aſſeſſing the ſame; and the Collectors to have and receive, for collecting and paying the ſame, as aforeſaid, the Sum of *One Shilling per Pound.*

CHAP. XV.
An Act for Regulating of Ordinaries.

FOraſmuch as there are great Exorbitances obſerveable in many places within this Province, occaſioned by Perſons ſelling Drink in private Houſes, and diſorderly keeping of Publick Houſes, to the diſhonour of God and impoveriſhing of the Common-wealth, *Be it therefore Enacted by the Governour, Council and Repreſentatives now in General Aſſembly met, And it is hereby Enacted by the Authority of the ſame,* That after the Publication hereof, no Perſon or Perſons within this Province ſhall draw or ſell, by Retail, any Rum, Brandy, Wine, or any other ſuch ſtrong Liquors, under the quantity of one Quart; nor any ſtrong Beer, Syder, Metheglin, or other ſuch Liquors, under the quantity of

C

Five

Five Gallons, directly or indirectly, upon the penalty of Twenty Shillings for every smaller quantity so drawn and sold, to be levyed upon the Offenders Goods and Chattels, by Warrant of Distress from any one Justice of the Peace ; provided the said Person be lawfully convicted by two Evidences, within one Moneth after the said Offence is committed, the one third part thereof to the Informer, and the other two Thirds to the Over-seers, for the use of the Poor of the Town or Precinct where such Offence is committed, excepting such Person or Persons that hath a Licence to sell Drink and keep Ordinary and Entertainment for Man and Horse, from the Justices of the Peace in their Sessions, or under the Hands and Seals of two Justices of the Peace out of Sessions, the one of them being of the Quorum.

And be it further Enacted by the Authority aforesaid, That all or any Justices granting Licences, as aforesaid, are hereby impowered and required to take Recognizance of Twenty Pounds, of all such Persons to whom such Licences are granted, for the keeping good Orders in their Houses ; and upon Default thereof, if lawfully convicted by two sufficient Evidences, that then the Penalty to be recovered upon the Offenders Goods and Chattels, by Action of Debt in any Court of Record within this Province, to be applyed to the Service of the *Queen,* her Heirs and Successors, towards the Support of the Government.

There was also passed at the same time the following Acts, viz.

Chap. 16. An Act for Support of this Her Majesties Government of *Nova Cæsarea* or *New-Jersey,* for One Year.   1722 *l.* 10 *s.* 4 *d.*
Chap. 17. An Act for settling the Militia of this Province.
Chap. 18. An Act for the Encouragement of the Post-Office within this Province.
[*Supplyed by an Act of Parliament.*]

Acts passed by the General Assembly of *New-Jersey* in *June,* 1709.

Chap. 19. An Act for raising Three Thousand Pounds for her Majestys Service in this present Juncture.
Chap. 20. An Act for Encouragement of Volunteers to go on the Expedition to *Canada.*
Chap. 21. An Act for enforcing the Currency of Bills of Credit for Three Thousand Pounds.

Acts passed by the General Assembly in *January,* 1709.

CHAP. XXII.

An Act for the better Qualifying Representatives to serve in General Assembly within this Province.

WHereas nothing can conduce more to the honour, safety and advantage of this Province, than the Members elected to serve in the General Aſſembly be perfectly acquainted with the true ſtate and Circumſtances of this Province; and many Ineonveniencies may ariſe by electing Perſons to ſerve in the ſaid General Aſſembly, who inhabit in another Province, altho' they may have ſome Intereſt or Eſtate in this, but their Concerns lying and being in ſome of the neighbouring Provinces, where they, with their Families do inhabit, they may thereby be ſwayed to have great regard to the Intereſt of the Province in which they with their Families ſo inhabit, than for the Wellfare and Proſperity of this. And whereas it is abſolutely neceſſary for the regular proceedings of the Repreſentatives, that the Houſe of Repreſentatives, when met, ſhould have, power over the ſeveral Members thereof, which the houſe cannot have if any of their Members are in any of the neighbouring Provinces. For the preventing of which, and many more Inconveniencies and Diſadvantages that may ariſe to this Province, by electing Perſons inhabiting elſe-where, *Be it Enacted by the Lieutenant Governour, Council and General Aſſembly now met and aſſembled, and by the Authority of the ſame,* That from and after the Diſſolution of this preſent Aſſembly, no Perſons ſhall be capable of being elected a Repreſentative to ſerve for any City, Town or County in the General Aſſembly within this Province, who is not inhabiting and uſually reſident himſelf, and likewiſe with his Family if any he hath) the day of the date of the Writ of Summons, and hath been ſo three Moneths before in ſome City, Town or County of that Diviſion in which he ſhall be elected.

Be it Enacted by the Authority aforeſaid, That after the Diſſolution of this preſent Aſſembly, no Perſon ſhall be capable of ſerving in the General Aſſembly of this Province, who hath not an Eſtate within the Diviſion in which he is elected, ſufficient to qualifie him, any Law or Uſage to the contrary nothwithſtanding. *See Chap.* 13.

CHAP. XXIII.

An Act for Dividing and Aſcertaining the Boundarys of all the Counties in this Province.

Whereas by the Uncertainty of the Boundaries of the Counties of this Province great Inconveniencies have ariſen, ſo that the reſpective Officers of moſt of thoſe Counties cannot know the Limits of them, For the preventing the ſame in time coming, and the better aſcertaining the Boundaries of them, *Be it Enacted by the Lieutenant Governour, Council and General Aſſembly, and by the Authority of the ſame,* That in the Eaſtern-Diviſion, the County of *Bergin* ſhall begin at *Conſtables-Hook,* and ſo run up along the Bay and *Hudſons-River* to the Partition Point between *New-Jerſey* and the Province of *New-York*; and ſo run along the Partition Line between the Provinces, and the Diviſion Line of the Eaſtern and Weſtern Diviſion of this Province to *Pequaneck-River,* and ſo to run down the ſaid *Pequaneck* and *Peſſaick-River* to the Sound, and ſo to follow the Sound to *Conſtables-Hoock,* where it began.

That

That the County of *Essex* shall begin at the Mouth of *Raway River,* where it falls in to the Sound, and so to run up the said *Raway River* to *Robesons* Banch ; thence West to the Division Line between the Eastern and Western Division aforesaid, and so to follow the said Division Line to *Pequaneck-River,* where it meets *Pessaick-River* ; thence down *Passaick-River* to the Bay and Sound ; Thence down the Sound to where it began.

The County of *Somerset,* begins where *Bound-Brook* empties it self into *Rariton River* thence down the Strand of *Rariton* to the mouth of a Brook known by the name of *Lawrances-Brook* ; thence running up the said *Lawrances Brook* to the great Road that leads from *Inians's* Ferry to *Cranbery-Brook* ; from thence South forty four Degrees Westerly to *Sanpinck-Brook* ; thence down the said *Sanpinck-brook* to the said Division Line of the Eastern and Western Division aforesaid, and so to follow the said division line to the Limits of the abovesaid County of *Essex* ; Thence East along the Line of *Essex County* to *Green-Brook,* and thence running down the said *Green-Brook* and *Bound Brook* to where it began.

Altered by an Act past 1713. vid. Chap. 59.

The County of *Middlesex* begins at the Mouth of the Creek that parts the Land of *George-Willocks* and the Land that was formerly Capt. *Andrew Bown's,* deceased ; thence along the said Capt. *Andrews* Line to the Rear of the said Land ; thence upon a direct Course to *Warn's* Bridge on the Brook where *Thomas Smith* did formerly live ; thence upon a direct Course to the South-East Corner of *Barcleys* Tract of Land that lies near *Martiniponex* ; thence to the most Southermost part of said Tract of Land, including the whole Tract of Land in *Middlesex County* ; thence upon the direct Line to *Sanpinck* Bridge on the High Road, including *William Jones, William Story, Thomas Richman* and *John Guyberson* in *Monmouth County* ; thence along the said Road to *Aarin Robins* Land ; thence Westerly along the said *Aarin Robins* and *James Lawrance* line to the Line of the Eastern and Western Division aforesaid, including the said *Robins* and *Lawrance* in *Monmouth-County* ; thence Northerly along the said line to *Sanpink* Brook, being part of the Bounds of the said *Somerset-County* ; thence following the lines of *Somerset* and *Essex Counties,* and so to the Sound, and thence down the Sound to *Amboy-Point,* and from thence to the Creek where it first began.

Altered by same Act, vid Chap. 59.

The County of *Monmouth* begins at the Mouth of the Creek aforesaid, that parts the Land of Capt. *Andrew Bowne,* deceased, and *George Willocks,* thence following the line of *Middlesex-County* to the line of the Eastern and Western Division aforesaid ; thence Southerly along the said Division line to the Sea ; thence along the Sea to the Point of *Sandy-Hook* ; thence up the Bay to the aforesaid Creek, where it first began.

The Line of Partition between *Burlington* and *Gloucester-County* begins at the Mouth of *Pensauquin,* alias, *Cropwell-Creek* ; thence up the same to the *Fork* ; thence along the Southermost Branch thereof (sometimes called *Cole-Branch*) until it comes to the head thereof, which is the Bounds betwixt

betwixt *Samuel Lipincotes* and *Isaac Sharps* Land; thence upon a strait line to the Southermost Branch of *Little-Egg-Harbour-River,* including the said *Sharp* his Land in *Gloucester-County*; thence down the said Branch and River to the Mouth thereof; thence to the next In-let on the South side of *Little-Egg-Harbour* most Southerly Inlet; thence along the Sea-Coast to the Line of Partition between *East* and *West-Jersey*; thence along the said Line of Partition by *Maidenhead* and *Hopewell,* to the Northermost and Uttermost Bounds of the Township of *Amwel*; thence by the same to the River *Delaware*; thence by the River *Delaware*, to the first mentioned station.

Gloucester-County begins at the Mouth of *Pensauquin-Creek,* thence up the same to the Fork thereof; thence along the said Bounds of *Burlington-County* to the Sea; thence along the Sea-Coast to *Great-Egg-Harbour-River*; thence up said River to the Fork thereof; thence up the Southermost and greatest Branch of the same to the head thereof; thence upon a direct line to the head of *Oldmans-Creek*; thence down the same to *Delaware* River to the place of beginning.

Salem-County begins at the Mouth of a Creek on the West side of *Stipsons Island,* commonly called *Jecak's Creek*; thence up the same as high as the Tide floweth; thence upon a direct line to the Mouth of a small Creek at *Tuckahoe,* where it comes into the Southermost Main Branch of the Fork of *Great-Egg-Harbour-River*; thence up the said Branch to the head thereof; thence along the Bounds of *Gloucester-County* to *Delaware-River*; then down *Delaware-River* and Bay to the place of beginning.

Cape-May-County begins at the Mouth of a small Creek on the West side of *Stipsons-Island,* called, *Jecak's* Creek; thence up the said Creek as high as the Tide floweth; thence along the Bounds of *Salem-County* to the Southermost Main Branch of *Great-Egg-Harbour-River*; thence down the said River to the Sea; thence along the Sea-Coast to *Delaware-Bay,* and so up the said Bay to the place of beginning.

And whereas at present there is not as yet a competent Number of Inhabitants in the County of *Somerset,* for holding of Courts, and for Jury's, *Be it therefore Enacted by the Authority aforesaid,* That the said County of *Somerset* shall and is hereby subject to the Jurisdiction of the Courts and Officers of the County of *Middlesex,* and that the Jury's for any Tryal whatsoever may be Promiscuously taken out of both or either of the said Counties, as has been usual for all Actions that are or shall be commenced in either of the said Counties, any Law, Custom or Usage to be contrary thereof in any wise notwithstanding.

The following Acts were also passed at the same time, viz.

Chap. 27. An Act for explaining and rendring more effectual an Act for Support of her Majesties Government of *North-Cæsar.a* or *New-Jersey* for one Year.

Chap. 28. An Act for the ascertaining the Place of the sitting of the Representatives to meet in General Assembly. Repealed

Chap. 29. An Act for Building and Repairing Goals and Court-Houses within this Province.

D　　　　　　　　　　　　　　　Chap. 30.

Chap. 30 An Act for ascertaining the Representatives Fees of General Assembly.

Chap. 31 An Act for Reviving and Continuing the Courts of Sessions and Common Pleas in the County of *Gloucester*, with the Proceedings of the same.

Acts passed by the General Assembly of the Colony of *New-Jersey*, in *January*, and *February*, 1710. being the Ninth Year of her Majestys Reign.

Chap. 32 An Act for Support of this Her Majesties Government of *Nova-Cæsarea* or *New-Jersey*. 944 *l.*

Chap. 33. An Act for Reviving the Militia Act of this Province.

Chap. 34 An Act for Amending and Explaining an Act of the General Assembly of this Province, Entituled, *An Act for the Currency of Bills of Credit for Three Thousand Pounds.*

Chap. 35 An Act for Reviving and Continuing the Courts of Common-Pleas in the County of *Gloucester*, with the Procedings of the same.

Chap. 36 *An Act for Enabling the Owners of the Meadows and Marshes, adjoyning to and on both sides of the Creek that Surrounds the Island of* Burlington, *to stop out the Tide form over-flowing them.*

Acts passed by the General Assembly of the Colony of *New-Jersey*, in *July*, 1711. being the tenth Year of her Majesties Reign.

Chap. 37 An Act for Levying and Raising Money, (viz. 5000 *l.*) for and towards the Encouragement, Pay, Provision, Transportation and other Charges of Volunteers to go on an Expedition against *Canada*, upon the Inhabitants of this Colony.

Chap. 38. An Act for the Currency of Bills of Credit in the Colony of *New-Jersey*.

IN the 10th and 11th year of King *William* the third, an Act of Parliament was passed, entituled, *An Act for preventing irregular proceedings of Sheriffs and other Officers in making the Returns of Members to serve in Parliament,* wherein (Sect. 3.) it is Enacted, That every Sheriff or other Officer or Officers aforesaid, who shall not make the Returns according to the true intent and meaning of this Act, shall Forfeit for every such Offence the Sum of Five hundred Pounds, one Moiety whereof shall be to his Majesty, and the other Moiety to him or them that shall sue for the same, to be Recovered by Action of Debt, Bill, Plaint or Information, in any of his Majestys Courts of Record at *Westminster*, wherein no Essoyn, Protection, Priviledge or Wager of Law shall be allowed, nor any more than one Imparlance.

Acts

Acts passed by the General Assembly of the Province of New-Jersey the 17th of March, 1713. in the 12th and 13th Years of Queen Anne.

CHAP. XXXIX.

An Act for preventing the Waste of Timber, Pine and Cedar Trees and Poles within this Province of New-Jersey, and to lay a Duty upon all Pipe and Hogshead Staves exported out of the same to any of the Neighbouring Colonies.

WHereas several ill disposed Persons of late have made very great Waste in destroying Timber, Pine Trees and Poles, by cutting, falling, working up and carrying away of Timber, as well as by boring, extracting of Turpentine, upon not only the Lands belonging to the Proprietors in General, but to others in particular within this Province, which unjust Practices will not only render the Lands, where such Wastes are committed, of little Value to the Owners, but will also prove a very great mischief to the Inhabitants of this Colony. And whereas the Exportation of Pipe and Hogshead Staves to the Neighbouring Provinces will not only be a means of destroying the Timber of this Colony, but is at present a very great Discouragement to the Trade thereof. For Preventing of which for the future,

Be it Enacted by the Governour, Council and General Assembly, and by the Authority of the same, That if any Person or Persons whatsoever, after Publication of this Act, shall presume to cut, sell, work up, or carry away any manner of Trees, Cedar or Pine Poles, standing or lying, or bore, box or extract Turpentine out of any Pine Trees, upon any Lands belonging to the said Proprietors, or others, within this Province, without leave first obtained from the Owner or Owners of the said Land, every such Person or Persons so offending, shall, for every Tree so cut, worked up, Boxed, Bored or carryed away, pay the Sum of Twenty Shillings, Proclamation Money, the one half thereof to the Owner or Owners of the said Land, and the other half to the Person or Persons that shall prosecute the same to effect, to be recovered by an Action of Debt; if Forty Shillings, or under, before any one Justice of the Peace; if above Forty Shillings in the inferiour Court of Common Pleas of that County, with Cost of Suit. And for every Pine or Cedar Pole so cut down or carryed away, shall pay the Sum of Ten Shillings, Money aforesaid, to the Uses above-said, and to be recovered in manner aforesaid. *Provided*, That such offenders shall be sued and prosecuted for every such Offence within six Months time after committing the same.

And it is also hereby further Provided and Enacted by the Authority aforesaid, That this Act shall not be construed or taken to extend to Inhibit any of the Freeholders of the Eastern-Division within this Province from cutting, felling or carrying away any Wood, Trees, Saplins or Poles, whatsoever, that are either standing, growing or lying upon the Land that remains undivided in Common amongst the Freeholders of that Town to which such Free-holder or Free-holders doth belong.

And be it Enacted by the Governour, Council and General Assembly, and it is

E

hereby

hereby Enacted by the Authority of the same, That there shall be paid unto Her Majesty, her Heirs and Successors, for and toward the Support of the Government of this Province, the Sum of thirty Shillings, Money of the value directed by her Majesties Proclamation, for every thousand Pipe-staves exported out of the Eastern-Division of this Colony, and transported into any of the Neighbouring Provinces, and Twenty Shillings Money aforesaid, for every Thousand of Hogshead-Staves exported as aforesaid, out of this Colony and transported into any of the neighbouring Provinces.

And for the better and more effectual Collecting the Duty of Thirty and Twenty Shillings aforesaid, and preventing the Exportation of the said Staves, contrary to the true intent and meaning of this Act, *Be it Enacted by the Authority aforesaid,* That every Master or Owner of any Sloop or other Vessel, shall, before he loads any Pipe or Hogshead Staves on board his said Vessel, yearly and every year, enter into Bond with the Collector of the said Eastern-Division, or his Deputy, with two sufficient Securities, Freeholders in this Province in the Sum of Two Hundred Pounds, to be paid to her Majesty, her Heirs and Successors, on Condition that he shall not within the term of one Year, load any Pipe or Hogshead Staves, or put them on board any Sloop, Boat, Flat or other Vessel, in order that they may be exported by the said Vessel out of the said neighbouring Province, or be loaded in the same, or make them into Raft, so as to land them, or any manner of way, directly or indirectly, Land, direct or Cause them to be landed in any of the neighbouring Provinces, contrary to the true intent and meaning of this Act. And any Master or Owner of any Sloop or other Vessel, or any other Person or Persons whatsoever, who shall any manner of way Transport from this Province any Pipe or Hogshead-Staves, into any of the neighbouring Provinces, without first having paid, or secured to be paid the Duty appointed by this Act to be paid for the same, shall for every such Offence forfeit the Sum of Twenty Pounds, Money as aforesaid, the one half to her Majesty, her Heirs and Successors, the other half to any Person who shall prosecute the same to effect, in any Court of Record within this Province. And any Pipe or Hogshead-Staves on board any Sloop or other Vessel whatsoever, the Master or Owner of which shall not produce a Certificate from the Collector, aforesaid, of her Majesties Customs, or his Deputy, that he has given such security, or paid such Duty as aforesaid, shall be forfeited, the One half to her Majesty, her Heirs and Successors, to the use aforesaid, the other half to any Person who shall prosecute the same to effect, in any Court of Record within this Province.

And be it further enacted by the authority aforesaid, That nothing in this Act shall be construed or taken to extend to inhibit to cut, fell or carry away any Wood or Timber within the bounds and limits of the High-ways, within this Province, for making and repairing of Bridges and High-ways, or for any other unavoidable Accident and Necessities, any thing in this Act to the contrary in any wise Notwithstanding.

CHAP.

CHAP. XL.

An Act for settling the Militia of this Province.

WHereas the Security and Preservation of this Province greatly depends upon the Militia being put into such Methods as may make the same most Useful for the Defence thereof, and the Honour of her Majesty, *Be it Enacted by the Governour, Council and General Assembly met and assembled, and by the Authority of the same,* That every Captain within this Province already appointed, or that shall hereafter be appointed, shall make a true and perfect List of all the Men that are at present, or that shall hereafter happen to be within the Districts or Precincts of which they are Captains, between the Age of Sixteen and Fifty Years, except Ministers, Physitians, School-Masters, Civil Officers of the Government, the Representatives of General Assembly, Millers, and Slaves, every one of which so Listed, shall be sufficiently Armed with one good sufficient Musquet or Fuzee well fixed, a Sword or Bagonet, a Cartouch-Box or Powder-Horn, a Pound of Powder, and Twelver Sizeable Bullets, who shall appear in the field so armed twice every Year, on the third *Friday* of *March*, and on the third *Friday* of *September*, yearly, at the Places appointed by their Captains or Superiour Officers, and to continue in Arms but one Day at each time, besides at other times when they shall be called together by an order in writing under the Hand of the Captain General or Commander in Chief, for the time being, at such Places as shall be by him appointed, to be taught the Use of their Arms, and the Discipline of War; and when under Arms, shall, and are hereby subjected to the Command of their proper Officer, and upon Disobedience shall and are hereby made liable to the Penalties and Punishments of the Martial Law, so that the Punishment does not extend to the taking away of Life or Member.

And be it Enacted by the Authority aforesaid, That every Person so Listed, and that doth appear at the times and places, as above, who shall not be armed and provided with Ammunition, as aforesaid, shall forfeit as followeth, *viz.* for want of a Musquet or Fuzee, *Two Shillings,* if not well fixed, *One Shilling;* for want of a Sword or Baggenet, *One Shilling;* for want of a Pound of Powder *One Shilling,* and so in Proportion; for want of twelve Sizeable Bullets, *One Shilling,* and so in Proportion; to be levied by the Serjeant or Corporal of the Company, by a Warrant from the Captain, upon their Goods and Chattles, if they refuse to pay their forfeitures, which forfeitures shall be applyed towards Providing the Company with Drums and Colours.

And be it further Enacted by the authority aforesaid, That it shall and may be lawful for the Captain General or Commander in Chief, for the time being, in Case of Invasion of an Enemy, to call all, or so many of the Persons aforesaid together, for Repelling the force of an Enemy, to order such Detachments for the common Defence, as he shall think fit, to follow and pursue the Enemy into any of the Neighbouring Governments for Expelling the Enemy and Preservation of her Majesties Subjects and Government.

And be it further Enacted by the Authority aforesaid, That every Person so Listed, that doth not appear at the Places appointed, as above, on the third *Fryday* of *March,* and on the the third Friday of *September,* shall contribute
and

and pay towards the Support of her Majesties Government in this Province, the Sum of *Five Shillings* for each of the said Days absence, to the Captain or the Commanding Officer, for the Time being, of their Respective Companies, excepting in case of Sickness, or any other Reasonable Excuse, to be allowed of by the Captain, which Sum so raised by the said Captain or Commanding Officer, shall, from time to time, be paid into the Treasurer of the Province. And if any Person or Persons shall refuse or neglect to pay, as aforesaid, the said Captain or Commanding Officer is hereby required and impowered to make out his Warrants to one of the Serjeants or Corporals, to make Distress upon every Persons Goods and Chattles so Neglecting or Refusing to pay, as aforesaid, Provided that such Distresses are made but once a year, for all the Defaults that have been Committed within the said year, before the time of such Distress, and shall expose the said Goods to a Publick Sale, and after Sale thereof, shall return the over-plus (if any be) to the owners thereof, after deducting *One Shilling* for his trouble, which he is hereby allowed to take.

And be it further enacted by the authority aforesaid, That the said Treasurer shall keep true and perfect Lists of all the Money collected, as aforesaid, and shall have for his the said Treasurers trouble *Ten Pounds* for every Hundred Pounds Received by virtue of this Act, and so in proportion for greater or lesser Sums, which Sum or Sums of Money are to be applyed to the Support of Her Majesties Government of this Province.

And be it further Enacted by the Authority aforesaid, That if the small Fines mentioned in this Act, for defraying the Charges of Drums and Colours, and other incidental Charges, are found insufficient, the Captain or Superiour Officer of each Company, who was at the Charge of furnishing them, shall be allowed by the Treasurer out of the other Fines, as much as will make up the small Fines sufficient to re-imburse them, any thing in this Act to the contrary notwithstanding.

And be it further Enacted by the Authority aforesaid, That it shall and may be lawful for such Captains or other Commanding Officers as live on or near the Sea side and Indians, on any Descent or Invasion by an Enemy, to call all, or so many of their several and respective Companies together, as shall be thought Necessary to expel the said Enemy.

And be it further Enacted by the Authority aforesaid, That when the Governour or Commander in Chief, for the time being, shall think fit to Direct, in time of War or Danger, any Watch to be kept in any Place or Places within this Province, the Colonel, Lieutenant Colonel, Major, or other Commanding Officer of the Regiment, to whom such Direction is signified, shall issue out his Orders to the several Captains under his Command, to appoint such and so many Men to appear with their Arms at such Time and Places as such Colonel or Commanding Officer shall appoint; which Watch so appointed, shall be equally Relieved by the Commanding Officers of said Company, and so equally through all the Companys of the said County; and every Person or Persons neglecting or refusing to Watch, during the Time, and at the Place appointed, shall forfeit the Sum of *Five Shillings* for each Offence, and any Person that shall leave the said Watch until Relieved by some other Persons appointed to Watch in his stead, every such Person so

leaving,

leaving, as aforesaid, shall forfeit the Sum of *Forty Shillings*, Money of the said Province, to be recovered before any Justice of the Peace of the County where the Offence is committed, one half to the informer who shall prosecute the same to effect, the other half to her Majesty, her Heirs and Successors, towards the Support of the Government, as aforesaid.

And be it further Enacted by the Authority aforesaid, That if any Person, appointed by the Captain to be a Serjeant or Corporal, shall refuse the said Office, every such Person so refusing shall forfeit the Sum of *Twenty Shillings*, to be recovered by Warrant from any one Justice of the Peace.

Provided always, That none be appointed Serjeants or Corporals but such as have or shall appear in Arms, as aforesaid; and any Serjeant or Corporal who shall refuse or neglect to Distrain, as aforesaid, shall forfeit the Sum of *Twenty Shillings* for each Default, to be Recovered before any one Justice of the Peace, and applyed to the Support of the Government, as aforesaid.

And be it further Enacted by the Authority aforesaid, That this Act shall Continue and be in Force for Seven Years after Publication thereof, and no longer.

CHAP. XLI.

An Act for Regulating of Slaves.

BE it Enacted by the *Governour, Council and General Assembly, and by the Authority of the same*, That all and every Person or Persons within this Province, who shall at any time after Publication hereof, buy, Sell, barter, trade or traffick with any *Negro, Indian* or *Mullatto Slave*, for any Rum, Wine, Beer, Syder, or other strong Drink, or any other Chattels, Goods, Wares or Commodities whatsoever, unless it be by the consent of his, her or their Master or Mistress, or the Person under whose care they are, shall pay for the first Offence *Twenty Shillings*, and for the second, and every other Offence, *Forty Shillings*, Money according to the Queens Proclamation, the one half to the Informer, the other half to the use of the Poor of that Place where the Fact is committed, to be recovered by Action of Debt before any one of Her Majesties Justices of the Peace.

And be it further enacted by the authority aforesaid, That all and every Person or Persons within this Province, who shall find or take up any Negro, Indian or Mullato Slave or Slaves, five Miles from his, her or their Master or Mistresses habitation, who hath not leave in writing from his, her or their Master or Mistress, or are not known to be on their service, he, she or they, so taken up, shall be Whipt by the party that takes them up, or by his order, on the bare back, not exceeding Twenty Lashes; and the Taker up shall have for his reward *Five Shillings*, Money aforesaid, for every one taken up as aforesaid, with reasonable Charges for carrying him, her or them home, paid him by the Master or Mistress of the Slave or Slaves so taken up; and if above the said five Miles, *six 'Pence per Mile* for every Mile over and above, to be recovered before any one Justice of the Peace, if it exceeds not *Forty Shillings*, and if more, by Action of Debt in the Court of Common Pleas in the County where the fact shall arise.

F

And

And be it further Enacted by the Authority aforesaid, That if any Negro, Indian or Mullatto Slaves, of or belonging to any other Province shall come into this Province without Licence under the Hand of his, her or their Master or Mistress, or that is not known to be upon his or her business, every such Negro, Indian or Mullatto Slave shall be taken up by any Person within this Province, and be whipt by the nearest Constable of the Place where the said Slave shall be taken up, not exceeding Twenty Lashes on the bare back, and to be committed by a Warrant from the next Justice of the Peace, to the Goal of that County, and the Person so taking them up, and carrying them to be whipt, shall have for his reward *Ten Shillings,* Money aforesaid, for each Slave, and the Constable *Three Shillings* for whipping each Slave, to be paid by the Master or Mistress of such Slave or Slaves, and to remain in Prison till it be paid, with all reasonable Charges that may accrue thereby.

Be it further Enacted by the Authority aforesaid, That all and every Negro, Indian or other Slave, who after the Publication of this Act shall Murder, or otherways kill (unless by Misadventure, or in Execution of Justice) or conspire or attempt the Death of any of Her Majesties Leige People, not being Slaves, or shall commit any Rape on any of the said Subjects, or shall willfully burn any Dwelling House, Barn, Stable, Out-House, Stack or Stacks of Corn or Hay, or shall willfully Mutilate, Mayhem or Dismember any of the said Subjects, not being Slaves, as aforesaid, or shall willfully Murder any Negro, Indian or Mullatto Slave within this Province, and thereof be convicted before three or more of Her Majesties Justices of the Peace, one whereof being of the *Quorum,* who are hereby required and impowred to hear and determine the same, in conjunction with five of the Principal Free-holders of the County wherein such Fact shall be committed, without a Grand-Jury, Seven of whom agreeing, shall give Judgment, and Sign the Execution, according to this Act, and he, she or they so offending, shall suffer the Pains of Death in such manner as the Aggravation or Enormity of their Crimes (in the Judgment of the Justices and Free-holders aforesaid) shall merit and require.

Be it further Enacted by the Authority aforesaid, That upon Complaint made to any one Justice of the Peace against any Indian, Negro or Mullatto Slave or Slaves, who have or are supposed to have committed any of the Murders, Rapes, Mayhems, &c. mentioned in this Act, the said Justice shall immediately issue out his Warrant to the next Constable, to apprehend the said Offender or Offenders, and for all or any Person or Persons to come before him, that can give Evidence, and if upon Examination it appears, that the Person or Persons are Guilty, he shall commit him, or them to Prison, and also shall Certify to the two next Justices the said cause, and to require them, by Virtue of this Act, to associate themselves to him, which the said Justices are hereby required to do, and they so associated, are to issue their Summons to five Free-holders, acquainting them with the cause, and appointing them the time and Place the same shall be heard and determined, at which Time and Place the Justices are hereby impowered to appoint some Person to prosecute the said Offender or Offenders, and the Person appointed shall prefer an Accusation in Writing, specifying the Time, Place and Nature of the Offence, as near as conveniently may be, to which Accusation the Offender or Offenders shall be obliged to

Plead,

Plead, and upon Refusal to plead, the like Judgment shall be given against the Person or Persons so accused, as if convict by Verdict or Confession. And upon Pleading thereto the Justices shall proceed to Tryal, in Conjunction with the said Free-holders so summoned as aforesaid, to which Free-holders no Peremptory Challenge shall be allowed. And if upon hearing the Matter (the said Free-holders being first Sworn by the said Justices, to Judge according to Evidence) they shall adjudge the Negro, Indian or Mulatto Slave or Slaves Guilty of the Offence complained of, they shall give Sentence of Death upon him, her or them, as aforesaid, and by their Warrant cause immediate Execution to be done by the common or any other Executioner, in such manner as they shall think fit. *Provided*, That the Evidence of Indian, Negro or Mullato Slaves shall be Admitted and allowed on Tryals of such Slaves, in all causes Criminal.

And whereas such Negro, Indian or Mulatto Slave is the Property of some of her Majesties Subjects in this or the neighbouring Provinces, *Be it therefore Enacted*, That any Master or Mistress of any Negro, Indian or Mulato Slaves, supposed to be Guilty, as aforesaid, may, upon their desiring the same, have a Jury to try the said Slave, Returned by the Sheriff, and the said Master or Mistress may have Liberty to make such Challenges to the Jury as is admitted to be made in other Cases of the like Nature.

And Whereas such Negro, Indian or Mullatto Slave so put to Death, will be a great Loss to the Owner of the same, who was no ways assisting, Countenancing or abetting his said Slave in the mischief done and perpetrated by the said Slave, and may induce the Owner to transport the said slave out of the Province, by which means the said Slave will be secured from the Punishment to be inflicted on him for his said Crime, and other Negro, Indian or Mullatto Slaves encouraged to do the like Mischief, in hopes of the same security. For preventing of which for the future, and that the owner of any Indian or Mullatto Slave may not be under any temptation of withdrawing and securing the said Slave from the prosecution of Justice, *Be it Enacted by the Governour, Council and General Assembly, and by the Authority of the same*, That every Owner of any Negro, Indian or Mullatto Slave (such owner Residing in this Province) shall for every Man Slave Executed for any of the Crimes aforesaid, receive the Sum of Thirty Pounds, Money according to the Queens Proclamation, and for every Woman Slave executed as aforesaid, the Sum of *Twenty Pounds*, Money aforesaid, to be Levyed, Collected and paid in manner following, *To wit*, The Constables of every Town or District within this Province shall deliver a List of all the Negro, Indian and Mullatto Slaves within their and each of their Several and Respective Districts, both Men and Women, above the Age of Fourteen, and under Fifty Years, which are not disabled or uncapable of performing their Master or Mistresses Service, unto the Justices at their Courts of General Quarter Sessions of the Peace in every County in the Months of *May* and *June*, Yearly and every Year, who shall Order the Clerk of the Peace to file the same, and when any Negro, Indian or Mullatto Slave shall happen to be Executed for any Crime, the Justices of the Peace of the County where the fact is committed, or any three of them, one being of the *Quorum*, at the desire of the Master or Mistress of such Negro, Indian or Mullatto Slave, shall meet together and call for the aforesaid List from the Clerk of
the

Error in paging of original edition. Text is complete.

the Peace, and according to said List they shall Assess the value of the said Slave or Slaves, so executed, equally on the Heads contained in the said List, *To wit, Thirty Pounds*, Money aforesaid, for a Man, and *Twenty Pounds* for a Women, or less, as the said Justices in their discretion shall think fit, and shall appoint a Collector to Collect and Receive the same, of which Assessment made as aforesaid, and the time of Payment thereof, the Constables shall give notice to the Masters or Mistresses of such Negro, Indian or Mullatto Slaves, within their and each of their several and respective Districts within said County, and upon refusal or delay of payment, the said Collector shall deliver a List of the said Deficients to any Justice of the Peace of the said County, who shall make out Warrants to the Constables of the several Towns and Districts to distrain for the same, and the said Distress to sell at a publick Out-Cry, and pay the said Assessment to the said Collector, and Eighteen Pence to himself for the Charges of such Distress, and return the over-plus (*if any be*) to the Owner; and the said Collector shall pay the said Money, so Collected, to the Master or Mistress of said Negro, Indian or Mullatto Slave so executed, as aforesaid, and take his or her Receipt for the same, which he shall deliver to the Justices at their next Sessions of the Peace to be filed by the Clerk of the said Court.

And the Justices of the Peace are hereby allowed *One Shilling* for every Warrant of Distress, as aforesaid, the Collector for his trouble shall have *One Shilling* in the Pound for all Money Collected and paid by him, by virtue of this Act, and each Constable shall have *Three Shillings* for giving notice as aforesaid.

And be it further Enacted, That if any Negro, Indian or Mullatto Slave shall attempt to Ravish any White Woman or Maid, or that shall presume to Assault or strike any Free-Man or Woman professing *Christianity*, any two Justices of the Peace are hereby authorized to Inflict such Corporal Punishment (not extending to Life or Limb) upon such Slave or Slaves so offending, as to the said Justices shall seem meet.

And be it enacted by the authority aforesaid, That if any Negro, Indian or Mullatto Slave shall steal to the value of *Six Pence*, or above, and under *Five Shillings*, and be thereof convicted before two Justices of the Peace, one whereof being of the *Quorum*, such Negro, Indian or Mullatto Slave shall be Whipt on the bare back at the publick Whipping-Place, with Thirty Lashes, by the Constable of such Township or Place where the Offence was committed, or by such Person as he shall appoint. And that if any Negro, Indian or Mullatto Slave shall steal to the value of *Five Shillings*, or above, such Slave shall be Whipt on the bare back with Forty Stripes, as aforesaid, by the Constable, as aforesaid, the which Constable shall receive for Whipping of each Slave, *Five Shillings*, to be paid by the Master or Mistress of the said Slave, and in default of Payment to be levyed by Warrant from any Justice of the Peace, out of the Goods of the said Master or Mistriss.

And be it Enacted by the Authority aforesaid, That every Justice of the Peace, Constable or other Officer Neglecting, delaying or refusing to perform their several Duties enjoyned by this Act, shall for every such Offence forfeit the Sum of *Five Pounds* to Her Majesty, Her Heirs and Successors, to be recovered by Action of Debt in any of the Inferiour Courts of Common Pleas within this Province; and every Free-holder and Jurors summoned, as
aforesaid,

aforesaid, and refusing to serve, shall forfeit *Twenty Shillings*, to be levyed by the Constable, by Warrant of Distress from two of the Justices of the Peace assembled to try the said Slave, who are hereby required immediately, upon such refusal, to issue their Warrant for levying the same accordingly.

Be it further Enacted by the Authority aforesaid, That no Person or Persons whatsoever shall hereafter imploy, harbour, Conceal or entertain other Peoples Slaves at their Houses, Out-Houses or Plantation, without the consent of their Master or Mistress, either signified to them Verbally, or by Certificate in writing under the said Master or Mistresses Hand, excepting in Distress of Weather, or other extraordinary Occasions, upon the forfeiture of *Forty Shillings,* for every Time they are so entertained and concealed, to be paid to the Master or Mistress of such Slave or Slaves (so that the Penalty for entertaining such Slave exceeds not the Value of the said Slave) And if any Person or Persons whatsoever shall be found Guilty so harbouring, entertaining or concealing of any Slave, or assisting to the conveying them away, if such Slave shall happen to be lost, Dead, or otherways rendered Unserviceable, such Person or Persons so harbouring, entertaining, concealing, assisting or conveying them away, shall be also liable to pay the value of such Slave to the Master or Mistress, to be recovered by Action of Debt in any Court of Record within this Province.

Be it further Enacted by the Authority aforesaid, That no Negro, Indian or Mullatto Slave, that shall hereafter be made free, shall enjoy, hold or possess any House or Houses, Lands, Tenements or Hereditaments within this Province, in his or her own Right in Fee simple or Fee Tail, but the same shall Escheat to Her Majesty, Her Heirs and Successors.

And Whereas it is found by experience, that Free Negroes are an Idle Sloathful People, and prove very often a charge to the Place where they are, *Be it therefore further Enacted by the Authority aforesaid,* That any Master or Mistriss, manumitting and setting at Liberty any Negro or Mullatto Slave, shall enter into sufficient Security unto Her Majesty, Her Heirs and Successors, with two Sureties, in the Sum of Two *Hundred Pounds,* to pay yearly and every year to such Negro or Mullatto Slave, during their Lives, the Sum of *Twenty Pounds.* And if such Negro or Mullatto Slave shall be made Free by the Will and Testament of any Person deceased, that then the Executors of such Person shall enter into Security, as above, immediately upon proving the said Will and Testament, which if refused to be given, the said Manumission to be void, and of none Effect.

CHAP. XLII.

An Act for Regulating of White Servants, and taking up Souldiers and Sea-men Deserting Her Majesties Service and coming into this Colony.

WHereas the Importation of White Servants into this Province would be a great benefit to the Country in General, by settling in and improving the same, but hath hitherto been much obstructed because several Ill minded Persons encourage and assist the said Servants to Run away and

G   absent

absent themselves from their Master or Mistresses Services, to the great Damage of the said Master and Mistresses. For Prevention whereof for the future,

Be it Enacted by the Governour, Council and General Assembly, and it is hereby enacted by the Authority of the same, That every Servant who shall depart or absent themselves from the Service of his or her Master or Mistress, without leave first obtained, shall by any one Justice of the Peace, before whom such Servant shall be brought, be adjudged to serve Double the Time he, she or they have so absented themselves, besides paying or serving for all Damages and Costs which such Master or Mistress shall be adjudged to have sustained by such unlawful Absence and Departure.

And be it further Enacted by the Authority aforesaid, That all and every Person or Persons whatsoever, who shall any way counsel, intice, aid or assist any Servant to Run away or absent themselves from their Master or Mistresses Service, as aforesaid, every such Person shall Forfeit the Sum of *Ten Pounds,* besides Costs, to be Recovered by the said Master or Mistress in any Inferiour Court of Common Pleas in this Province.

And be it further Enacted by the Authority aforesaid, That all and every Person or Persons, who shall knowingly conceal, entertain or harbour any Servant, unless in necessity, every such Person so offending shall pay the Sum of *Ten Shillings* for every Days Concealment, Entertainment or Harbouring, to the Master or Mistress of such Servant, to be recovered, if under *Forty Shillings,* before any Justice of the Peace, and if above *Forty Shillings,* by Action of Debt in any Inferiour Court of Common Pleas within this Province

And be it further enacted by the authority aforesaid, That every Person or Persons who shall take up any Servant, Run away or absenting, and carry back, or return said Servant to his or her Master or Mistress, every such Person shall have *Fifteen Shillings* for his Trouble and pains, besides *six Pence for every Mile,* from the Place where taken up, to the said Master or Mistresses Habitation, to be paid by the said Master or Mistress ; and upon Refusal to be recovered, if under *Forty Shillings,* before any Justice of the Peace ; if above, by Action of Debt in any Inferiour Court of Common Pleas within this Province, besides Costs ; for which the said Servant shall pay and satisfie, as aforesaid.

And whereas not only Servants do absent themselves from the Service of their Masters and Mistresses, and Run away and escape into the Neighbouring Provinces, but the Souldiers and Seamen of her Majestys Garrisons and Ships of War do sometimes Run away and Desert her Majestys Service, coming into, abiding in, and passing through this Province. For Preventing of which for the future,

Be it further Enacted by the authority aforesaid, That all Sea-Men, Souldiers, Servants, and other Labourers and suspected Persons, who shall travel in and through this Province, without a Pass from one or more Justices of the Peace of this or the neighbouring Provinces, signifying that he, she or they are free Persons, it shall and may be Lawful for any Constable or other Person or Persons whatsoever, to take up all such Vagrant Persons, Travelling without Passes, as aforesaid, and him, her or them to carry before any Justice of the Peace of this Province, who shall strictly Examine all such

Persons

Perfons fo brought before him, and all fuch as can give no good account of Themfelves, and the Caufes and Reafons of their Travelling, fhall be by the faid Juftice committed to the common Goal of the County where taken up, there to remain till thence delivered by order of their Captain, Mafter, Miftrefs, or other due Courfe of Law.

And be it enacted by the authority aforefaid, That any Boat-man or Ferry-man who fhall carry or tranfport into or out of this Province, or over any Ferry within the fame, any of the Perfons above-mentioned, without Paffes, as aforefaid, or any Keeper of a Publick-Houfe who fhall entertain fuch Servants, Sea-men or Souldiers, as aforefaid, not having Paffes, and not apprehend the faid Perfons and fecure them, fo as the faid Perfons may be brought before fome of her Majeftys Juftices of the Peace, Every Perfon fo offending, contrary to the true Intent and Meaning of this Act, fhall, for every fuch Offence, Forfeit the Sum of *Forty Shillings,* to be recovered by the Captain or other Commanding Officer of fuch Souldier or Sea-man, the Mafter or Miftrefs of fuch Servant, or any others injured by fuch Carriage, Ferriage, Tranfportation or Entertainment, before any Juftice of the Peace of faid Province, as aforefaid.

CHAP. XLIII.

An Act for Preventing Corruption in the Courts of Juftice within this Province.

For the more effectual Preventing of Corruption in the Courts of Juftice within this Province, it is humbly propofed, and prayed, That all the Laws and Statutes now in force in that part of her Majeftys Dominion of *Great Britain,* formerly her Majeftys Kingdom of *England,* and wherein Provifion is made againft the taking of Bribes, Gifts, or any unlawful Fee or Reward by Judges, Juftices of the Peace, or any other Officers, either Magifterial or Minifterial, may be declared to be in Force in this her Majeftys Province of *New-Jerfey.*

It is therefore Enacted and Declared by the Governour, Council and General Affembly, and by the authority of the fame, That all the Laws and Statutes now in Force in that Part of her Majeftys Dominion of *Great Britain* formerly called *England,* wherein Provifion is made againft the taking of Bribes, Gifts, Unlawful Fees or Rewards, or any other Male-Adminiftration by Judges, Juftices or any Officers, Magifterial or Minifterial, be, from the Publication of this Act, in force in this her Majeftys Colony of *New-Jerfey,* effectually to all the Intents, Conftructions and Purpofes expreft, meant and intended in and by the faid Laws and Statues.

And be it further Enacted by the Authority aforefaid, That every Judge and Juftice that hereafter fhall adjudge and determine any Suit or Action before them, as Judges or Juftices in any of the Inferior Courts of Judicature within this Province, and that fhall take upon them to hear, adjudge and Determine the fame Action or Suit again, as a Judge or Juftice, in any of the Superiour Courts, where they are alfo Judge or Juftice; every fuch Judge and Juftice offending contrary to the true intent and meaning of this Act, fhall forfeit the

Sum

Sum of *Forty Pounds*, the one half to her Majesty, her Heirs and Succeffors, and the other half to fuch Perfon as fhall Profecute the fame ; To be Recovered by Action of Debt in any Court of Record within this Province; wherein there fhall be no Effoyn, Protection or Wager of Law, nor any more than one Imparlance ; and every fuch Judgment, fo given by the faid Judge or Juftice, to be void and of none effect.

C H A P. XLIV.

An Act for preventing Malicious Profecutions by Informations.

BE it *Enacted by the Governour, Council and General Affembly, and it is hereby Enacted by the Authority of the fame,* That from and after the Publication hereof, No Perfon or Perfons whatfoever fhall be troubled, vexed or difturbed in his or their Liberty or Eftate by the Queens Attorney General, or any other Perfon or Perfons whatfoever, upon pretence of any Mifdemeanour committed, otherwife than by Prefentment of the Grand Jury, or by Information by an Order from the Governour, for the time being, figned in Council, for fuch Profecution, and the party or parties fo profecuted fhall be brought to Tryal the fecond Court after fuch Information filed, or be difcharged the Court without paying of any Fees, any Law, Ufage or Cuftom to the contrary notwithftanding.

And be it further Enacted by the Authority aforefaid, That any Perfon or Perfons profecuted by Information, as aforefaid, and brought to Tryal the fecond Court, as aforefaid, and acquitted by the Verdict of Twelve Men, fhall be difcharged the Court without paying of any Fees.

And be it further enacted by the authority aforefaid, That if the Attorney General, or any other Perfon, fhall profecute any Perfon or Perfons contrary to the true Intent and meaning of this Act, (excepting on fuch Penal Statutes as include the Plantations, or where it is otherways provided for by Acts of General Affembly of this Province) fhall forfeit *Fifty Pounds* for every fuch Offence, to be recovered by Action of Debt in any Court of Record within this Province, the one half to the Perfon or Perfons who fhall profecute the fame to Effect, and the other half to Her Majefty, Her Heirs and Succeffors.

C H A P. XLV.

An Act for Afcertaining the Qualification of Jurors within this Province.

BE it *Enacted by the Governour, Council and General Affembly, met and Affembled, and by the Authority of the fame,* That from and after Publication hereof all Grand and Petty Juries fhall be Summoned by the High-Sheriff of each County, or his Deputy or under Sheriff, or (in cafes where either of them are concerned, or of other Lawful Challenge) by the Coroner, and that either Perfonally, or by Summons in Writing, left at every mans Houfe fo Summoned,

Summoned, Respectively, four Days, at least, before the first day of the Court, which Persons so Summoned, shall be of good Fame, Credit and Reputation, and Free-holders of the County for which they shall serve.

And be it further Enacted by the Authority aforesaid, That all Persons so Summoned to serve upon Grand Inquests, shall be returned by the said High-Sheriff, and shall each of them be worth, at least, One Hundred Pounds in Real Estate, in the County for which they shall serve. And that all Persons Summoned to serve on all Petty Juries, also, be returned by the said High-Sheriff, or in cases where he or his Deputy are concerned, or of other Lawful Challenge, by the Coroner without the direction or advice of any other Person or Persons whatsoever, and shall each of them be worth One Hundred Pounds in Real and Personal Estate, in the County for which they shall serve.

And be it further Enacted by the Authority aforesaid, That in case any Sheriff or Coroner shall return any Person or Persons to serve on Juries, not qualified, as directed by this Act, every Plantiff or Defendant may have his Challenge against such Persons. And in case any Debate or Controversy arises concerning the Qualification of the Person or Persons so Challenged, it shall be determined by any two Persons that are sworn on such Jury, as the Law in such cases directs.

CHAP. XLVI.

An Act Confirming Letters of Administration, granted, and to be granted, within this Province.

WHereas Her Sacred Majesty hath reserved to her respective Governours or Commanders in Chief of this her Colony of *New-Jersey* the Collating to Benefices, granting Lisences for Marriages, Probates of Wills, and granting Letters of Administration,

Be it therefore Enacted by the Governour, Council and General Assembly, and by the Authority of the same, That all Letters of Administration that heretofore have been granted by the present or any preceeding Governour or Commander in Chief, or by any other Person or Persons that heretofore have been impowred to grant the same, or that hereafter shall be granted within this Colony by the present or any succeeding Governour or Commander in Chief, or by any other Person or Persons impowered by him or them, All such Letters of Administration heretofore granted, or hereafter to be granted by the Authority aforesaid, shall only be, and are hereby declared to be, and at all times hereafter shall be taken, deemed and Esteemed to be good and vallid in the Law, to all intents and purposes, according to the true intent and design of them, and every of them respectively, and shall not be Superceded or Reversed by any other Administration whatsoever granted or to be granted for Estates within this Colony, excepting by such Administration as shall be granted by the Authority aforesaid.

H   CHAP.

CHAP. XLVII.

An Act Concerning Swine.

BE it Enacted by the Governour, Council and General Assembly, and by the Authority of the same, That all and every Free-holder within this Province, Himself, Servants or Tenants for years, may kill any Swine trespassing on any part of his or their Land, and shall give the Owner of the Swine notice thereof, if he can easily be found, otherwise he shall (within fifteen Hours after) give notice to one of the Over-seers of the Poor, who shall dispose of the same to the best advantage for the use of the Poor of that Town or Precinct; but if any Free-holder or Tenant for years finding any Swine Trespassing on his or their Land, shall not think fit to kill them, as aforesaid, he may put them into his Yard or other Inclosure, and send word to the Owner, who shall pay double Damage to the Person injured, as it shall be appraised by two honest Neighbours to be chosen by the party Injured, to be recovered by Action of Debt; if Forty Shillings, or under, before any Justice of the Peace; if above Forty Shillings, in the inferiour Court of Common Pleas of that County, with cost of Suit.

And be it enacted by the authority aforesaid, That if any Free-holder, his Servants or Tenants for years, shall kill any Swine not Trespassing on his or their Land, he shall pay double Damage to the Owner, to be recovered by Action of Debt; if Forty Shillings, or under, before any Justice of the Peace; if above Forty Shillings, in the Inferiour Court of Common Pleas of that County, with Costs of Suit.

And be it further enacted by the authority aforesaid, That if any Person or Persons (who are not Free-holders, their Servants or Tenants for years) shall Range the Woods or Fields, Hunt, Mark or kill any Swine, every Person or Persons so ranging, hunting, marking or killing, contrary to the true intent and meaning of this Act, shall pay double the value of each Swine so killed, mark't or drove away, to the Owner of the same; to be recovered as aforesaid. And if any such Persons, not Free-holders, their Servants or Tenants for years, shall drive, carry away and convert to his own Use any Swine whatsoever and wheresoever within this Province, such Person or Persons shall also Forfeit the Sum of Forty Shillings for each Offence, to be Recovered before any one Justice of the Peace, on the Testimony of one Evidence, with other Circumstances, one Third part to the Informer that shall prosecute the same, the other two Thirds to the Over-seer, for the Use of the Poor of that Town or Precinct.

And be it enacted by the authority aforesaid, That if any Person or Persons, convicted, as aforesaid, of Killing, Marking or Driving away any Swine, as aforesaid, shall not within three Hours after such his Conviction, pay the said Forty Shillings, that then and in such case he shall receive Ten Lashes on the bare back.

And be it Enacted by the authority aforesaid, That all the Acts here-to-fore made concerning Swine, shall be, and are hereby Repealed, to all intents and purposes.

CHAP.

CHAP. XLVIII.

An Act for Regulating Fences.

WHereas for the preventing Differences and Trespasses among Neighbours, it is Necessary that Fences shall be kept in good Repair, *Be it therefore enacted by the Governour, Council and General Assembly, and it is hereby Enacted by the authority of the same,* That all Fences that are and shall be esteemed good and lawful, shall be Four Foot and six Inches High, and close, strong and sufficient to prevent Horses and Neat Cattel, great and small, going thorow or under such Fences.

And be it further Enacted by the Authority aforesaid, That all such Cattle and Horses that shall Iump over or break down any such Fence, shall be Pounded, and the Owner of the Beast shall pay the Damage to the Person Damnified, which shall be appraised by two sufficient Men of the Neighbourhood, chosen by the party Damnified by such Creatures, who shall also view the sufficiency of the Fence. And it shall and may be lawful for the Person injured to Pound such unruly trespassing Horses and Cattle within his Field or Yard the space of Twenty Four Hours, he giving notice thereof to the Owner of the said Trespassers, if known or easie to be found, and if they are not Redeemed within the said Twenty four hours space, then he shall lead or drive them to the Town or Precinct Pound, where the Pound-Keeper shall receive and keep them till the Damages and Charges of the Trespass, driving and pounding is paid. And the Pound-keeper shall have for letting in and out of the Pound *Two Pence per head,* and for feeding, pounding and tending, *six Pence per head* for every Twenty four Hours they shall continue in the Pound.

And be it Enacted by the Authority aforesaid, That where any Person sets his Fence in the Partition Line between him and his Neighbour, and his Neighbour improves the Land or Meadow adjoyning thereto, by inclosure, for Tillage, Mowing or Pasturage, they shall make and maintain the said Division-Fence equally between them; and if either of them refuse or neglect so to do, then the other may make and repair the said Division Fence wholly, and shall recover half the Charges of the party refusing, by Action of Debt within any Court of Record, as it shall be valued by two honest Men of the Neighbourhood, indifferently chosen by both Parties; but if the Person Neglecting to make or Repair the said Fence, shall refuse to chuse one of the said Appraisers, then the other may chuse them both himself. And where any Persons do agree to fence their Land in common, such Fences shall be made and maintained according to their several proportions of Land, and benefit they receive thereby.

And be it Enacted by the Authority aforesaid, That when any Stray Cattle or Horses are Impounded for Trespassing, as aforesaid, the said Pound-keeper is hereby required forth-with to give notice to the Owner, if known, or to set up Papers at the most publick places within the Township and County to which the Pound belongs, and the three next adjoyning Towns, giving Publick Notice and Description of the said Strays; And if the Owner of such

Stray,

Stray, or some Person by his Order, do not appear and redeem them within two Months after such publick Notice given, the Pound-keeper shall sell such Strayes at Publick Out-cry (he seting up Papers on said Publick Places) giving notice of the time and Place of Sale, six days before the Sale) and out of the Money received for such Strays, he shall pay for the Trespass, as aforesaid, and other incident Charges, and return the over-plus to the Owner of the said Stray, or to his order, provided he appear and demand the same within one year after such Sale ; and if the Owner, or some Person by his Order, doth not appear within the time aforesaid, then the Pound-keeper shall pay the said Over-plus Money to the Overseers, for the use of the Poor of that Town or Precinct.

And be it enacted by the authority aforesaid, That if any owner or possessor of Land within this Province shall neglect or refuse to make and keep in good Repair the Fence and Fences about his Land, in manner as is herein before prescribed, and for Default thereof the Horses or Cattle of any other Person shall break in or enter into or upon the said Land, over or thorow such Fence, that the Owner of the said Cattle or Horses shall not be liable to any Action, nor the Cattle or Horses be Impounded for any Damage committed; and if any Action be commenced thereon, that then the Owner of such Cattle or Horses do plead the General Issue, and give this Act in Evidence to Justify the same.

And be it Enacted by the Authority aforesaid, That where there is not a Pound kept within the Town or Precinct, then the Person Damnified by such Cattle or Horses Trespassing, as aforesaid, may Pound them in his own Field or Yard till redeemed : and he shall act in such cases, in all things as the Pound-keeper should or ought to have done by this Act, any thing herein to the contrary notwithstanding.

And be it Enacted by the Authority aforesaid, That the Act, Entituled, *An Act for Regulating Fences,* made in *January,* One Thousand Seven Hundred and Nine, be and is hereby Repealed, to all Intents and purposes.

CHAP. XLIX.

An Act for raising of Money for Building and Repairing of Goals and Court-Houses within each respective County of this Province.

WHereas Goals and Court-Houses are absolutely necessary for the Administration of Justice, and puting the Laws in Execution;
Be it Enacted by the Governour, Council and General Assembly, and by the Authority of the same, That the Inhabitants of each Town and Precinct within each County shall Assemble and meet together on the second *Tuesday* in *March,* yearly, and every Year, at the most publick place of each respective Town and Precinct, and by the Majority of Voices chuse two Free-holders for every such Town and Precinct for the ensuing Year, which Free-holders, so chosen, or the Major part of them, together with all the Justices of the Peace of each respective County, or any three of them (one whereof being of the *Quorum*) shall meet together,

Fo

(For the County of *Bergin*, near to the *Dutch* Church, by *Hackensack-River*. For the County of *Essex*, at *Newark*. For the County of *Middlesex*, at *Perth-Amboy*. For the County of *Sommerset*, at the most convenient place of the County, which shall be agreed upon by the Major part of the Free-holders that inhabit there. For the County of *Monmouth*, at *Shrewsberry*. For the County of *Burlington*, at *Burlington*. For the County of *Gloucester*, at *Gloucester*. For the County of *Salem*, at *Salem*. For the County of *Cape-May*, near to the Prison there. And agree upon such Sum and Sums of Money as shall be needful for Repairing such Goals and Court Houses as are already built, and for Building such as are wanting, (*viz.*) In the County of *Bergin*, near to the *Dutch Church* by *Hackensack-River*. In *Essex*, at *Newark*. In *Middlesex*, at *Perth-Amboy*. In *Sommerset*, at the most convenient place which the Free-holders Inhabitants, shall agree upon. In *Monmouth*, near the House of *John Okeson* of *Freehold*. In *Burlington* County, at the Town of *Burlington*. In *Salem* County, at the Town of *Salem*. In *Gloucester* County, at the Town of *Gloucester*. In *Cape-May County*, near the present Prison there.) And shall appoint Assessors and Collectors, which said Assessors, so named for each Town and Precinct, shall meet together at the Places above-mentioned within each County, on or before the fourth *Tuesday* in *March* yearly, to Assess the Inhabitants within each Town and County equally, and make a fair List of the said Assessments, and deliver the same to the respective Collectors, at or before the first *Tuesday in April* yearly, which Collector shall deliver a true Copy thereof to the Constable of each Town and Precinct, Who is hereby required immediately, on Receipt thereof, to give notice to the several Inhabitants within their Respective Districts, of the Sums they are to pay, which Sums shall be paid to each Collector at or before the fourth *Thuesday* in *May* yearly. And upon non-payment, then the Collectors are hereby required to deliver a List of the Delinquents to any one Justice of the Peace of the County where the Default is, who is hereby required, forth-with, to Issue his Warrant or Warrants to the several Constables, Commanding them to Levy the same by Distress on the Goods and Chattles of each Delinquent, and expose the same to Sale, and to pay their respective Sums to the Collector or Collectors, at or before the second *Tuesday* in *June*, yearly, and return the over-plus, if any be, to the owner, deducting Twelve Pence to himself for each Distress, and six Pence to the Justice for the Warrant.

And be it Enacted by the Authority aforesaid, That the Justices of Peace and Free-holders appointed and elected, as aforesaid, are hereby required to appoint Mannagers to do and see done, such Things and Works as they shall agree upon to be done and performed, which said Mannagers are hereby Authorized and Impowered to draw Warrants on the Collectors respectively, for Payment of the Work and Materials needful in Building and Repairing Goals and Court Houses, as aforesaid, not exceeding the Sum or Sums appointed by the Justices and Free-holders aforesaid, for that purpose, which Warrants the Collectors are hereby required to answer and pay. And all the Assessors, Collectors and Mannagers shall be accountable to the said Justices and Free-holders, when called thereunto, the Allowance for their Pains and Trouble shall be, for the Assessors *Four Pence per Pound*, the Collector *Four*

J

Pence

Pence per Pound, The Conftables (for giving notice of the Sums and time of payment) *two Pence per Pound*, The Mannagers *Ten Pence per Pound*.

And be it Enacted by the Authority aforefaid, That if any Perfon or Perfons appointed or elected, as aforefaid, fhall neglect or refufe to act, do and perform whatfoever is required of them by this Act, fuch Perfon or Perfons fo neglecting or refufing fhall forfeit the Sum of Twenty Shillings for each, Offence, to be levyed by Diftrefs on each Defaulters Goods and Chattels, as aforefaid, to be applyed towards Building and Repairing the refpective Goals and Court Houfes. And in cafe of Death, Abfence or Refufal of any Perfon or Perfons, nominated and appointed, as aforefaid, any three Juftices of the Peace, one being of the *Quorum*, fhall appoint a Perfon or Perfons in his or their ftead, and who fhall in cafe of neglect or refufal, alfo be liable to all the Penalties above-mentioned.

And be it Enacted by the Authority aforefaid, That if the Inhabitants of any Town or Precinct fhall neglect to meet and chufe Freeholders, as aforefaid, then it fhall and may be lawful for the Juftices at their next Court of Quarter-Seffions, to appoint two Free-holders refiding in each fuch Town or Precinct that fhall fo neglect or refufe, as aforefaid, and who fhall, in cafe of Neglect or refufal, alfo be liable to the Penalties above-mentioned, any thing contain'd herein to the contrary notwithftanding.

And be it Enacted by the Authority aforefaid, That the Act, entituled, *An Act for building and repairing Goals and Court-Houfes* within this Province, made in the Month of *January*, One Thoufand Seven Hundred and nine, in the eighth year of Her Majefties Reign, be and is hereby Repealed, and every Claufe and Thing therein contained, to all intents, Conftructions and Purpofes. And Whereas there was, by Virtue of that Act of Affembly, thereby Repealed, an Affefsment made, and part of the Money collected and expended towards the building a Goal in the County of *Monmouth*,

Be it therefore Enacted by the authority aforefaid, That the Juftices and Free-holders aforefaid, fhall, and are hereby impowred to examine and compute the Money fo Collected and expended, and raife fo much over and above the Sum they determine to raife on their County of *Monmouth* aforefaid, for the Building a Court-Houfe and Goal, by the directions of this Act, as was Collected and expended by virtue of the Act hereby Repealed, and the Perfons that have paid their former Affefsments, as aforefaid, are hereby impowered to ftop the Sum fo paid by them, out of their proportions of the Affefsment which fhall be made, as aforefaid, and the Collector or Collectors are hereby required to allow the fame.

And be it further Enacted by the Authority aforefaid, That if any of the Juftices and Free-holders aforefaid, fhall neglect or refufe to meet at the time or times appointed by this Act, or refufe to do what is required of them, then any three of the Juftices in each refpective County (one being of the *Quorum*) fhall appoint fuch time or times, as they fhall think proper, to meet and act as aforefaid; and every Perfon Neglecting or refufing to meet and act at fuch time or times fo appointed, provided publick Notice be put up by the faid Juftices, in writing, Eight days before, in fome Publick place in each refpective Town or Precinct, fhall be liable to the Penalties before mentioned in this Act, as if they had neglected or refufed to meet and act at the time or Times before mentioned in this Act,

CHAP.

CHAP. L.

An Act for Establishing a Ferry from the Town of *Burlington*, to the Town of *New-Bristol*.

BE it Enacted by the Governour, Council and General Assembly, and it is hereby Enacted by the Authority of the same, That a Ferry shall be kept and plyed from the Town and Island of *Burlington*, over *Delaware-River*, unto the Town of *New-Bristol* in the Province of *Pennsilvania*; and that the said Ferry shall be kept and managed by such Person or Persons as the Governour or Commander in Chief, for the time being, shall Lisence and appoint, and that such Ferry-Man, or Ferry-Men, so Lisenced (and no other) shall and may demand and have the Fees or Ferriages following, and no other, *To wit*, For every single Person, carried over the said River, Three Pence; if above one Person, Two Pence half Penny for each. For each Man and Horse, Nine Pence. For every Ox, Cow, Steer or Hiefer, One Shilling. And for every Sheep or Hog, Three Pence, all Money according to the Queens Proclamation.

And be it Enacted by the authority aforesaid, That the Ferry-Man or Ferry-Men so Lisenced, as aforesaid, shall keep good and sufficient Boat or Boats, for carrying Men, Horses and Cattle, and shall well and duly attend the Service of the said Ferry at all times, under the penalty of *Twenty Shillings,* Money aforesaid, for every such default, to be Recovered by Action of Debt by any Person or Persons whatsoever that shall sue for the same, for his or their own use, before any one Justice of the Peace within the County of *Burlington* aforesaid.

And be it Enacted by the authority aforesaid, That every Person who shall Ferry Over, for Fee or Reward, any Person or Persons, Horse or Horses, Cattle, Sheep, Hogs, Goods or Merchandize, from the said Town or Island of *Burlington*, over the said *Delaware-River*, unto the said Town of *New-Bristol*, or unto any place near the same, without the Consent of the Ferry-Men Lisenced as aforesaid, shall forfeit the Sum of *Twenty Shillings*, Money aforesaid, for every such Offence, to be Recovered by the Ferry-Man or Ferry-Men Lisenced as aforesaid, to his or their own use, by an Action of Debt, before any one Justice of the Peace within the said County of *Burlington*, any Custom or Usage to the contrary in any wise notwithstanding.

CHAP. LI.

An Act for Confirming of Conveyances of Lands made and to be made by Wills and Powers of Attorney, and declaring what Exemplifications of Records and other Things shall be holden and received for good Evidence of Estates of Inheritance, and for Transfering of Uses into Possession.

WHereas on and several Years after the first settlement of this Colony, the great distance of Plantations, and scarcity of Inhabitants
was

was fuch, That it was difficult to get more then two Witneffes to be prefent at the figning, fealing and acknowledging of laft Wills and Teftaments, which induced the then Legiflature of the Province of *Eaft-Jerfey,* now the *Eaftern-Divifion* of this Province, in the Year One Thoufand fix Hundred and Eighty Two, to make a Law declaring, That all Wills in Writing, attefted by two credible Witneffes, fhall be of the fame force to convey Lands, as other Conveyances.

And whereas Purfuant to the faid Law, many Wills have been made, Bequeathing and Devifing Lands, figned by the Teftator, and attefted only by two fubfcribing Witneffes.

Be it therefore Enacted by the Governour, Council and General Affembly, and by the Authority of the fame, That all laft Wills and Teftaments heretofore made in writing, figned by the Teftator, in prefence of two fubfcribing Witneffes, and proved according to the cuftom heretofore ufed in either the *Eaftern* or *Weftern-Divifions* of this Province, by which any Lands, Tenements or Hereditaments have been given, devifed or bequeathed unto any Perfon or Perfons whatfoever, every of the faid laft Wills and Teftaments fhall at all times hereafter be held, taken, deemed and eftemed as good, valid and fufficient Title in the Law, to all Intents, Conftructions and Purpofes, as if the Teftator had conveyed the fame away in his Life time, and fhall forever Bar any Perfon or Perfons claiming or to claim Eftate under any fuch Teftator, contrary to the true intent and meaning of fuch Will or Teftament; and the faid Will being proved as aforefaid, and the Books of Regifters of either of the *Eaftern* or *Weftern-Divifions* of this Province in which they were entred, being proved as aforefaid, may be given, and fhall be received in Evidence, any Law or Cuftom to the contrary notwithftanding.

And be it Enacted by the Authority aforefaid, That all Wills and Teftaments which hereafter fhall be made in writing, figned and publifhed by the Teftator, in prefence of three fubfcribing Witneffes, and regularly proved and entred upon the Books of Records or Regifters in the Secretarys Office of this Province, or any proper Office for that purpofe, fhall and are hereby declared, and forever hereafter fhall be taken, accepted, deemed and efteemed fufficient to devife, bequeath and convey any Lands, Tenements, Hereditaments, or other Eftates whatfoever, within this Province, as effectually to all intents, conftructions and purpofes whatfoever, as if the Teftator had conveyed the fame away in his life time; and the Books in which they are Regiftred or Recorded may be given in Evidence, and fhall be accepted of and be fufficient Evidence at all times and Places where the faid Wills or Teftaments may be requifit to be given in Evidence, any Law or Cuftom to the contrary notwithftanding.

And be it Enacted by the Authority aforefaid, That the Copies of any laft Will or Teftament whatfoever heretofore made, or hereafter to be made within any part of the Kingdoms of *Great Britain* or *Ireland,* by which any Lands, Tenements, Hereditaments or other Eftate within this Province, are devifed or bequeathed, certified under the Seal of fuch Office where fuch Will or Teftament is proved and lodged, may be given, and fhall be received in Evidence before any of the Courts of Judicature within this Province, and be efteemed as valid and fufficient as if the original Will or Teftament were then and there produced and proved.

Anc

And be it Enacted by the Authority aforesaid, That the Copy of any Will or Testament made in any other of Her Majesties Colonies, by which any Lands, Tenements, Hereditaments or other Estates within this Province is given, devised or bequeathed, being proved according to the Custom of such Colony, certified under the great Seal of such Colony, may be given, and shall be received in Evidence in any of the Courts of Judicature within this Province, and be esteemed as valid and sufficient as if the original Will or Testament were then and there produced and proved.

And be it Enacted by the Authority aforesaid, That all Deeds, Grants, Sales, Leases, Assurances, or other Conveyances whatsoever, heretofore made by Virtue of Letters of Agency, Powers of Attorney, or other Powers or Authorities whatsoever, that have been entred on the Publick Books of Records of this Province, or the publick Books of Records of the *Eastern* or *Western Divisions* thereof, whereby any Lands, Tenements or Hereditaments whatsoever within this Province, have been granted, sold, conveyed, assured, released or transferr'd to any Person or Persons, pursuant to such Powers and Authorities whatsoever, shall be and are hereby declared as good, vallid and sufficient Title in the Law, to all Intents, Constructions and purposes whatsoever unto the said Grantees, their Heirs and Assigns, as if the Constituent or Constituents had then and there sold and Conveyed the Land or Lands, and had executed Deeds (according to the true Intent and meaning of such Grants, Deeds or Conveyances) which said Grants, Deeds or Conveyances shall be of force against, conclude and bind all and every the Constituents, Imployers, Grantors of such Powers and Authorities, and their, and all and every of their Heirs, and all and every other Person or Persons claiming or to claim Estate from or under them or any of them, severally and respectively; and all Lands, Tenements or other Hereditaments, that for the time to come shall be sold, conveyed or disposed of by virtue of such Powers or Authorities, as aforesaid, such Powers shall be first proved and entred upon the Publick Records, after which all Grants and Conveyances made pursuant to the Powers thereby Granted, shall be deemed, taken and Esteemed as good, vallid and sufficient Titles against all and every the Constituents, Imployers and Grantors of such Powers and Authorities, and against all claiming or to claim Estate under them, severally and respectively, aforesaid, as if the Constituent or Constituents had then and there sold and Conveyed the same Land or Lands.

And be it Enacted by the Authority aforesaid, That the Exemplification of any Deeds or Writings relating to Estates Real or Personal, within this Province, proved and certified under the City Seal of *London* or *Edinburgh* in the Kingdom of *Great Britain,* or under the Seal of the City of *Dublin* in the Kingdom of *Ireland,* or under the Great Seal of any of Her Majesties Colonies in *America,* and any of the publick Books of Records or Registers of this Province, or of either of the Divisions thereof, shall be received in Evidence in any Court of Record within this Province, and shall be esteemed as sufficient as if the Originals were then and there produced and proved.

And be it enacted by the Authority aforesaid, That all and every Person or Persons to whom the use or uses of any Tract or Tracts of Land within this Province have been Sold, Given, Limited, Granted, Released or Conveyed

K

by

by Deed, Grant or any other Legal Conveyance whatſoever, or that ſhall hereafter be granted by any Deed or Conveyance whatſoever, ſuch Grantees, their Heirs and Aſſigns ſhall be Deemed, Taken and Eſteemed to be in as Full and Ample Poſſeſſion of ſuch Lands, Tenements and Hereditaments, to all Intents, Conſtructions and Purpoſes as if ſuch Grantees, their Heirs and Aſſigns were poſſeſſed thereof by ſolemn Livery of Seiſin and Poſſeſſion, any Uſage or Cuſtom to the contrary notwithſtanding.

Provided always, That nothing in this Act ſhall be conſtrued to Extend to make Good, Vallid and Effectual any Fraud or Forgery made or uſed in or about any Power of Agency or Letter of Attorney, or other Deeds, Writings or Records, Laſt Will and Teſtaments, or any Bargain and Sale, or other Conveyances of any Eſtate of Inheritance, grounded upon ſuch Fraudulent or Forged Power of Agency or Letter of Attorney, or other Deeds, Writings or Records, and Laſt Wills and Teſtaments.

CHAP. LII.

An Act for ſhortening of Law Suits, and Regulating the Practice of the Law.

BE it Enacted by the Governour, Council and General Aſſembly, and it is hereby Enacted·by the Authority of the ſame, That every Perſon on whom a *Capias* is ſerved by the Sheriff, or other proper Officer, ſhall enter his Appearance at the Court to which the ſaid *Capias* is Returnable, or give in ſpecial Bail to the Action, as the Law and the nature of the Cauſe requires, and in caſe ſuch Perſon does neglect or refuſe to enter ſuch Appearance, or give ſuch ſpecial Bail, as aforeſaid, the Bail Bond ſhall be aſſigned, unleſs the Court does think fit to allow a further time for the puting in of ſpecial Bail, which they may do at their Diſcretion·; *Always Provided*, Such time ſhall not exceed the Term of Twenty Days in the Supream Court, and Ten Days in the Inferiour Courts.

And be it Enacted by the Authority aforeſaid, That every Plantiff ſhall file his Declaration in the Clerks Office during the ſitting of the Court, to which ſuch *Capias* is Returnable ; or in caſe time is allowed by the Court at or before the Expiration of ſuch time ſo allowed, and ſhall give Oyer of the Specialties or other Inſtruments mentioned in the ſaid Declaration, together with Copies of the ſame, to the Defendant or his Attorney, or leave them in the Clerks Office, on penalty of being Non-ſuited, in caſe the Plantiff or his Attorney neglect to do the ſame.

And every Defendant ſhall file his Plea in the Clerks Office, and give Oyer of ſuch Inſtruments as are mentioned in the ſaid Plea, together with Copies of the ſame, to the Plantiff or his Attorney, or to the Clerk of the Court in which the Declaration is filed, within ſuch time as is hereafter directed, That is to ſay, To the Clerk of the Supream Court within Twenty Days after ſuch Declaration is filed, and to the Clerk of any of the Inferiour Courts of Common Pleas, within Twenty Days after the Declaration is filed ; and if the Defendant ſhall neglect or refuſe to enter his ſaid Plea within the times by this Act directed and appointed, that then and in ſuch caſe

Judgment

Judgment fhall be entered againft him for fuch his Default.

And if it fo happen that Replications or Rejoynders are neceffary to be made, fuch Replication fhall be filed by the Plantiff in the Clerks Office of the Supream Court, within Twenty Days after the time appointed by this Act for filing the Plea, and in the Clerks Office of any of the Inferiour Courts of Common Pleas, within twenty Days after the time appointed by this Act for filing the faid Pleas, or be Non-fuited: And the Rejoynder fhall be filed by the Defendant in the Clerks Office of the Supream Court within Twenty Days after the time appointed by this Act for filing of the Replication; and in the Clerks Office of any of the Inferiour Courts of Common Pleas, within Twenty Days after the time appointed by this Act for filing the faid Replication: and if the Defendant neglect or refufe to file fuch Rejoynder within the time prefcribed by this Act, then Judgment fhall be entered againft the faid Defendant fo neglecting, for fuch his Default: and where further Pleadings are not neceffary, Iffue fhall be joyned, and the Cafe Tryed the next Court after that to which the *Capias* was returned; and where further Pleadings are neceffary, the time of fuch Pleadings fhall be appointed by the next Court following.

And be it further enacted by the Authority aforefaid, That the Plantiff fhall come to Tryal the next Court after Iffue joyned, or be Non-fuited, unlefs the Court fee caufe to the contrary; And if the Defendant does not appear upon the Tryal, the Plantiff fhall Proceed in his Default.

Provided always, and it is hereby further enacted by the authority aforefaid, That in cafe of a Non-fuit, or Judgment by Default, no Execution fhall Iffue thereupon-till after the next Court following fuch Non-fuit or Judgment by Default.

And be it Enacted by the Authority aforefaid, That every Perfon defiring the fame, fhall be permitted and allowed to enter Appearance, and plead his own Caufe or Caufes himfelf, or by his Attorney, or by both, in any Court of Record within this Province.

And be it Enacted by the Authority aforefaid, That all Procefs fhall be Sealed by the refpective Clerk of each Court of Record within this Province, and that Writs of *Capias* fhall be figned underneath on the right Hand by the Clerk, and on the left by the Plantiff or his Attorney, otherwife the Writ fhall abate.

And be it Enacted by the Authority aforefaid, That every Attorney on filing a Declaration or Plea in any Caufe, fhall enter his Warrant of Attorney, and leave a Copy thereof in the Clerks Office, under the Penalty of paying all the Cofts, and the Action fhall difcontinue. And every Attorney having undertaken, or that fhall undertake to Plead a Caufe or Caufes, fhall manage the fame, until it be fully Determined (unlefs difcharged by his Imployer) under the Penalty of paying all the Coft and Damage that fhall be fuftained by his Imployer or Imployers, if the Caufe fhall happen to mifcarry through his Default, to be recovered by fuch as fhall be agrieved, from fuch Attorney or Attorneys, by Action of Debt in any Court of Record within this Province.

And be it Enacted by the Authority aforefaid, That when any Non-Refident of the County where the Action fhall be brought, fhall take out a Writ of *Capias* againft an Inhabitant, he fhall give Bond unto the Defendant, with Security dwelling in the faid County, in the Penalty of Ten Pounds, upon
condition

condition to pay the Cofts, if caft, non-fuited, difcontinue or with-draw his Suit without confent of the Defendant, which Bond fhall be left with the Clerk of that Court in which the Action is Commenced. And when any Non-Refident of this Province fhall take out a Writ or *Capias* againft any Perfon within this Province, he fhall give Bond unto the Defendant, with Security, dwelling in the faid Province, in the Penalty of Ten Pound, upon condition to pay the Coft, if Caft, Non-fuited, Difcontinue or with-draw his Suit without the confent of the Defendant, which Bond fhall be left with the Clerk of the Court in which the Action is Commenced. And any Clerk neglecting to take fuch Security, fhall pay the Defendants Cofts, to be reco-vered, as aforefaid. And in all Actions above the Value of Ten Pounds, the Defendant fhall give Special Bail, if required, except in Actions of *Slander*, *Quare claufum fregit*, *Affault and Battery*, unlefs it be otherwife ordered by the Court.

And be it Enacted by the Authority aforefaid, · That no Perfon or Perfons what-foever, after Publication hereof, fhall commence, fue or profecute any Suit or Action whatfoever in the Supream Court of Judicature of this Province, wherein the true and real caufe of Action fhall not exceed the Sum of Twenty Pounds of Money according to the Queens Proclamation, over and above all the Coft and Charges of the Suit (Except where Titles of Land are any ways concerned) under the Penalty of paying to the Defendant all his Cofts and Damages which fhall acerue by fuch Profecutions, to be recovered by Action of Debt in any of the Inferiour Courts of Common Pleas within this Province.

And be it further Enacted by the Authority aforefaid, That no Suit or Action whatfoever (except where Titles of Land are concerned) fhall be removed from the Inferiour Courts of Common Pleas of any County within this Pro-vince, by *Habeas Corpus*, or any otherwife, unlefs by *Writ of Error* after Judgement given, except where the Sum or Value of the Suit or Action commenced, as aforefaid, fhall exceed the Sum of Twenty Pounds, Money according to the Queens Proclamation. And if any Perfon or Perfons fhall remove any Action contrary to the true Intent and meaning of this Act, he, she or they fo offending fhall pay to the party or parties injured all the Coft and Damages fuftained by fuch Removal, to be recovered as aforefaid, any Law, Cuftom or Ufage to the contrary notwithftanding.

And be it further enacted by the authority aforefaid, That if any Perfon or Perfons fhall bring a *Writ of Error* upon a Judgment obtained in any of the Inferiour Courts of Common Pleas, Returnable to the Supream Court, fuch Perfon or Perfons fhall give Security, within Ten Days after the *Writ of Error* is brought, to profecute his *Writ of Error* to Effect, and to pay double the Cofts of the other party, if the Judgment given in the faid inferiour Courts fhall be affirmed.

Provided always, That no Execution fhall Iffue upon fuch Judgment of the Court of Common Pleas, after the Plantiff in Error hath given notice to the Defendant, by shewing him or his Attorney the faid Writ, unlefs he shall neglect to give in Security as aforefaid.

And be it further Enacted by the authority aforefaid, That all Procefs, Pleadings, Entries and Proceedings Whatfoever, in all the Courts of Judicature within this Province, fhall be in the *Englifh Tongue.*

CHAP.

CHAP. LIII.

An Act for Settling the Bounds between the Counties of *Sommerset, Middlesex* and *Monmouth*.

BE it Enacted by the Governour, Council and General Assembly, and by the Authority of the same, That the Boundary Line between *Sommerset* and *Middlesex* Counties shall be and begin where the Road Crosseth the River *Rariton* at *Inians's* Ferry, and Runs from thence along the said Old Road by *Judadiah Higgens's* House, leading towards the Falls of *Delaware*, so far as the *Eastern-Division* of this Province extends.

And be it Enacted by the Authority aforesaid, That the Boundary Line between *Middlesex* and *Monmouth* County shall be and begin at the Mouth of the Creek that parts the Land of *George Willocks* and the Land that was formerly Capt. *Andrew Bowns*, deceased, Thence along the said Capt. *Andrew Bowns* Line to the Rear of the said Land; Thence upon a direct Course to *Warnes* Bridge, on the Brook where *Thomas Smith* did formerly live; Thence upon a direct Course to the South-East Corner of *Barclays* Tract of Land, that lies near *Matchiponix*; Thence to the most Southermost part of said Tract of Land, including the whole Tract of Land in *Middlesex* County; Thence upon the direct Line to *Assanpinck* Bridge on the High Road, including *William Jonas, William Story, Thomas Ruckman* and *John Guyberson* in *Monmouth* County; Thence along the said Road to *Aaron Robbins* Land; Thence Westerly along the said *Aaron Robbins* and *James Lawrance* Line, to the Line of the *Eastern* and *Western Division* aforesaid, including the said *Robbins* and *Lawrence* in *Monmouth* County.

And be it Enacted by the Authority aforesaid, That the Boundary Lines between the said Counties, settled by Act of General Assembly of this Province, past in *January* One Thousand Seven Hundred and Nine, so far, and no further, as the same is altered by this Act, shall be and is hereby Repealed to all Intents and Purposes.

CHAP. LIV.

An Act to prevent the concealing of Stray Cattle or Horses.

WHEREAS Great and many Inconveniences has happened to the Inhabitants of this Province by reason of Cattle and Horses straying from their owners to other Plantations or Towns, and no Law to enforce the Publishing of Cattle and Horses so straying; and in a much as Ill Minded Persons have and may conceal and convert such Cattle and Horses to their owne use,

Therefore be it Enacted by the Governour, Council and General Assembly, and by the Authority of the same, That all Persons who have, or hereafter shall have, at any time between the sixteenth of *November*, and the first of *April*, any stray Cattle or Horses upon his or their Improv'd Land, shall give notice in Writing set up in the most publick Place of that Town or Precinct, of every such stray, with their Age, Colour, natural and Artificial Marks, as near as

L

may

may be, within Ten Days after any such Cattle or Horses coming on his or
their Improv'd Land ; and for so doing, he or she shall be paid *Three Shillings*
by the Owner of such Cattle or Horses ; and in case of Refusal, to be Recovered by Action of Debt before any one Justice of Peace. And if an Owner
do not appear within Ten Days after such Publication, but afterward shall
claim any such Cattle or Horse, he shall pay all reasonable Charges, and also
the *Three Shillings* for publishing as aforesaid.

And be it Enacted by the Authority aforesaid, That if any Person whatsoever,
that has or hereafter shall have any Stray Cattle or Horse at or upon his or
their Improv'd Land, at any time between the sixteenth of *November* and
the first of *April*, and shall not publish and give notice thereof, in Writing set
up, as aforesaid, shall forfeit the Sum of *Twenty Shillings* to the Owner of
every such stray, to be recovered by Action of Debt before any one Justice
of the Peace of the County where such strays are taken up, any Law, Custom
or Usage to the contrary in any wise notwithstanding.

CHAP. LV.

An Act for Acknowledging and Recording of Deeds and Conveyances of Land within each respective County of this Province.

WHEREAS the Inhabitants of this Province are under great Inconveniences, and put to much trouble and Charges by reason there
is no Records of Deeds and Evidences of Lands kept within the respective
Counties thereof. For the Remedying of which,

*Be it Enacted by the Governour, Council and General Assembly, and it is hereby
Enacted by the Authority of the same*, That all Deeds, Conveyances and Evidences of Lands shall be acknowledged by the Grantor, or proved by one or
more of the Witnesses, either before any of the Justices of the Supream Court,
or one of her Majesties Council, or the Judge, or any two of the Justices of the
Inferiour Court of Common Pleas within their respective Counties, and in-
dorsed on the said Deeds, before they shall be Recorded.

And it is hereby further Enacted by the Authority aforesaid, That the Clerk
of the Common Pleas of each respective County within this Province, shall
keep a Book or Books, wherein all Deeds, Conveyances and Evidences of
Lands, lying within the same County, already made, or hereafter to be
made, shall, or may be Recorded by him, he giving sufficient Security, in
the Sum of five Hundred Pounds lawful Money of the said Province, for the
good and Faithful Discharge of the said Office, and that all Persons concerned
may have recourse to the said Records, as they shall have occasion, paying
the lawful Fees ; the Records of which Deeds, Conveyances and Evidences,
so acknowledged or proved, produced by the said Clerk in any Court shall be
as good, vallid and effectual in the Law, to all intents, constructions and purposes whatsoever, as if the Original were then and there produced and proved in Court, any Law, Custom or Usage to the contrary notwithstanding.

Provided always, and is it hereby further Enacted, That neither this Act nor
any Clause thereof shall be construed to debar the Secretary of this Province
from Recording or Registring any Deeds or Evidences relating to Titles of
Land

Land in his said Office, the said Deeds and Evidences being first proved, as above directed; which Register or Record shall be admitted to be good and lawful Evidence in any Court within this Province, any thing in this Act to the Contrary notwithstanding.

And be it further Enacted by the authority aforesaid, That in the County where the Secretarys Office is, or shall be for the future, kept, Deeds and Evidences relating to Titles of Land, shall only be Recorded in the said Secretary's Office.

CHAP. LVI.

An Act Encouraging the killing of Wolves, Panthers & Red Foxes.

BE *it Enacted by the Governour, Council and General Assembly, and by the Authority of the same,* That the Justices of the Peace and Free-holders chosen Yearly in each Town and Precinct of every County, for raising Money for the Building and Repairing of Goals and Court Houses, shall also raise such Sum and Sums of Money as shall be found necessary for defraying the Charge of killing of Wolves, Panthers and Red-Foxes, yearly, and shall also nominate and appoint Assessors and Collectors to assess and collect the same.

And be it Enacted by the Authority aforesaid, That every Person or Persons who shall kill any Wolf, Panther or Red Fox, and carry the Head of such Wolf, Panther or Red Fox to any Justice of the Peace, such Justice of the Peace shall give him or them a Certificate (after he has cut off the Ears thereof to the Collector, who upon sight thereof shall pay to the Person bringing such Certificate, the Sum and Sums of Money hereafter expressed.

And be it Enacted by the Authority aforesaid, That every Person or Persons who shall kill any Wolf, Panther or Red Fox, and procure a Certificate, as aforesaid, shall be paid by the respective Collector, for every Wolf or Panther, the Sum of Fifteen Shillings, and for every Whelp of Wolf or Panther, which cannot prey, the Sum of Four Shillings, and for every Red Fox *Two Shillings.*

And be it Enacted by the Authority aforesaid, That if any the Justices, Free-holders, Assessors, Collectors, or any others, shall refuse or Neglect to perform the Duty and Services required of them by this Act, such Refusers or Neglecters for each fault shall Forfeit the Sum of Forty Shillings, to be Levyed on the Goods and Chattels of the Defaulters, by the Constable having Warrant from any Justice of the Peace, one third part to the Informer, the other two thirds to be paid to the Collector, for and towards paying for killing of Wolves, Panthers and Red Foxes, as aforesaid.

And be it Enacted by the Authority aforesaid, That if any Person or Persons shall neglect or refuse to pay their Assessments to the Collector who shall be appointed by the said Justices and Free-holders, the same shall be Levyed by Warrant from any Justice of the Peace on the Goods and Chattles of such Delinquents, by the Constable, and immediately paid to the Collector. The Fees of the Assessors shall be *six Pence per Pound,* of the Justices and Freeholders, Twelve Pence *per Pound*; of the Collectors, Twelve Pence *per Pound,* and the Constable, Twelve Pence for each Distress. Provided, that all the
Money

Money mentioned in this Act, be, and is hereby declared to be according to the Queens Proclamation.

And be it further Enacted by the authority aforesaid, That all the Laws here-tofore made concerning Wolves, be and is hereby Repealed.

CHAP. LVII.

An Act for laying a Duty on Negro, Indian and Mullatto Slaves imported and brought into this Province.

BE it Enacted by the Governour, Council and General Assembly, and it is hereby Enacted by the Authority of the same, That every Person or Persons that shall hereafter Import or bring in, or cause to be imported or brought into this Province, any Negro, Indian or Mullatto Slave or Slaves, every such Person or Persons so importing or bringing in, or causing to be imported or brought in, such Slave or Slaves, shall enter with one of the Collectors of her Majesties Customs of this Province, every such Slave or Slaves, within Twenty Four Hours after such Slave or Slaves is so Imported, and pay the Sum of *Ten Pounds,* Money as appointed by her Majestys Proclamation, for each Slave so Imported, or give sufficient Security that the said Sum of *Ten Pounds,* Money aforesaid, shall be well and truly paid within three Months after such Slave or Slaves are so Imported, to the Collector or his Deputy of the District into which such Slave or Slaves shall be Imported, for the use of her Majesty, her Heirs and Successors, towards the Support of the Government of this Province.

And be it enacted by the Authority aforesaid, That if any Person or Persons shall neglect or refuse to enter with the Collector within twenty four hours, as aforesaid, and pay or secure to be paid for each Slave so imported, the Sum of *Ten Pounds,* Money as aforesaid, within the space of Three Months, as aforesaid, after the Importation of such Slave or Slaves, it shall and may be lawful for the Collector or his Deputy, or any other Person or Persons whatsoever, to take and apprehend the same Slave or Slaves so brought or Imported, and not entered according to the true intent and meaning of this Act, and deliver him, her or them to the Custody of the Sheriff of the County where they are apprehended, who shall bring him, her or them to the first Court of Record within the said County, which Court shall order the same to be sold by Publick Vendue to the highest Bidder, one Third part of which shall go to the Informer who shall prosecute the same to effect, the other two Thirds to her Majesty, her Heirs and Successors towards the Support of the Government of this Province, after paying the Charges of apprehending, keeping and Sale, such Sum of Money as shall be directed by the said Court.

Provided always, and be it further Enacted by the authority aforesaid, That this Act, nor any thing therein contained, shall be construed to debar any Master or Mistress of a Family, who shall come into and settle in this Province, to import along with them what number of Negro, Indian or Mullatto Slaves they shall think fit, for his or their own use and Service, and not for Sale, nor to debar any Traveller or Travellers to bring what number of such Slaves as

they

they think fit, to attend his, her or their Perfons, during their ftay in this Province, or to carry through the fame from any of the neighbouring Plantations.

And be it enacted by the authority aforefaid, That this Act fhall be in full Force from and after the firft Day of *June*, which fhall be in the Year of our Lord One Thoufand Seven Hundred and Sixteen; and no fooner, and from thence until the Full Term and Time of Seven Years next enfuing, and no longer.

Provided always, That any Perfon or Perfons that fhall bring into this Province, or caufe to be brought in, any Negro or other Slave or Slaves, from and after the firft Day of *June* next enfuing the publication hereof, and before the firft Day of *June*, One Thoufand Seven Hundred and Sixteen, and not directly from *Africa;* fhall pay for each Slave fo brought into this Province, the Sum of *Ten Pounds,* as aforefaid, excepting fuch as are excepted in this Act.

Provided always, and be it further Enacted, That this Act nor any thing therein contained, fhall be conftrued to debar any Perfon or Perfons poffeffing a Tract or Tracts of Land or Plantation within this Province, and having Negro, Indian or Mullatto Slaves in any of the neighbouring Provinces, to import and remove into this Province all or any the faid Negro, Indian or Mullatto Slaves, for his or their own Ufe and Service, to Cultivate and Improve the faid Tract or Tracts of Land and Plantation, and not for Sale, any thing to the Contrary notwithftanding.

CHAP. LXIV.

An Act that the Solemn Affirmation and Declaration of the People called Quakers, fhall be accepted Inftead of an Oath in the Ufual Form, and for Qualifying and Enabling the faid People to ferve as Jurors and to Execute any Office or Place of Truft or Profit within this Province.

WHereas in the *Weftern Divifion* of this Province the greateft Part of the Inhabitants are of thofe People called *Quakers,* who are and were for fome time paft, not admitted to ferve on Jurys, or to Exercife fome of the Places of Truft or Profit therein, becaufe they make a Religious Scruple of taking or giving an Oath in the ufual Form, by reafon of which the burden of ferving on Jurys, and in other Places of Truft, has lain upon the fmalleft part of the Inhabitants, as well to the great hurt and damage of that fmall part of the faid Inhabitants, as to the great Detriment and Inconvenience of the other more Numerous and Wealthy part of the faid Inhabitants, called *Quakers,* who have evinced their Loyalty to her Majefty by their readinefs to Support her Government. And whereas her Majefty has been gracioufly pleafed to direct, for the eafe of the faid People, called *Quakers,* That an Act be paft by the General Affembly of this Province of *New-Jerfey,* That the Solemn Affirmation and Declaration of the People called *Quakers,* fhall be accepted inftead of an Oath in the Ufual Form ; And has been further pleafed to Direct, That they might be admitted into Places of Truft or Profit. To Remidy therefore the Inconveniencys before mentioned, and in Obedience to her Majeftys Commands,

Be it Enacted by the Governour, Council and General Assembly, and by the Authority of the same, That from and after the Publication hereof, all *Quakers,* or reputed *Quakers,* within her Majestys Province of *New-Jersey,* may take an Affirmation in these words following. *viz.*

I A. B. *Do Declare in the Presence of Almighty GOD the Witness of the Truth of what I say.*

Which Affirmation shall be admitted, allowed and taken instead of an Oath in the usual Form, and is hereby Enacted and Declared to be of the same Force and Effect, to all Intents, Constructions and Purposes in all Courts of Justice, and in other places where, by Law, an Oath is required within this Province of *New-Jersey.* And the said *Quakers,* or reputed *Quakers,* being lawfully summoned, and having taken the Affirmation aforesaid, may and shall be admitted to serve on all Inquests, Grand and Petty Jurys (except on Petty Jurys in Causes Criminal) any Law, Custom or Usage to the contrary thereof in any wise notwithstanding.

Be it further Enacted by the Authority aforesaid, That all *Quakers* taking and signing the Declaration of Allegiance in the same Form which has been used by the said People in England, with a solemn Declaration for their true Discharge of their respective Trusts, as the case is, and as the nature of the Office may require, shall be, and are hereby declared to be capable (when Elected or Appointed) to serve in the General Assembly, or in any other Post, Place or Office of Trust or Profit within this Province.

And be it further Enacted by the Authority aforesaid, That if any Quaker or reputed Quakers taking the aforesaid Solemn Affirmation, and shall be Lawfully Convicted of having willfully, falsly and corruptly Affirmed and Declared any matter or thing, which, if the same had been in the usual Form of an Oath, would have amounted to willful Perjury, he, she or they, so offending, shall incur the same Penalties and Punishments as, by the Laws, Persons Convict of willfull Perjury are appointed to suffer.

And be it further Enacted by the Authority aforesaid, That this Act shall be and continue in force Eleven Years after Publication, and from thence to the end of next Sessions of Assembly, and no longer.

CHAP. LXV.

An Act for Erecting the upper Parts of the Western-Division of New-Jersey, into a County.

WHEREAS the Inhabitants of the upper parts of the said *Western-Division,* have, by their Petition, set forth, That for many years last past their frequent attending the several Courts held in *Burlington,* being at a very great distance from most of their Habitations, inconvenient and troublesom, as well as chargeable to the Inhabitants of the said Upper parts of the *Western-Division,* aforesaid, and to the great Detriment and Damage of the said Inhabitants. For the Removing of which Inconveniencys, and making of the said People more easie for the time to come, it is Humbly proposed, and prayed that it may be Enacted.   *And*

And be it Enacted by the Governour, Council and General Assembly, and by the Authority of the same, That all and singular the Lands, and upper parts of the said *Western-Division* of the Province of *New-Jersey,* lying northwards of or scituate above the Brook or Rivolet, commonly called *Assunpink,* be erected into a County, and it is hereby Erected into a County, Named, and from henceforth to be called, *The County of Hunterdon*; and the said Brook or Rivolet, commonly known and called by the Name of *Assunpink,* shall be the Boundary Line between the County of *Burlington,* and the said County of *Hunterdon.*

And be it Enacted by the Authority aforesaid, That the said County of *Hunterdon* shall have and enjoy all the Jurisdictions, Powers, Rights, Liberties, Priviledges and Immunities whatsoever, which any other County within the said Province of *New-Jersey* doth, may or ought of Right to Enjoy, excepting only the choice of Members, to Represent the said County of *Hunterdon,* in General Assembly, which liberty is hereby suspended until Her Majesties Pleasure be further known therein, or that it shall be otherwise ordered by Act of Assembly.

And be it enacted by the Authority aforesaid, That until such time that the said County of *Hunterdon* shall be allowed the Priviledge of chusing Representatives of their own to serve in General Assembly, it shall and may be lawful to and for the Free-holders of the said County being qualified according to law) from time to time, as occasion shall be, to appear at *Burlington,* or else-where in the said County of *Burlington,* and there to vote and help to elect and chuse Representatives for the said County of *Burlington,* after the same manner as formerly, before the making of this Act, they were accustomed to do; and their said Votes shall be as good, and of the same validity and effect, as if the Persons so Voting were properly Free-holders of the said County of *Burlington*; any Law, Custom or Usage to the contrary thereof notwithstanding.

And be it Enacted by the authority aforesaid, That all Taxes and Arrearages of such Taxes, that are already laid by Acts of General Assembly of this Province, which are already assessed or that are hereafter to be assessed, shall be assessed, collected and paid according to the Directions of the said Acts formerly past for that purpose, and that all Persons concerned therein shall be under the same Restrictions and Penalties as are exprest in the said Acts, to all Intents, Constructions and Purposes, as if this Act had never been past.

CHAP. LXVI.

An Act Enforcing the Observation of the Ordinance for Establishing Fees within this Province.

WHereas his Excellency the Governour hath, by and with the advice and Assistance of her Majestys Council, established an Ordinance for Regulating of Fees in these words following, *viz. An Ordinance for Regulating and Establishing Fees within this her Majestys Province of* Nova Cæsarea or New-Jersey, By his Excellency *Robert Hunter,* Esq; Captain General and Governour in Chief in and over the Provinces of *New-Jersey, New-York* and all the Territories and Tracts of Land depending thereon in *America*, and vice Admiral of the same, this tenth Day of *March* in the Thirteenth Year of the Reign of our Soveraign Lady *Anne*, by the Grace of God of *Great Britain*, *France* and *Ireland*, Queen, Defender of the Faith, &c. *Annoq; Domini* One Thousand Seven Hundred and Thirteen. His Excellency the Governour, by and with the advice and Assistance of Her Majestys Council for the said Province, and by virtue of the Power and Authority to him given by Her Majestys Letters Patents under the Great Seal of *Great Britain*, by and with the advice and assistance aforesaid, doth hereby Ordain and Declare, That from and after the Publication hereof, no Officer or other Person or Persons whatsoever, for any Service or Services by him or them to be done and performed in their respective Office or Offices, or for and in respect of his or their said Office or Offices, for any Fee, Perquisite or other Benefit or Reward, shall exact, demand or ask any greater or other Fee or Fees, Sum or Sums of Money, for the discharge of his or their several and respective Duty or Dutys, in his or their respective Offices, other than what herein after is allowed and established for the same; *viz.*

The Governours Fees, in Money according to her Majesties Proclamation.

Every Lisence for Marriage, *Ten Shillings.*
The Seal to every Letter of Administration, or Probate of a Will, *Nine Shillings.*
A Certificate or Register, that a Vessel was built and belongs to her Majesties Subjects, *Ten Shillings,*
A Certificate under the Governours Hand and Seal to go beyond Sea, *Ten Shillings.*
A Lisence to purchase Lands of the Indians, *Two Pounds Ten Shillings.*
A Bill of Health, *Twelve Shillings,*
Fixing the Seal to a Patent for a Town ship, *One Pound.*
The great Seal for a Confirmation or renewing a Patent, *Twelve Shillings.*
Every *Writ of Error* for removing a Cause before the Governour in Council, *Three Shillings.*
The first Rule in every Cause in Error, *Eight Shillings.*
Lisencing every Attorney, *One Pound.*

Justices Fees of the Supream Court.

All Civil Causes, to be paid on the first Rule, to the Judge that makes the Rule, *Six Shillings.*
All Causes Criminal, *Six Shillings.*
The allowance of every *Writ of Error*, *Certiorari*, *Habeas Corpus*, or any other Writ, *Three Shillings.*
Taking every Affidavit, *One Shilling.*
Every Supercedeas, *Six Shillings.*
Taking the Acknowledgment of a Deed, *Three Shillings:*
Taxing Costs, *Four Shillings.*
Taking Bail on a *Writ of Error*, or any other Writ, *Three Shillings.*

Attorney General Fees.

All Criminal Causes, &c. or Indictment found by the Grand Jury, *Fifteen Shillings.*

All

All Informations preferred by Order of the Governour in Council, if convicted, Fifteen Shillings.
All Capital Caufes, *One Pound Ten Shillings.*
Every *non vult ulterius profequi*, &c. *Ten Shillings.*

Secretarys Fees.

A Patent for a Town-fhip, *Three Pounds.*
  A Patent for Confirmation, wherein no new Grants are contained, *One Pound ten Shillings.*
Every Petition to the Governour in Council, and Order, *Four Shillings.*
Every Order in Council, and Copy, *Two Shillings.*
Every Certificate under the Governours Hand and Seal, Counter-figned by the Secretary, *Three Shillings.*
A Bill of Health, *Four Shillings.*
Entring Deeds and other things on Record, the firft Sheet containing twenty four Lines, and eight Words to a Line, *One Shilling and Nine Pence.*
Every fheet more, *One fhilling.*
Every Copy of the fame, and of all other Papers whatfoever, out of the Office, every fheet containing as aforefaid, *Seven Pence.*
Every Commiffion for a Place of Profit, *Nine fhillings.*
Every Bond taken in the Office, *Two fhillings and fix Pence.*

Fees of the Prerogative Office.

FOr Engroffing a Will and Probate, to be done in Parchment, for each fheet containing twenty four Lines, and eight Words to a Line, *One Shilling and Six Pence.*
Taking the Depofitions to a Will, and Recording the Will, each fheet containing twenty four Lines, and eight Words to a Line, *One Shilling.*
Swearing or Attefting the Witneffes and Executor, for each, *Nine Pence.*
Drawing every Fiat or order for Adminiftration, and for Swearing or Attefting the Adminiftrator, *Three Shillings.*
  Engrofing the Letters of Adminiftration, each fheet containing Twenty four Lines, and eight Words to a Line, *One Shilling.*
Recording the fame, per Sheet, *One Shilling.*
Drawing the Adminiftration Bond, *Two Shillings and fix Pence.*
Filing the original Will, *Nine Pence.*
Filing the Fiat of Adminiftration, *Nine Pence.*
Recording an Inventory, *per* fheet, each fheet to contain twenty four Lines, and eight Words to a Line, *One Shilling.*
Filing the Inventory, and fwearing the Executor, *One Shilling and fix Pence.*
Entring a Caveat, *One Shilling.*
Every Quietus, *Nine Pence.*
Recording the fame, *Nine Pence.*
Auditing all Accompts of Adminiftrators and Executors, *One Shilling.*
Drawing and fetting up Notice, in order to their paffing their Accompts, *One Shilling.*
Every Lifence of Marriage, *nine Shillings.*

Clerk of the Supream Court.

SEaling every *Capias* or any other Writ, *One Shilling.*
  Filing every Indictment, *Six Pence.*
Entering every Action, *Nine Pence.*
Copying every Indictment, Declaration, Plea, &c. twenty four lines to a
                   Sheet

Sheet, and Eight words to a line, *Nine Pence.*
Every Copy of a Plea, Replication, or any other Process, *six Pence.*
Entring every Appearance of the Defendant, *six Pence.*
Taking and entring every Verdict, *six Pence.*
Entring every Judgment, *six Pence.*
Reading every Evidence, *six Pence.*
Every Rule of Court, *Nine Pence.*　　Copy thereof, *six Pence.*
Reading a Petition and Order thereon, *Nine Pence.*
Copy thereof, *six Pence.*
With-drawing an Action, Discontinuance or Entring a *non Prosequi*, *Nine Pence.*
For every Recognizance, *One Shilling.*
Searching the Records, *Nine Pence.*
Filing the Roll for every Action, *One shilling.*
Swearing every Jury and Constable, *Three Shillings.*
Discharging by Proclamation, *One shilling.*

Sheriffs Fees in all Courts.

SErving a Writ or Capias, taking into Custody, without any pretence of Riding, *Ten shilling.*
Returning the Writ. *Nine Pence.*
Taking a Prisoner into Custody by Order of the Court or Justice of the Peace, *Four Shillings.*
Discharging the same, *Nine Pence.*
Serving a *Venire Facias*, and Return, *Four shillings and six Pence.*
Serving every Execution under Fifty Pounds, *six Shillings.*
All above Fifty Pounds, *Three Pence per Pound.*
Every Writ of Possession and Return, *One Pound.*
Every *scire Facias* and Return, *Two shillings and six Pence.*
For taking every Bail Bond, *One shilling.*
Victualing every Prisoner, *per Day six Pence.*
Every Writ of Inquiry and Return, *Fifteen shillings.*

Justices Fees in or out of Sessions.

EVery Warrant of appearance, *One shilling.*
Taking every Recognizance, *Eighteen Pence.*
A Lisence for Selling Drink, *Four Shillings and six Pence.*
The Justices Clerk, for a Bond for the same, *Eighteen Pence.*
A Pass, *Ten Pence.*
A Mittimus, *One shilling.*
Taking examinations, each Sheet containing twenty four Lines, and Eight words in a line, *One shilling.*
Every Oath or Attestation, *six Pence.*
Actions Tryed in the Sessions, each Action *three Shillings.*

Judge and Justices Fees in the Court of Common Pleas.

ACknowledging every Deed, and endorsing the same, *Two Shillings*
All Actions tryed, to the Bench, *Three Shillings.*
Any Action called, where there is a Rule made in the Cause, and not tryed, *Eighteen Pence.*
Taking special Bail, to the Judge, *Eighteen Pence.*
Settling and allowing every Bill of Costs, *One Shilling.*
Allowance of every Writ of Error, *One Shilling and Eight Pence.*

Actions

Actions of Forty Shillings or under.

A Summons, *Six Pence.*
A Warrant to take into Custody, *One Shilling.*
A Judgment, *Nine Pence.*
Administring every Oath, *Four Pence.*
A Summons for Evidence, *six Pence.*
Every Execution, *One Shilling.*
Every Evidence subpœna'd, and attending, *Two Shillings per Day,* and so in Proportion for a longer or shorter time.

Fees for the Clerk of Sessions and common Pleas.

DRawing a *Capias,* or any other Writ, *One Shilling.*
Sealing the same, *One Shilling.*
Entring every Action, *six Pence.*
Filing a Declaration Plea, Rejoynder, &c. *six Pence.*
Copy of a Declaration, or any other Pleadings, for each sheet containing twenty four Lines, and eight Words to a Line, *Nine Pence.*
Every *venire facias, One shilling.*
Sealing every Subpœna, each Writ not exceeding four Names, *Nine Pence.*
Entring the Defendants appearance, *six Pence.*
Entring Plea, *non vult, six Pence.*
Entring every Verdict, *six Pence.*
Entring every Judgment, *One Shilling.*
Entring every Rule or Order of Court, *six Pence.*
Reading every Petition and order thereon, *Nine Pence.*
Entring every *non pros. Retraxit,* Discontinuance, &c. *six Pence.*
Calling and swearing the Jury and Constable, *One Shilling* and *six Pence.*
Every Evidence sworn or attested, *Four Pence.*
Entring every allowance of *Habeas Corpus, Writ of Error,* &c. *One Shilling.*
Every Recognizance taken in Court, *One Shilling.*
Copy of every Rule of Court, *six Pence.*
Recording every Deed for the first sheet containing twenty four Lines, and eight Words to a Line, *One Shilling* and *Nine Pence.*
Every sheet more, *nine Pence.*
Copy of the same, each sheet, *Seven Pence.*
Searching the Records, *nine Pence.*
Recording Ear Marks, *six Pence.*
Discharging by Proclamation, *One Shilling.*

Jurys Fees.

IN all causes tryed, *Twelve Shillings.*
For a Writ of Enquiry. *Twelve Pence per Man.*
Jurys Fees in every cause, when the Jury is summoned and the cause not tryed, half Fees *six Shillings.*

Cryers Fees.

CAlling every Action, every Term not exceeding three Terms, *Eight Pence.*
Calling the Jury in each cause, *Eight Pence.*
Calling every Evidence. *Three Pence.*
Every one discharged by Proclamation, *six Pence.*

Coroners

Coroners Fees.

VIewing a Dead Body, *Twelve Shillings.*
  A Warrant to summon the Inqueſt, *Two Shillings.*
Swearing or atteſting the Jury, *Two Shillings.*
Swearing or Atteſting every Witneſs, *Four Pence.*
Drawing and Returning the Inquiſition, *ſix Shillings.*
Executing every Proceſs, *Ten ſhillings.*
Returning every Writ, *nine Pence.*
Serving every Venire and Return, *Four ſhillings* and *ſix Pence.*
Every man on the Inqueſt, *One ſhilling.*
Taking every Bail Bond, *One ſhilling.*

Practitioners of the Law.

MAking out every Proceſs, Writ or Capias, *Two ſhillings and ſix Pence.*
  Drawing every Declaration, *Five ſhillings.*
Every Copy of a Declaration ſerved on a Perſon committed for want of
  Bail, or in Ejectment, *Two ſhillings.*
Drawing every Affidavit, *One ſhilling.*
Every Common Plea, Replication or Rejoynder, &c. *One ſhilling.*
Every Term Fee, *Six ſhillings.*
Drawing every Special Plea, Replication, Rejoynder, &c. twenty four Lines
  to a Sheet, and eight words to a Line, *Eighteen Pence* for each ſheet.
Entring Declaration, Plea, &c. on the Roll, *per ſheet,* as aboveſaid, *Eigh-
  teen Pence.*
Every Warrant of Attorney, *nine Pence.*
Drawing every Breviate, *three ſhillings.*
Every Continuance of the Cauſe after Iſſue, *One ſhilling.*
Drawing up the Judgment, and Entring the ſame on the Roll, *Five ſhillings.*
Every ſpecial Motion, allowed to be a motion in *Weſtminſter Hall,* *ſix Shillings.*
Arguing a Demurer or ſpecial Verdict, *Fourteen ſhillings.*
Fee upon every Tryal, *Fourteen ſhillings.*
Copy and Service of every Rule of Court, *Two Shillings* and *ſix Pence.*
Drawing every Bail peice, and attending the Judge, *Three Shillings* and *ſix
  Pence.*
Every Ticket for a Subpœna, *ſix Pence.*

Conſtables Fees.

SErving every Warrant or Summons, *One ſhilling.*
  Serving every Execution, *Eighteen Pence.*

Serjeant at Arms.

SErving every Order, *ſeven ſhillings.*
  Travelling Charges *per Mile,* *ſix Pence.*
Taking every Perſon committed into Cuſtody *Two ſhilling and ſix pence.*
Every Days Attendance on any Perſon after Commitment, *Two Shillings.*

Fees due on the Removal of any Cauſe out of the Supream Court to the Governour in Council.

TO the Chief Juſtice or ſecond Judge, for making the Return, ſealing the
  ſame, and attending with the Record and tranſcript, and examining
    the

the fame in Council, and returning the Record into the Supream Court, *Three Pounds.*

To the Clerk of the Council.

Aking out the Fiat for the great Seal, to be affixed to every Writ of Error, filing the fame, Sealing the Writ, and finding Wax and Parchment, *Three Shillings and fix Pence.*

Entring the Caufe on the Council Book, and making out the Docquet for the Governour, *Nine Pence.*

Transcribing the Record in Parchment, twenty four Lines to a Sheet, and Eight Words to a Line, *One Shilling and fix Pence.*

Examining the Record in Council, *One Shilling.*

Entering the Plantiff and Defendants appearance, *Nine Pence.*

Every Rule made in the Caufe, and Copy, *Two Shillings.*

Entring Judgment on the Minutes, and Copy, *Two Shillings.*

Entring every *non profequi, Difcontinuance,* &c. *Two Shillings.*

Filing the Errors, and all other Pleadings or Writs of Error, each *Nine Pence.*

All other Writs, the fame Fees as on a Writ of Error.

Making out Paper Books for the Governour, and the Gentlemen of the Council, each fheet containing twenty four Lines, and eight words to a line, *One Shilling.*

He Practitioners of the Laws Fees to be the fame as in the Supream Court.

To the Clerk of the Council for Reading every private Bill, each time, *Three Shillings.*

Attending the Committee each time, *Three Shillings.*

Engrofing the Bill in Parchment, and affixing the Seal, per Sheet, *Three Shillings.*

To the Speaker.

FOr every Private Bill, *One Pound.*

To the Clerk of the Affembly.

REading the Petition, and entring the Order or Anfwer thereof in the Minutes, each time, *One Shilling.*

Copy of each Order, *fix Pence.*

Reading a private Bill, each time, *One Shilling.*

Engrofing every Bill in Parchment, per fheet, twenty four Lines to a fheet, and Eight Words to a line, *One Shilling and fix Pence.*

The Door-keeper.

EVery Private Petition, *One Shilling.*
Tending the Houfe *per Diem, Two Shillings and fix Pence.*

For the Collectors of the Customs.

ENtring every Ship or other Veſſel of Sixty Tuns and upwards, inwards and outwards,   *One Shilling and ſix Pence.*

Liſence to load or unload,   *One Shilling and ſix Pence.*

A Bill of ſtore,   *Eighteen Pence.*

A Certificate of Goods Landing, where Bond is given abroad,   *Eighteen Pence.*

For a Clearing,   *ſix Shillings.*

Entring all Veſſels under Sixty Tuns, for entring in or out,   *Nine Pence.*

Liſence to load or unload,   *Four pence half penny.*

A Bill of ſtore,   *Nine pence.*

A Certificate,   *Nine Pence.*

Clearing in or out,   *Two Shillings.*

A Cocket after clearing,   *One Shilling and a penny half penny.*

The ſight of every Certificate, and Bond given, and entring them in the Queens Books,   *Nine pence.*

Cancelling a Bond, filing a Certifitate, and making it returned in the Queens Books,   *Nine pence.*

Regiſtring a Veſſel,   *ſix Shillings.*

Endorſing the Regiſter,   *Nine pence.*

Every Bond for Ennumerated Goods,   *One ſhilling and ſix pence.*

And it is hereby further ordained and Declared by the authority aforeſaid, That all and every Officer and Officers, Perſon and Perſons whatſoever that ſhall at any time hereafter exact, demand or ask any greater or other Fee or Fees for or in reſpect of any of the Services herein before mentioned, other then ſuch which herein now are, or which at any time hereafter ſhall by the Authority aforeſaid be eſtabliſhed and allowed for them, ſhall be deprived of his or their ſaid Office or Offices, and be liable to ſuch other Fines and Penalties as the utmoſt Rigour of the Law can inflict.

And it is further Ordained and declared by the Authority aforeſaid, That the ſaid Chief Juſtice and Judges of the Supream Court of this Province, all Juſtices of the ſeveral Courts of Seſſions of the Peace, and all Judges of the Inferiour Courts of Common Pleas within the ſeveral Counties of this Province, do tax and allow all Bills of Coſts accruing within their ſeveral Courts, for Services hereafter to be done, according to the Table of Fees herein before eſtabliſhed, and not otherwiſe, as they will anſwer the ſame at their Peril, any Law, Uſage or Cuſtom in their reſpective Courts, for Services hereafter to be done, according to the Table of Fees herein before eſtabliſhed, and not otherwiſe, as they will anſwer the ſame at their Peril, any Law, Uſage or Cuſtom in their reſpective Courts to the Contrary thereof in any wiſe Notwithſtanding. Given by his Excellency *Robert Hunter,* Eſq; Captain General and Governour in Chief in and over the Province of *Nova Caeſarea* or *New-Jerſey, New-York,* and all the Territories and Tracts of Land depending thereon in America, and vice Admiral of the ſame, in Council, at the Town of *Burlington* in the ſaid Province, this tenth Day of *March, Annoq; Domini* One Thouſand Seven Hundred and Thirteen, and in the thirteenth Year of her Majeſtys Reign.

For the betrer enforcing the Obfervation of the above recited Ordinance.

BE it *Enacted by the Governour, Council and General Affembly, and by the Authority of the fame,* That all and every Practifer of the Law, who fhall Refufe to ferve for or upon account of the Fees mentioned in this Ordinance and Act, fhall be and are hereby declared uncapable of practifing the Law in any Court of Judicature within this Province.

And be it further Enacted by the authority aforefaid, That all Contracts, Promifes and Agreements made contrary to the true intent and meaning of this Ordinance and Act, and all Security thereupon given, fhall be Null, void and of none effect.

And be it enacted by the authority aforefaid, That if any Attorneys, or other Perfon, fhall at any time fplit or divide Caufes, and bring feveral Actions where one might have been fufficient, that then no more Fees be allowed in the faid feveral Caufes than ought to have been allowed if one Action only had been brought for the fame.

And be it enacted by the authority aforefaid, That if any Practitioner of the Law fhall take or exact any more or greater Fees than is limited in this Ordinance and Act, fhall forfeit the Sum of *Fifty Pounds,* Money according to Her Majeftys Proclamation, and forever be Debarred from Practifing in any Court within this Colony, one half of which Forfeiture to Her Majefty, Her Heirs and Succeffors, towards Support of the Government of this Province, the other half to any Perfon or Perfons that fhall fue for the fame in any Court of Record within this Colony.

And be it enacted by the Authority aforefaid, That if any Perfon or Perfons Whatfoever fhall exact or take any greater Fees of any Perfon or Perfons for his or their fervice, in the Execution of his or their Office refpectively, than is afcertained in this Ordinance and Act, for any of the Services mentioned in the faid Ordinance and Act, all or any fuch Perfon or Perfons fo offending fhall for every fuch offence forfeit *Fifty Pounds* Money aforefaid, to be recovered and applyed as aforefaid.

An Ordinance for eftablifhing Courts of Judicature within the Province of *New-Jerfey.*

By his Excellency Robert Hunter, *Efq; Captain General and Governour in Chief in and over the Provinces of* New-Jerfey, New-York, *and all the Territories and Tracts of Land depending thereon in* America, *and Vice Admiral of the fame, &c. in Council.*

HIs Excellency the Governour, by virtue of the Power and Authority to him given by her Majefties Letters Patents under the great Seal of *Great Britain,* by and with the Advice and Affiftance of her Majefties Coun-

cil

cil for the said Province of *Nova Cesarea*, doth hereby Ordain and Impower every Justice of the Peace residing within any Town or County within this Province of *Nova Cesarea* to have Cognizance of all Causes and Cases of Debt or Trespass, to the value of *Forty Shillings* or under, all which Causes and Cases shall and may be heard, tryed and finally Determined, without a Jury, by any of the said Justices of the Peace, as aforesaid, excepting such Cases where Titles of Land are or may be any way concerned.

And be it ordained by the Authority aforesaid, That the Process of Warning against a Free-holder or Inhabitant, shall be by Summons under the Hand of any of the said Justices of the Peace, directed to the Constable of the Town or Precinct, or to any deputed by him, where the party complained against does dwell or reside, which Summons shall be served upon the Person or left at the House or place of abode of the Defendant, four Days at least before the Time appointed for the hearing of the Plaint. And in case the Defendant does not appear at the Time appointed, the Justice granting such Summons may proceed to hear such Cause or Causes, and Determine the same in the Defendants absence (unless the said Justice, for good reason see cause to the contrary) and grant Execution thereupon, directed to the said Constable, or his Deputy, to be levyed upon the Defendants Goods and Chattels, or for want thereof upon the Person of the Defendant, which he is hereby directed and required to execute accordingly.

And be it ordained by the Authority aforesaid, That the Process against an Itinerant Person, Inmate or Forreigner, shall be by Warrant from any one Justice of the Peace, to be served by any Constable or his Deputy, within that County, who shall, by virtue thereof, arrest the Party, and him safely keep till he be carryed before the said Justice, who shall and may immediately Hear, Try and finally Determine all such Causes and Cases of Debt and Trespass, as aforesaid, to the value of *Forty Shillings*, or under, by awarding Judgment and Execution. And if payment be not immediately made, the Constable shall deliver the said Party to the Sheriff of that County, who is hereby required to take him into Custody, and him safely keep till Payment be made of the same, with Charges.

Provided always, and it is hereby further Ordained, That an Appeal to the Justices of the same County at the next General Court of Sessions of the Peace held, shall be allowed for any Sum upwards of *Twenty Shillings* in all Causes and Cases whatsoever.

And it is hereby further Ordained by the Authority aforesaid, That there shall be kept and holden a *Court of Common Pleas* in each respective County within this Province of *New-Jersey* aforesaid, at such places where the General Courts of *Sessions of the Peace* are usually held and kept, to begin immediately after, or the next Day after the *General Sessions of the Peace* ends and terminates, and then to hold and continue for any time, not exceeding Three Days. Which several and respective Courts of *Common Pleas* shall have Power and Jurisdiction to Hear, Try, and finally Determine all Actions or Causes of Action, and all Matters and Things Tryable at Common Law, of what nature and kind soever.

And it is hereby further Ordained by the Authority aforesaid, That the General Courts of Sessions of the Peace shall be held and kept in each respective County within this Province, at the Times and Places herein after-mentioned, That is to say,

The

The firſt Court of Seſſions to be held after the Publication hereof, at the Times and Places to which the ſaid Courts were laſt adjourned, and thereafter yearly and every year,

For the County of *Bergin*, at the Town of *Bergin*, until the Court-Houſe and Goal, for ſaid County be built, on the firſt Tueſdays in *February* and *Auguſt*, and the third Tueſdays in *April* and *October*, and there-after at the Court-houſe of the ſaid County on the Days and Times before-mentioned.

For the County of *Eſſex*, at *Newark*, the ſecond Tueſday of *February* and *Auguſt*; and the fourth Tueſday in *April* and *October*.

For the County of *Middleſex* and *Sommerſet*, at the Town of *Perth-Amboy*, the third Tueſday of *February*, *May*, *Auguſt* and *November.*

For the County of *Monmouth*, at *Shrewsberry*, until the Court-houſe and Goal for ſaid County be built, and there-after at the Court-houſe in the ſaid County, on the fourth Tueſday of *February*, *May*, *Auguſt* and *November.*

For the County of *Hunterdon*, at *Maidenhead* the firſt Tueſday in *June* and *December.* And at *Hopewell* the firſt Tueſday in *March* and *September*, until the Court-houſe and Goal for ſaid County be built, and then after at the Court-houſe of ſaid County only.

For the County of *Burlington* at the Town of *Burlington*, on the ſecond Tueſday of *March*, *June*, *September*, and *December.*

For the County of *Glouceſter*, at the Town of *Glouceſter*, on the third Tueſday in *March*, *June*, *September*, and *December.*

For the County of *Salem*, at the Town of *Salem* on the fourth Tueſday in *March*, *June*, *September*, and *December.*

For the County of *Cape-May* at *Cape-May*, the firſt Tueſday in *April*, *July*, *October* and *January.*

Which General Court of Seſſions of the Peace ſhall hold and continue for any time not exceeding two Days.

And it is hereby further ordained by the authority aforeſaid, That there ſhall be a *Supream Court* of Judicature held and kept at *Burlington* on the firſt Tueſday of *May* next, to which Time and Place it was laſt adjourned, and on the firſt Tueſday of *November.* And yearly and every year at *Burlington* on the firſt Tueſdays of *May* and *November.* And yearly and every year at *Perth-Amboy* on the ſecond Tueſday of *May*, and ſecond Tueſday of *November.*

Which Supream Court ſhall continue for any Term not exceeding five days, and is hereby fully Impowered to have Cognizance of all Pleas, Civil, Criminal and Mixt, as fully and amply to all intents and purpoſes whatſoever, as the Courts of *Queens Bench, Common Pleas and Exchequer* in *England* have or ought to have. In and to which Court all and every Perſon and Perſons whatſoever, ſhall and may commence and proſecute any Action or Suit, the real Debt or Damages thereof being *Twenty Pounds*, or upwards, and ſhall or may by *Certiorari, Habeas Corpus, Writ of Error,* or any other lawful Writ, remove out of any of the ſaid reſpective Courts of Seſſions of the Peace, any Information, Preſentment or Indictment there depending, or Judgment thereupon given, or to be given in any Criminal Matter whatſoever, cognizeable before them, or any of them, as alſo all Actions, Pleas or Suits, Real, Perſonal or Mixt, depending in any of the ſaid Courts of Common Pleas, and all Judgments thereupon given, or to be given. *Provi-*

P   *ded*

ded always, That the Action or Suit depending, or Judgment given be of the Value of *Twenty Pounds,* or upwards, or that the same be of, for or concerning the Right or Title of any Lands, Tenements and Hereditaments whatsoever.

And it is hereby further Ordained and declared by the Authority aforesaid, That the Office of the said *Supream Court* of Judicature shall be kept by the Clerk thereof, or his sufficient Deputy, at *Perth-Amboy* aforesaid, for the *Eastern,* and at *Burlington* aforesaid for the *Western-Division,* under the Penalty of Deprivation, and such other Fines as the Law can inflict. Out of which Office of *Perth-Amboy* and *Burlington* aforesaid, all Process shall issue for each Division respectively, under the Test of the Chief Justice of said Province, for the time being; and unto which Office all Returns shall be made respectively.

And it is hereby further Ordained and Declared by the authority aforesaid, That all and every the Justices and Judges of the said several Courts are sufficiently Impowered and Authorized to make, order and establish such Rules and Orders for the more Regular Proceedings in the said Courts, as Justices and Judges in *England* may lawfully do, any former Ordinance or Establishment of Courts of Judicature to the contrary hereof in any ways notwithstanding; All which are from hence-forward declared to be Null and Void by these Presents.

Given under my Hand and Seal in Horsumus *the* 17*th Day of* April, *in the Thirteenth year of her Majesties Reign,* Annoq; Domini 1714.

Ro. Hunter.

CHAP. LXVII.

An Act to Enable *Thomas Gordon,* Esq; Treasurer of this Province, to pay the Sum of Nine Hundred Ninety Nine Pounds thirteen Shillings and three Pence, towards the Support of the Government, and for Discharging the said Treasurer thereof.

WHereas upon strict Examination of the Accounts of the said *Thomas Gordon,* Treasurer of this Province, it appears that there is remaining in his hands the Sum of Nine Hundred Ninty Nine *Pounds* Thirteen *Shillings* and Three *Pence,* Money of the value appointed by the Queens Proclamation, being the Ballance of Twelve Thousand five hundred Ounces of Plate, lately raised by Act of General Assembly of this Province, in Bills of Credit, *Be it therefore Enacted by the Governour, Council and General Assembly, and by the Authority of the same,* That the said *Thomas Gordon,* Esq; Treasurer of this Province, shall Pay unto his Excellency the Governour and other Officers of this Province, pursuant to such Warrants as shall be unto him directed, signed by the Governour in Council, the said full and just Sum of Nine hundred Ninty nine *Pounds* Thirteen *Shillings* and three *Pence,* Money aforesaid, for the Support of this Her Majesties Government from the twenty third day of *June,* One thousand Seven hundred and twelve, to the twenty third Day of *September,* One thousand Seven hundred and thirteen. *And*

And be it enacted by the authority aforesaid, That upon the said *Thomas Gordon,* Esq; his paying the Sum of Nine hundred ninty nine *Pounds* thirteen *Shillings* and three *Pence,* according to the Warrants aforesaid, he the said *Thomas Gordon,* his Heirs, Executors and Administrators, and his and their Lands and Tenements, Goods and Chattles are and shall be forever hereafter acquited, exonorated and discharged of and from the Twelve thousand Five hundred Ounces of Plate aforesaid.

The following Acts were also passed at the same time.

An Act for the Support of this her Majestys Government of *Nova Cæsaria* or N. *Jersey* for two years, (25050 *l.*)

An Act for Collecting the Arrearages of Taxes since the year 1708.

An Act to Continue and Revive the Currency of Bills of Credit appointed to be sunk in the years 1712, and 1713. and to enable *Thomas Gordon,* Esq; Treasurer of this Province, or the Treasurer for the time being, to pay in the said Bills of Credit the several Sums of Money due from the Government to several Persons having Warrants or proper Orders for the same; And also to enable the said Treasurer to pay the said Bills in Exchange for the Bills of Credit issued out on the first Expedition against *Canada.*

An Act for Reviving and Continuing the Courts of Sessions and Common Pleas in the County of *Cape-May,* with the Proceedings of the same.

Private Acts.

An Act to enable the Executors of *Miles Forster,* late of *Perth-Amboy* in the County of *Middlesex,* Merchant, deceased, to sell Lands to pay Debts and Legacys, according to the last Will and Testament of the said deceased.

An Act to Naturalize *Peter Bard,* native of *France.*

An Act to Naturalize *Stephen Chalmas* and *Peter Romuer,* Natives of *France.*

An Act to enable *Thomas Lambert* (one of the Principal Creditors of *John Easton,* late of *Nottingham* in the County of *Burlington,* deceased, and Administrator of the Goods, Rights and Credits of the Estate or Estates of Inheritance within the County of *Burlington* and the County of *Salem* in the Province of *Nova Cæsaria,* for and towards the payment of his just Debts.

An Act to enable *Sarah Edwards* Sole Executrix and late widdow of *Robert Edwards,* deceased, by and with the consent of *William Cuttler,* her present Husband, to make a good and lawful Conveyance of a Tract of Land sold by the said *Robert Edwards* in his Life time to one *Tunis Tuns,* by Articles of Agreement, and to receive the Remainder of the Money due for the said Land, according to the last Will and Testament of the said *Robert Edwards,* deceased.

An Act to enable certain Trustees to Sell and Dispose of a small Estate of Inheritance in the County of *Burlington.*

An Act for Confirmation of a Patent granted by his Excellencys *Robert Hunter,* Esq; Capt. General and Governour in Chief of *New-Jersey,* and *New-York,* and all the Territories and Tracts of Land depending thereon in *America,* and Vice-Admiral of the same.

An Act to enable the Owners of the Meadows and Marshes adjoyning to and on both sides of *Maneton Creek,* to stop out the Tide from overflowing them.

An Act for enabling the Owners of the Meadows adjoyning to the Lands of *Sarah Mickle, John Dole, John Kaighn, Tobias Griscomb,* &c. adjacent to *Delaware River* in the Township of *Newtown* and County of *Gloucester,* to stop the Tide from overflowing them.

An Act to enable the Owners of the Meadows and Marshes belonging to the Town of *Salem,* to keep out the Tides from overflowing the same.

The following Act was passed in January 1716.

An Act to Naturalize *Jacob Arents* and his three Children, to wit, *Nicholas Arents, Mary Arents* and *Margaret Arents.*

WHereas *Jacob Arents* and his three Children, to wit, *Nicholas Arents, Mary Arents,* and *Margaret Arents* were born under the Allegiance of the Emperor of *Germany,* and being of the *Protestant Religion,* have Transported themselves and Effects unto his Majestys Colony or Plantation of *Nova Caesaria* or *New-Jersey* in *America*; and duly considering the happy Constitution of this Province, being govern'd as near as may be to the Laws of *England*; and the said *Jacob Arents* and his three Children, *Nicholas Arents, Mary Arents,* and *Margaret Arents* being desirous to be made partakers of those Advantages and Priviledges which the natural born Subjects thereof do enjoy, the said *Jacob* has prayed leave by his humble Petition, to bring in a Bill to this Assembly, for Naturalizing himself and his three Children.   And whereas the Increase of People is the means of advancing the Wealth and strength of any Government, and the encouragement hereby given to the said *Jacob Arents* and his three Children, *Nicholas Arents, Mary Arents* and *Margaret Arents* may induce others to transport themselves and Estates into this Colony, *Be it therefore Enacted by the Governour, Council and General Assembly, and by the Authority of the same,* That the said *Jacob Arents* and his three Children, *Nicholas Arents, Mary Arents* and *Margaret Arents* be made, and are hereby, they and each of them declared to be his Majesties Natural born Subjects; and for all times hereafter shall be deemed, adjudged and taken to be his Majesties Natural born Subjects of this Province, to all intents, constructions and purposes whatsoever, as fully and amply as if they had been born, or were born within this Province of *New-Jersey*; and that the said *Jacob Arents* and his three Children, *Nicholas Arents, Mary Arents* and *Margaret Arents* may take, receive, enjoy and be entituled to all the Rights, Priviledges and Advantages of natural born Subjects, as fully to all intents, constructions and purposes whatsoever, as any of his Majesties Natural born Subjects of this Colony, can, do or ought to enjoy, by virtue of their being his Majesties natural born Subjects of this Province.

Acts paſſed by the General Aſſembly

of the Province of *New-Jerſey*, in *January* 1716. in the Third Year of the Reign of our Soveraign Lord *George*, by the Grace of God, King of *Great Britain*, *France* and *Ireland*, &c.

An Act for the more Regular Chuſing and Electing Aſſeſſors and Collectors in the reſpective Towns and Counties in this Province.

TO the end that the Publick and neceſſary Charge in each County within this Province may be duly Defrayed, *Be it Enacted by the Governour, Council and General Aſſembly, and it is hereby Enacted by the Authority of the ſame*, That the Freeholders and Inhabitants, Houſe-holders of every Town, Diviſion, Precinct and Diſtrict within the ſeveral Counties of this Province, ſhall meet together on the Second Tueſday in *March*, yearly and every Year, and by Plurality of Voices Chuſe one Aſſeſſor and one Collector for each Town, Diviſion, Precinct or Diſtrict within this Province; to be Aſſeſſor and Collector for the Town, Diviſion, Precinct or Diſtrict for which they are choſen for the enſuing year; which ſaid Aſſeſſors and Collectors ſhall within Ten Days, after choſen, repair to ſome Juſtice of the Peace within the County, and take an Oath, or Atteſtation, if *Quakers*, for the True performing of their Office. And if it ſhould ſo happen that the Free-holders of any Town, Diviſion, Precinct or Diſtrict within any of the Counties of this Province ſhould neglect or refuſe to meet and chuſe one Aſſeſſor and one Collector, according to the Intention of this Act, then the Conſtable or Conſtables of the Town, Diviſion, Precinct or Diſtrict ſo neglecting or refuſing, ſhall give notice to the Juſtics of the Peace of the ſaid Counties, or any three of them; one whereof to be of the *Quorum*, who ſhall and may, and they are hereby Required and Commanded forth-with to nominate and appoint one Aſſeſſor and one Collector for the ſaid Town, Diviſion Precinct or Diſtrict ſo neglecting or refuſing ; which Aſſeſſor and Collector ſo choſen and appointed, ſhall be under the ſame Regulations, and ſubject to the ſame Penalties as the Aſſeſſors and Collectors, choſen, as aforeſaid, are ſubject to.

And be it further Enacted by the Authority aforeſaid, That when a Provincial Tax ſhall be raiſed by Act of Aſſembly of this Province, That every Aſſeſſor, choſen as aforeſaid, ſhall go to all the Inhabitants in the Town, Diviſion, Precinct or Diſtrict for which he is choſen ſeverally and reſpectively, and take an exact Account of what every Perſon is poſſeſſed of, that is Rateable, and ſhall meet together in the moſt convenient Place in the ſeveral Counties, and aſſeſs the Inhabitants Equally, according to the Rateable Eſtates they hold, to make up the Quota appointed to be raiſed on every County, ſeverally, by Act of Aſſembly, within the Time or Times limited by the ſaid Act. And when the Inhabitants are ſo aſſeſſed, the Aſſeſſor of every Town, Diviſion, Precinct or Diſtrict ſhall make a

B

Liſt

List of every Persons Tax as Rated, and deliver one to the Collector of the County appointed by Act of General Assembly, and one to the Collector of each Town, Division, Precinct or District, which said Collector shall gather in the said Tax, and pay it to the Collector of each respective County appointed by Act of Assembly, at such Days and Times as the said Act appoints; which said Collector is also hereby Required to pay the same at such Days and Times, and to such Persons and Uses as is and shall be appointed by Act of General Assembly of this Province. Which said Assessors shall have for their Trouble for assessing the same, *Nine Pence per Pound*, and the Collector for Collecting, gathering and paying to the Collector of the County to be appointed by Act of Assembly, *Six Pence per Pound*, and the Collector of the County for Receiving and paying the same, *Six Pence per Pound*. And if any Person or Persons shall neglect to give an Account, or conceal any of his Rateable Estate from the Assessor, he or they shall forfeit *Two Shillings per Pound* for every such Neglect or Concealment, To be Recovered by any Person who will sue for the same by Action of Debt before any one Justice of the Peace within the County where such Concealment is made, one half to his own use, the other half towards the Support of the Government. And if any Person or Persons shall refuse or neglect to pay his Tax to the Collector or Collectors when demanded, the Collector or Collectors shall make out a List of the Names and Sir-Names of such Delinquents, with what Sums he, she or they are to pay, and make Return thereof to any one Justice of the Peace in said County, who is hereby Impowered and Required to make out his Warrant to the Constable of such Town or Precinct, to make Distress on the Offenders Goods and Chattles; and make Sale of the same at a publick vendue, in any Town or County within the said Province, and pay the Tax or Taxes for which such Distress or Distresses is or are made, unto the Collector or Collectors of such Town, Division or Precinct, and after payment made, deducting *One Shilling* for the Warrant, to be paid the Justice of the Peace that makes out the same, if but one Person be named in the Warrant, but if more; *Three Pence* for every other Name mentioned in the said Warrant; and *Eighteen Pence* to the Constable for each Distress, the overplus to be Returned to the Owner, if any be. And where Goods and Chattles cannot be found, the Constable or Constables of such Towns or Precincts are hereby Impowered and Required to take the Body or Bodies of him or them, if to be found in said County, and deliver them to the Sheriff of such County or Counties, who is hereby Impowered and Required to receive and keep them in safe Custody until payment be made, and all Charges accrewed thereby, defrayed. And if any of the Assessors or Collectors chosen as aforesaid, or Justices, refuse or neglect to perform their services Required by this Act, he or they shall Forfeit the Sum of *Forty Shillings* for each Offence, to be Recovered by any Person who will sue for the same by Action of Debt before any three Justices of the Peace of the said County (*Quorum unus*) one half thereof to his own use, the other half to be applyed towards support of the Government.

And be it further Enacted by the Authority aforesaid, That if any of the Assessors or Collectors chosen as aforesaid, happen to dye, remove or refuse to serve, any two Justices of the Peace of said County, one of which being of the *Quorum* are hereby Impowered and Required to appoint others in the Room and Place of them so deceased, removed or refusing,

and

and for their Services ſhall have the ſame Fees before allowed by this Act, and upon Refuſal or neglect ſhall Forfeit the Penalties before mentioned in this Act.

And be it further Enacted by the Authority aforeſaid, That if any Perſon or Perſons find or think themſelves Wronged by being over aſſeſſed, ſuch Perſon or Perſons ſhall or may make his or their Appeal to the next Court of Quarter-Seſſions held in that County ; or in caſe the ſaid Tax be appointed to be paid before the Court of Quarter-Seſſions, any Three Juſtices in the ſaid County, one of which being of the *Quorum* ; which ſaid Court of Quarter-Seſſions or three Juſtices aforeſaid, are hereby Impowered and Required to make ſuch abatement of ſaid Tax as they find to be Equal. And if it be made to appear before ſuch Court or Juſtices, that any of the Inhabitants be not aſſeſſed ſo high as their Rateable Eſtate will amount unto, They are hereby Authorized, Impower'd and Required to add to the ſaid Tax ſo much as will make it Equal.

And be it Enacted by the Authority aforeſaid, That when a Tax is found neceſſary to be Raiſed within any of the Counties within this Province, for Defraying the Publick and neceſſary Charge of ſaid County, That it ſhall be aſſeſſed and Collected in manner as is before mentioned in this Act, and be Paid to the Collector of each County, to be applyed to ſuch ſervices as ſhall be appointed by the Juſtices of each County, with the Free-holders choſen by the Inhabitants, according to the Directions of an Act of Aſſembly of this Province, Entituled, *An Act for Raiſing of Money for building and Repairing Goals and Court-houſes,* &c.

And be it further Enacted by the Authority aforeſaid, That the Collector of each County within this Province, appointed or to be appointed by Act of General Aſſembly, ſhall keep a fair Account of what Money he ſhall receive from the ſeveral Collectors of the Towns, Diviſions, Precincts or Diſtricts within the ſaid County, and ſhall deliver the ſaid Accounts, with an Account of what Deficiencies are in each Town, Diviſion, Diſtrict or Precinct, the Quota's of the County in general, and of each Town, Diviſion, Diſtrict or Precinct in particular, to the Treaſurer or Receiver General, for the Time being, for all Money Raiſed towards ſupport of the Government, and for what Money he ſhall receive for the Uſe of the ſaid County, before the Court of Quarter-Seſſions once in every Year ; and if ſaid Collectors have any publick Money remaining in his or their Hands, over and above the Quota appointed to be paid by ſaid County, it ſhall Remain in the Hands of the ſaid Collector, to be Imployed to the publick uſe of ſaid County.

An Act for laying an Exciſe on all ſtrong Liquors Retailed within this Colony of *New-Jerſey.*

BE it Enacted by the Governour, Council and General Aſſembly, and by the Authority of the ſame, That there ſhall be given and granted to his Majeſty, his Heirs and Succeſſors, an Exciſe on all ſtrong Liquors, to wit, for all Rum, Brandy, Wine, and other Spirits, Retailed, or to be Retailed, under the Quantity of Two Gallons, throughout this Province, *Twelve Pence per Gallon,* Proclamation Money,

And

And the Sum of *Four Shillings and six Pence,* Money aforesaid, for every Barrel of Syder so Retailed, by Land or Water, under the Quantity of Five Gallons ; And for every Barrel of Beer, Retailed, as aforesaid, *Two Shillings,* Money aforesaid ; And for every Gallon of Syder-Royal and Metheglin, *Six Pence per Gallon,* Money aforesaid. Which Excise shall be paid yearly, and every year, from the first Day of *March* next, to the first Day of *March* in the Year of our Lord One Thousand Seven Hundred and Twenty One, as herein after mentioned, for and towards the Support of the Government of this Province, to be disposed of as shall be appointed by the Governour, Council and General Assembly.

To the end therefore that the said Duty of Excise may be orderly Collected and managed to the best Advantage, for and towards the Uses aforesaid, *Be it Enacted by the Authority aforesaid,* That the aforesaid Duty of Excise, hereby given and granted to his Majesty, shall be Farmed Out, and the said Duty of Excise is hereby Hired and to Farm-Letten to *David Lyell* and *William Bradford,* Esqrs. Their Heirs, Executors, Administrators or Assigns, for and during the full Term of Five Years, from the aforesaid First Day of *March* next ensuing, To the first Day of *March,* which shall be in the Year of our Lord 1721. To have and to hold to them the said *David Lyell* and *William Bradford,* their Executors, Administrators or Assigns, or the Survivors of them, the said *David Lyell* and *William Bradford,* or either of them, the said Duty of Excise, and all the Fines, Forfeitures, Profits, Benefits and Advantages arising thereon, for and during the aforesaid Term of Five Years, They the said *David Lyell* and *William Bradford,* or either of them, their, or either of their Heirs, Executors, Administrators or Assigns, *Yeilding* and *Paying* to his Majesty, his Heirs and Successors, the Sum of Three Hundred Pounds, Proclamation Money, on the Twenty Fifth Day of *March,* yearly and every year, for and during the said Term of Five Years, they also giving sufficient Sureties, living and having Estates within this Province, either by Bond or Recognizance to his Majesty, his Heirs and Successors, to be approved of by his Excellency the Governour, for the due and true Payment of the said Sum of Three Hundred Pounds, Money aforesaid, yearly and every year, to the Receiver General of this Province, who is hereby Required to Receive the same; for the use of his Majesty, his Heirs and Successors, to be disposed of as before directed.

And be it further Enacted by the Authority aforesaid, That in order to Enable the said Farmers of the aforesaid Duty of Excise, their or either of their Heirs, Executors and Administrators or Assigns, to Collect the said Duty, it shall and may be Lawful for the said Farmers, or either of them, or their Deputies, to enter into all, any or every Retailer or Retailers of strong Liquors aforesaid, their Houses, Ware-houses, Cellars, or any other place, to Guage and take an Account of all such strong Liquors aforesaid, from time to Time, for and during the aforesaid Term of Five Years, from the aforesaid first Day of *March,* and when such account of the Quantity of the aforesaid strong Liquors is so taken by said Farmers, or either of them, the said Retailer or Retailers of such Liquors shall and are hereby Required to enter into Bond, with sufficient Sureties, to pay to said Farmers, or either of them, the said Duty of Excise, given and granted by this Act, within the Term of Three

Months

Months from the Day of the Date of such Bond. And if such Retailer or Retailers shall deny, delay or Refuse to enter into or give such Bond, or pay the said Duty, it shall and may be Lawful for the said Farmers, their or either of their Executors, Administrators or Assigns, to seize all such Liquors, and condemn the same before any three of his Majesties Justices of the peace (one whereof to be of the *Quorum*) who are hereby Required, Authorized and Impowered to Hear, Try and Finally to Determine the same.

And be it further Enacted by the Authority aforesaid, That all such Retailers of strong Liquors within this Province, shall, upon all and every of their Receipts of all such strong Liquors before expressed, and Exciseable, come to the said Farmer or Farmers of the said Excise, or such as they shall appoint under their Hands and Seals in each and every County of this Province, and there Enter the Quantity and Quality of all such Liquors as they shall then receive into their Houses, Warehouses, Cellars, or other Places, without paying any Fee for Entering the same, the Time when Received and by what Conveyance it came, and of whom brought and Purchased, and on Default thereof, all such Liquors as shall be found in any Retailers House, Ware-house, or other Place, he, she or they so offending shall Forfeit all such Liquors, and three Times the value thereof, to be Recovered before any Two Justices of the Peace of the County (one whereof to be of the *Quorum*) where said Offence is committed, who are hereby Required and Impowered, summarily, to Hear, Try and Determine, and to issue forth their Warrant for seizing all such Liquors so Forfeited, as aforesaid, and for Committing to the Sheriff of the said County where the said Offence is Committed, all such Retailers of Liquors who have not Entered and Paid, or secured to be paid, the Duties of Excise aforesaid, and shall be so Convicted thereof, there to Remain without Bail or Mainprize until he, she or they shall satisfie and make payment of Three Times the value of such Liquors seized and Forfeited, as aforesaid; which Sheriff is hereby Authorized, Required and Commanded to receive the Body or Bodies of such Retailer or Retailers, and him or them to commit to the common Goal of the said County; and if the said Sheriff shall either wilfully or negligently suffer the said Person or Persons so committed to him, to escape out of the said Goal, he shall be liable to an Action in the same manner as if the said Person or Persons had been committed to him in Execution, by Process out of any Court of Record within Province.

And be it further Enacted, That if any such Retailer of any the aforesaid strong Liquors shall deny, delay or refuse to let the said Farmers, or either of them, or their Deputies to have free Recourse into his, her or their House, Out-House, Cellar, or other Place, to Guage and take an Account of all Liquors Exciseable by this Act, that are found in their said Houses, Out-Houses or Cellars, or other Place, and thereof be Convicted, he, she or they so offending shall Forfeit the Sum of *Ten Pounds* for each and every such Refusal, To be Recovered by Action of Debt before any Court of Record in this Province, wherein there shall be no Essoyn, Protection or Wager of Law, or any more than one Imparlance.

And be it further Enacted by the Authority aforesaid, That if any Person

C or

or Perfons within this Province fhall prefume to difpofe of any ftrong
Liquors made Excifeable by this Act, under the notion of Selling, or taking Money or other effects, for Pipes, Tobacco, or any other thing
whatfoever, whereby to evade the paying the faid Duty of Excife intended by this Act, he, fhe or they fhall for every fuch Offence Forfeit the
Sum of *Five Pounds,* to be Recovered by Action of Debt in manner and
form aforefaid.

And be it further Enacted by the Authority aforefaid, That the faid Farmer or Farmers of the faid Excife, their Heirs, Executors, Adminiftrators
or Affigns fhall be, and are hereby Required, obliged and Commanded, at
the Expiration of the faid Term of Five Years, to give the Governour,
Council and general Affembly, for the Time being, a juft and true Account,
upon Oath, of all fuch Sum or Sums of Money he or they fhall have
annually Received for the faid Excife, and from whom they have received
the fame in each and every County within this Province.

And to prevent the Taking, Exacting or Receiving of Exorbitant
Prices for Provifions or Liquors by any publick Houfe-keepers or Re-
tailers of Liquors within this Colony, or felling by lefs Meafures than
Ale and Wine Meafures, as appointed by the Laws of *Great Britain.*

Be it Enacted by the Authority aforefaid, That the Juftices of the Peace in
the Quarter-Seffions held in each refpective County in this Colony, are
hereby Authorized and directed, impowered and commanded to fix the
Prices of all ftrong Liquors Excifeable by this Act, and of all Provifions
and Accomodations for Man and Horfe, and fhall publifh the fame at the
Court of Quarter Seffions; and every publick Houfe-keeper or Perfon
Lifenced to Retail ftrong Liquors, Excifeable by this Act, are hereby
Required and Commanded to procure a Copy of the Rates of Provifions
or Liquors fo fetled by the Juftices in the refpective Courts of Quarter
Seffions, figned by the Clerk of the Peace of the refpective Courts of
Quarter-Seffions, and fhall affix the fame in fome publick Place in his, her
or their Houfes, that all Perfons concerned may fee the fame; and fhall
not prefume to ask, demand or receive any more or greater Sums of Money
for their faid Provifions, Liquors or Entertainment of Man or Horfe than
is expreffed in the Rates fo fettled, under the Penalty of Forfeiting their
Recognizance, to be fued for, Recovered and applyed, as aforefaid.

An Act for the better laying out, Regulating and Preferving Publick Roads and High-ways thro'-out this Province.

BE it Enacted by the *Governour, Council and General Affembly, and by
the Authority of the fame,* That all the Roads and High-ways of Six
and Four Rods broad, which have been laid out and afcertained by
virtue of an Act of the General Affembly of this Province, entituled,
*An Act for laying out, Regulating, Clearing and Preferving publick Common
Roads and High-ways through-out this Province,* are hereby Confirmed to be
and remain Common Publick Roads and High-ways, Excepting fuch
Roads and High ways as have been, are and fhall be laid out from the
Twentieth Day of *November* laft, to the Publication hereof, all which
Roads and High-ways in that time laid out, are hereby declared void and
null as if they had never been laid out.   *And*

And be it further Enacted by the Authority aforesaid, That the Free-holders and Inhabitants of each respective Town, Division and Precinct within this Province, shall meet and Assemble together on the second *Tuesday* in *March,* Yearly and every Year, at the most publick Place in each respective Town, Division or Precinct within this Province, and thereby Plurality of Voices Elect and chuse four Persons fit for Surveyors of the High-ways, who shall be presented to the next General Court of Quarter-Sessions of the Peace for the said County, out of which said Four Persons the Justices of the said Court shall Nominate such two as they shall think fit, to be Surveyors of the High-ways for that Town, District or Precinct for the ensuing year. *Provided always, and it is hereby further Enacted,* That because the County of *Hunterdon* have no Commissioners of the High-ways at present for said County, Therefore *It is hereby Enacted,* That the several Townships of the said County shall and may meet together on the first Day of *March* for this present year, and elect and chuse Four Persons, out of which the Justices of the next Court of Quarter-Sessions shall chuse two Surveyors for each Township, as aforesaid, who shall serve until the usual time of others being elected, chosen and appointed in their Places, as appointed by this Act.

And be it further Enacted by the Authority aforesaid, That upon application made by the Inhabitants of any of the Towns, Divisions or Precincts within this Province, to the Surveyors appointed, as aforesaid, for any Road or Roads to be laid out from one Town or Division to another, or to any publick Landing place, or Market, or Mill, or from any Town to the Kings High-way, that then the said Surveyors so applyed to shall call to their assistance the two Surveyors of the two next adjacent Towns, Divisions or Precincts, and lay out all such Roads and High-ways as shall be necessary for the respective Town, Division or Precinct so making application; which Roads so to be laid out, shall be of four Rods broad, and laid out to the best Conveniency of the Inhabitants of the adjacent Towns, Divisions or Precincts, and with as little Disadvantage to the Owner or Owners of the Lands through or by which any Road shall be laid out, or run through, according as the aforesaid six Surveyors, or the Major part of them, shall agree.

And be it Enacted by the Authority aforesaid, That the Justices of the Peace of each respective County within this Province shall once in every Year, in their Court of Quarter Sessions, in the Months of *February, March* and *April,* nominate and appoint Two Inhabitants in each respective Town, Division or Precinct (Patented Towns only excepted, wher provision for the Chusing of Over-seers, is already made in the said Patents) to be Overseers for making and keeping in good Repair all publick Roads and High-ways within each respective Town, Division or Precinct for which they are appointed Overseers.

And be it further Enacted by the Authority aforesaid, That the said Overseers of each respective Town, Division or Precinct within this Province, shall once in every Year, and so often as there shall be occasion, call together so many of the Inhabitants (the Surveyors only excepted) of each respective Town, Precinct or District, for the mending and Repairing all such High-ways, Bridges and Cause-ways as have been heretofore laid out by the Commissioners appointed by Law, or shall be hereafter laid out as this Act directs, as they think necessary. And if any Person or

Perfons fo fummoned by faid Overfeers to work on faid High-ways, do not by themfelves or a fufficient Labourer meet at the Time and place appinted, and perform fuch Services as by the faid Overfeers fhall be Required, every fuch Defaulter fhall forfeit *Four Shillings and Six Pence* Proclamation Money, for every Days neglect, to be Levyed on the offenders Goods and Chattles, by Warrant from any one Juftice of the Peace, who is hereby required to grant the fame, directed to the Conftable of the Town or Diftrict to make Diftrefs and Sale of faid Offenders Goods and Chattles at a publick Vendue, returning the Over-plus, after payment of fuch Forfeiture, and what Charge accrues thereon, to the Owner. And every Team with Cart or Waggon, and a Man to mannage the fame, which the faid Overfeers, or any of them, fhall have occafion to imploy, fhall be efteemed in place of two Days Labour of one working Man; and the Forfeiture of a Team and a Man, with Cart or Waggon, not coming and Performing the Service required by the refpective Overfeers, fhall be proportionable, and Recovered from any Defaulter by Warrant from any one Juftice of the Peace, in manner aforefaid, all which Forfeitures fhall be paid by the faid Conftables or Defaulters to the faid Overfeers, and by them applyed to the making and maintaining the publick High-ways of faid Town. Diftrict or Precinct.

And be it Enacted by the Authority aforefaid, That upon the Application of any Perfon or Perfons to the aforefaid Surveyors for a Road to be laid out from or to the faid Perfons Plantation, or to any other Plantation, the Surveyors of the faid Town, Divifion, Precinct or Diftrict where fuch Road is required, and two Surveyors of the next Town if they judge it neceffary, fhall lay out the fame Road one or two Rod wide, as they or the major part of them fhall think fit, in fuch manner as may be moft Commodious for the adjacent Plantations, and with as little Difadvantage as may be to the Owner of the Land through which faid Road fhall be laid out. All fuch Roads that are or fhall be laid out purfuant to this Act of one or two Rods wide, fhall be Cleared and maintained by the Inhabitants who require the fame. And if the Owner of faid Land, through which any of the faid Roads of one or two Rod wide fhall find it for his advantage to hang Swinging Gates in faid Road, he may have Liberty to do the fame.

And be it further Enacted by the Authority aforefaid, That if any Perfon or Perfons fhall ftop, leffen, narrow or incroach on any Road or High-way, laid out by direction of the Laws of this Province, fhall forfeit the Sum of *Forty Shillings* for every offence, to be Recovered by Action of Debt by the Overfeers of fuch refpective Town, Divifion or Precinct, before any one Juftice of the Peace within the County where fuch Offence is committed, to be applyed to the Repairing of the High-ways of the faid Town, Diftrict or Precinct.

And be it further Enacted by the Authority aforefaid, That the Overfeers of every Town, Divifion or Precinct within this Province fhall make up their Account of what Money is in their Hands for Forfeitures, by way of Diftrefs, or otherways, to the Overfeers for the enfuing Year, and pay the fame into their Hands, to be imployed to fupporting the High-ways.

And be it Enacted by the Authority aforefaid, That if any of the Survey-ors, chofen, as aforefaid, fhall refufe or neglect to perform their Duty required by this Act, fhall Forfeit the Sum of *Forty Shillings* for each

Offence,

Offence, to be Recovered by Action of Debt before any one Justice of the Peace by any Person who will prosecute the same. And if any of the Overseers, so appointed, shall Refuse or neglect to perform their Services herein Required, shall Forfeit *Forty Shillings*, for every Offence; to be Recovered by Action of Debt before any Justice of the Peace within the County where the Offence is committed; To be Recovered by any one who will prosecute the same in manner aforesaid. All which Fines and Forfeitures arising by any Person or Persons neglecting to perform their Services required by this Act, shall be Imployed one half to the use of the Persons who shall prosecute the same to effect, and the other half to Repairing the High-ways and Bridges, by the Overseers of the Town or Precinct where the Forfeiture becomes due.

And be it Enacted by the Authority aforesaid, That if any of the Surveyors or Overseers chosen and appointed by this Act, shall happen to dye or remove in the Time of their said Service, or neglect, or refuse to perform their respective services aforesaid, any Two Justices of the Peace within the County where it shall or may so happen, are impowered, and hereby required to appoint Persons instead of such removing, refusing or neglecting, who shall have the same Power and Authority as if chosen and appointed by this Act, and who shall perform the respective Duties required by this Act, under the same Penalties and Forfeitures, as aforesaid.

And whereas there is several Sums of Money in the Hands of some of the Constables, or in the Hands of some other Persons who were formerly Constables of several Towns, Divisions or Precincts within this Province, that were taken by Distress, or otherways, from several Persons neglecting to work on the High-ways, *Be it Enacted by the Authority aforesaid,* That all Constables, or any other Person or Persons whatsoever, that have any Money or Goods taken or received, as aforasaid, shall immediately upon Publication hereof pay the same to the Overseers of the High-ways, for the Time being, of the Town, Division or Precinct where such Money or Goods were taken, as aforesaid. And if any such Constable, or other Person or Persons having such Money or Goods in his or their Hands, shall refuse or neglect to pay in such Money or Goods, taken, as aforesaid, it shall and may be Lawful for the Overseer or Over-seers of the High-ways in any Town, Division or Precinct within this Province, to commence an Action of Debt against him or them so neglecting or Refusing, in any Court of Common-Pleas within this Province, if above *Forty Shillings,* and if *Forty Shillings,* or under, before any Justice of the Peace of said County, and Recover all such Money or Goods, and double Costs of suit. And all such Sums of Money so Recovered by the Overseers, shall be laid out for making or Repairing the publick Roads in the Town, Division or Precinct for which the said Distresses were made.

And be it Enacted by the Authority aforesaid, That all Roads which are Discommodious to the adjacent Towns or Precincts, or goes through Swamps, or Ground not sufficient for High-Roads, or is over-much Disadvantagious to the Owners of the Lands where said Roads go through, shall be liable to Regulation and Alteration by the Surveyors which shall be Chosen, Elected and appointed, according to the Directions of this Act, to wit, six of the said Surveyors of the said County

D

where

where the said Alteration is to be made, and six of the Surveyors of the next adjacent County, who are most concerned in the said Alteration, all being agreed, may Alter and Amend Roads of Four Rod Broad, where it is necessary, and Six of the Surveyors of the said County being agreed, may alter Roads of Two or One Rod broad; which said Surveyors are hereby required to alter and lay out the same, when application is to them made by any injured Person, Town, Division or Precinct, where it is required, as will be most Commodious for Travellers and Carriages and the least Disadvantagious to the Owners of the Lands where such Roads will go through. And the Overseers to be appointed by the Directions of this Act, are hereby Required to Summons as many of the Inhabitants as they think necessary to Clear and make good and sufficient all Roads so altered, and making Bridges and Cause-wayes where said Overseers shall appoint; which said Overseers are hereby Required to Imploy the Inhabitants equally in their Respective Towns, Divisions or Precincts, both in these and all other Roads; and all Persons who refuse or neglect to do their Duty, as herein required, shall suffer the Penalties and Forfeitures before mentioned in this Act.

And whereas it may happen in some Towns or Precincts, that there may not be occasion to Imploy all the Inhabitants equally in the year, Therefore *Be it further Enacted by the Authority aforesaid*, That the Overseers shall every year give an Account to the succeding Overseers, of all such Persons that have not wrought their equal part on the High-ways the preceeding year, and the new Overseers shall first imploy those Persons on the High-ways.

And whereas the Counties of *Sommerset* and *Cape-May* are not divided into Townships, *Be it therefore Enacted by the Authority aforesaid*, That the Inhabitants of each of the Counties of *Sommerset* and *Cape-May*, (until they shall be divided into Townships or Districts, and then to chuse as is otherways directed in this Act) shall meet at the most convenient places in each of their Counties, at the times before mentioned in this Act, yearly, and shall chuse, by plurality of Voices, Twelve Persons fit for Surveyors of the High-ways, for each of the said Counties, who shall be presented to the next General Court of Quarter-Sessions for each of the said Counties, out of whom the Justices of each of the said Courts shall nominate and appoint Six Persons for their respective Counties, to lay out, alter and amend Roads within their Counties, according to the Directions of this Act, who are Re uired to Act accordingly, when application is to them made. And all Over-seers of the High-ways which shall be appointed, are hereby required to Summons so many of the Inhabitants as they think needful, to clear, make good, build Bridges and make Cause-ways, where they are necessary in any of the Roads and High-ways so laid out or altered; and all Persons refusing or neglecting to perform their Duties hereby required, shall be under the same Penalties before mentioned in this Act.

And whereas the Road to *Cape-May*, as it is now used, either by *Egg-Harbour* or *Prince-Maurice-River*, by reason of the many Swamps and Creeks it passeth through, is at some Seasons altogether Impassible, and the said Inhabitants having found out a more convenient Road, which they desire they may have liberty to lay out and clear, *Be it further Enacted by the Authority aforesaid*, That the Inhabitants of the said County of *Cape-May* be, and are hereby authorized and impowered to meet together at such time and place as they shall think fit, and by plurality of Voices chuse six Surveyors, who are hereby authorized, impowered and appointed to lay out the said Road or High-way from *Cedar Swamp Bridge* to *Tuckahoe*, and so (the most convenient way) to the Town of *Gloucester*, and direct the said Road to be Cleared, and convenient Bridges to be made, for the ease and benefit of the said Inhabitants. Which Road, when made, shall be Maintained and Repaired, and subject to the same Regulations as all other Publick Roads in this Province are appointed to be by this Act, any Law, Custom or Usage to the contrary in any wise notwithstanding.

And forasmuch as the Bridge in *Salem* Road, over *Gloucester-River*, is now very much out of repair, and almost impassible, and that the Charges of Amending, Repairing and Maintaining the same are very great, and too heavy to be born by the Towns in which the said Bridge is, *Therefore be it Enacted by the Authority aforesaid*, That the said Bridge be forth-with amended and repaired, and that the said Bridge over *Gloucester-River* shall at all times after the Publication hereof, as need shall require, be Re-builded, Amended and Repaired at the publick and general Charge of the said County of *Gloucester*, and that the Money for defraying the Expence and Charge thereof shall, from time to time, be assessed, levyed and raised on the Inhabitants of the said County after such manner, and by the same Assessors and Collectors appointed in and by an Act of Assembly made *Anno* 1713. entituled, *An Act for raising of Money for building and repairing of Goals and Court-houses within each respective County of this Province, &c.* and that the respective Officers for assessing, levying and collecting of the said Charges be subject to the Fines, Forfeitures and Penalties in the said Act mentioned, and that the said Fines and Forfeitures becoming due by reason of any Delinquency or Default, be levyed as the said Act directs, and applyed towards Repairing and Amending the Bridge aforesaid.

And whereas the Bridge over *South-River*, in the great High-Road between *Amboy* and *Burlington*, is too great a Charge to be born by the Towns of *Amboy* and *Piscattaway* adjoyning thereto, *Be it therefore Enacted, and it is hereby Enacted by the Authority aforesaid*, That the said Bridge over *Sout-River* on the said great high-Road between *Amboy* and *Burlington*, shall be maintained, repaired, kept up and re-built, as occasion requires, at the general Cost and Charges of the County of *Middlesex*, after the same way and manner as is above-mentioned, expressed and appointed for the said Bridge over *Gloucester-River*, as aforesaid.

And be it further Enacted by the Authority aforesaid, That all Persons who are desirous to have Swinging Gates on any Drift-ways and other Roads going through their Plantations, to other Plantations, or to the High-Road, may apply themselves to any two of the Surveyors of the High-ways of the County where they live, by whose consent and approbation they may make, maintain and keep in good repair, at their own cost and charge, such Swinging-Gates as they desire.

And whereas several Persons in Clearing of their Lands, through which the Publick High-ways run, have only killed the Trees. and left them standing, which Trees, so killed, on every high Wind, are

Subject

subject to fall a croſs the Roads, and are thereby Dangerous to both Man and Beaſts, that are travelling and feeding in the ſaid Roads, *Be it therefore Enacted by the Authority aforeſaid,* That if any Perſon within this Province ſhall kill any Tree or Trees within one Chain of any publick Road or High-way, and not fall the ſame within one year after it be killed, ſhall Forfeit the Sum of *Five Shillings* for every Tree ſo killed, to be recovered before any one Juſtice of the Peace, the one half to be applyed towards Repairing the High-ways, and the other half to the Proſecutor.

And be it further Enacted by the Authority aforeſaid, That a former Act, entituled, *An Act for laying out, regulating, clearing and preſerving publick common High-ways throgh out this Province,* be, and is hereby Repealed to all intents and purpoſes whatſoever.

An Act to Prevent Unſeaſonable Burning the Woods.

WHereas by continual Experience, Firing the Woods in the Fall and Winter, is found very Prejudicial and Dangerous to the Inhabitants of this Province, *Be it therefore Enacted by the Governour, Council and Repreſentatives in General Aſſembly met and convened, and by the Authority of the ſame,* That if any Perſon ſhall Fire the Woods at any time whatſoever, excepting between the Fourteenth Day of *February* and the Fourteenth Day of *April* next following, of every year, ſhall Forfeit the Sum of *Forty Shillings,* Proclamation Money, for every ſuch Offence, To be recovered by Action of Debt by any Perſon who will ſue for the ſame, to his own uſe, before any one Juſtice of the Peace of the County where the Fact is committed,

And be it further Enacted by the Authority aforeſaid, That if any Perſon ſhall preſume to fire the Woods at any other time than, as aforeſaid, whereby any Perſon or Perſons are Damnified, the Perſon ſo firing the Woods ſhall pay all Damages done unto any Perſon or Perſons ſo Injured, if under *Forty Shillings,* to be Recovered by Action of Debt before any one Juſtice of the Peace, and if above *Forty Shillings,* to be Recovered by Action of Debt in any Court of Common-Pleas within this Province, with Coſt of Suit.

And be it further Enacted by the Authority aforeſaid, That neither this Act, nor any thing therein contained, ſhall be taken or conſtrued to hinder any Perſon from firing the Woods upon his own Land, Provided ſuch Perſon do not ſuffer the ſaid Fire to run of the ſame, upon Pain and Penalty of Paying the Damage aforeſaid.

An Act to Repeal part of an Act of General Aſſembly of this Province, entituled, *An Act for preventing the waſte of Timber, Pine and Cedar Trees and Poles within this Province of* New-Jerſey, *and to lay a Duty upon all Pipe and Hogſhead ſtaves Exported out of the ſame to any of the Neighbouring Colonies.*

WHereas there was an Act paſſed in the Twelfth and Thirteenth
Year

Year of her late Majesty, entituled, *An Act for preventing the waste of Timber, Pine and Cedar Trees, &c.* and that part of the said Act which relates to Hogshead Staves being found by Experience to be Prejudicial to the Inhabitants of this Province, *Be it therefore Enacted by the Governour, Council and General Assembly, and by the Authority of the same,* That so much of the said Act as relates to Hogshead Staves, shall be, and is hereby Repealed, Anulled and made Void, and so much of every Article and Clause in said Act as relates in any manner of way to Hogshead Staves or laying a Duty thereon, is hereby Repealed accordingly, any Act, Law or Custom to the contrary thereof in any wise notwithstanding.

An Act for the better Enforcing an Ordinance of his Excellency *Robert Hunter,* Esq; Captain General and Governour in Chief of the Provinces of *New-Jersey, New-York, &c.* Entituled, *An Ordinance for the further establishing of Fees and Ferriages.*

WHereas his Excellency, by and with the Advice and Consent of his Majesty's Council for this Province, hath established an Ordinance for the Regulating of Fees and Ferriages in the words following, *viz.*

BY His Excellency *Robert Hunter,* Esq; Captain General and Governour in Chief in and over the Provinces of *New-Jersey* and *New-York,* and all the Territories and Tracts of Land depending thereon in *America,* and Vice-Admiral of the same, this 16th Day of *January,* in the Third year of the Reign of our Soveraign Lord *George,* King of *Great Britain, France* and *Ireland,* Defender of the Faith, *&c. An Ordinance for further Regulation of Fees and Ferriages.*

WHereas several Fees are omitted in the former Ordinance. For Remedy whereof, and for Regulation of Ferriages, *&c.* His Excellency the Governour, by virtue of the Power and Authority to him given by his Majestys Letters Patents under the Great Seal of *Great Britain,* and by and with the Advice and Assistance of his Majesty Council for said Province of *New-Jersey,* Doth Declare and Ordain, and it is hereby Declared and Ordained, That no Officer, Boatman or other Person whatsoever shall ask, demand or receive any other Fees or Ferriages for the Services herein after-mentioned, but according to what hereafter is expressed.

Fees when *Titles* of *Land* are concerned.

TO the Practitioners of the Law, for drawing every Declaration in Ejectment, Ten Shillings.
Retaining Fee, Ten Shillings. Fee on the Tryal, Twenty Shillings. Jurors coming out of their County, *&c.* sworn, for every Day of their Attendance, Four Shillings.
For every Juror not Sworn, *per Diem* Three Shillings.
Every Evidence that comes out of their County, shall have *per Diem* Three Shillings.

E

Rates

Rates of the Ferry to and from Amboy and New-York.

PAssage-Boat Hire from *Amboy* to *New-York*, Twelve Shillings.
    Passenger in Company, Man and Horse, if above two, Five Shillings.
Common Passenger, Fourteen Pence.
Flower per Barrel, Five Pence.
Beer, Syder, and other Liquors per Barrel, Ten Pence.
Rum, Mallosses, &c. per Hogshead, Four Shillings and six Pence.
Wine per Pipe, Five Shillings and six Pence.
Every thing per Bushel, Two Pence.
Iron per hundred Weight, Four Pence half Penny.
Beef per Quarter, Nine Pence.
Hogs, Sheep, &c. per Head, Nine Pence.
Dry Goods per Ton, Eight Shillings,
    And so in Proportion for greater or smaller Quantities.

Redford's Ferry to and from *Amboy*, and to & from Capt. *Billops*.

MAn and Horse, Neat Cattle, &c. to *Amboy*, One Shilling.
    Single Person, Four Pence
Man and Horse, Neat Cattle, &c. to Capt. *Billops*, One Shilling & 9 Pence.
Single Persons, Eight Pence.
Sheep, Hogs, &c. to *Amboy*, per head, Three Pence.
All Barrels and half Barrels of Flower, Two Pence.
Pipes and Hogsheads of Liquor or Mallosses, Eighteen Pence.
Sheep, &c. to *Billops*, Six Pence.
Barrels, &c. Four Pence. Pipes, &c. Three Shillings.
    From *Amboy* to *Billops* the same as from *Redfords* to *Amboy*.

Wechank Ferry.

MAn and Horse to or from *New-York*, Eighteen Pence.
    Single Person, One Shilling.
If above Three Persons, *per piece* Three Pence.
Every thing per Bushel, One Penny.
Hogs, Sheep, &c per head Two Pence.
Beef per Quarter, Three Pence. Barrels, Four Pence.
Hogsheads, One Shilling. Pipes, Eighteen Pence.

Inian's Ferry.

HOrse and Man, Four Pence.
    Single Person, Two Pence.

Burlington, &c.

FRom the Falls to *Burlington* for Freight of Wheat and Flower, &c
    per Bushel, Three half Pence.

Casks

Casks of Flower from the Falls to *Burlington,* per Ton, Six Shill. 8 Pence.
From *Farnsworth's* to *Burlington,* for Wheat Meal, *&c.* per Bush. 3 half Pence:
Casks of Flower from *Fernsworth* to *Burlington,* per Ton, Four Shill. 6 Pence:
Barrels of Pork, Syder, *&c.* Nine Pence.

Ferry to and from *Philadelphia* and *Burlington.*

Hire of a Boat in the Winter, (from *Michaelmas* to *Lady Day,*) for a single Passenger, Five Shillings and Nine Pence:
Single Passenger in Company, One Shilling.
In the Summer, Four Shillings and Six Pence.
Single Passenger in Company, Nine Pence.
Flower per Ton, Six Shillings and Eight Pence.
Bread per Ton, Five Shillings and Nine Pence.
Rum per Hogshead, Two Shillings and Three Pence.
Flower per Ton from *Farnsworths* to *Philadelphia,* Ten Shillings.
Wine per Pipe, Three Shillings and Nine Pence.
Every thing per Barrel, Nine Pence.
Iron per Hundred Weight, Four Pence half Penny.
Beef per Quarter, Seven Pence half Penny.
Hogs, Sheep, *&c.* per head, Seven Pence half Penny.
Meal, Salt, &c. per Bushel, Two Pence.

All the above Fees and Ferriages to be paid in Proclamation Money.

And his said Excellency, by virtue of the Power and Authority, and by and with the Advice and Assistance aforesaid, Hath Ordained, and Doth hereby Ordain, All keepers of the said Ferrys, Wherries or Passage Boats, immediately after the Publication hereof, to repair to the Secretarys Office of the said Province, and there give in Bond to his said Excellency for the due Observance of their parts of the said Ordinance, And thereupon to obtain a Lisence from the said Office for Plying the said Ferrys. And a Copy of such part of this Ordinance as concerns them, under the Hand of the said Secretary, they are hereby Ordained always to keep affixt in one of the most publick Places in their House, or near the said Ferring-Place.

By His Excellency's Command   Ro. *Hunter.*
     Ja. Alexander

BE it therefore Enacted by the Governour, Council and General Assembly, met and Assembled, and by the Authority of the same, That if any Person shall pretend to carry Goods or Passengers for Hire, to or from any of the Places mentioned in the said Ordinance, without first having obtained a Lisence for the same from the Governour of this Province, for the time being, and giving such Security as by the said Ordinance is Required, he, she or they shall Forfeit the Sum of *Forty Shillings,* Money according to her late Majesty's Proclamation.

And be it further Enacted by the Authority aforesaid, That if any Person or Persons shall take or exact greater Fees or Rewards for his or their Services than is ascertained in the Ordinance and Act, for any of the Services mentioned in the said Ordinance and Act, all and every Person and Persons so Offending, shall, for every such Offence, Forfeit the Sum of *Ten Pounds,* to be Recovered by Action of Debt in any Court of Record in this Province, and be forever hereafter barr'd from following the said Practice.

And whereas the Security appointed to be given by Persons not Residet in this Province, who shall take out a Writ or Capias, or file any Declaration in Ejectment, against any person within this Province, are not sufficient to pay the Costs of the Defendant, if the said plantiff should be Cast, Non-suited, Discontinue or with-draw his Suit, without the Consent of the Defendant, *Be it therefore Enacted by the Authority aforesaid,* That if any non-Resident of this Province hath already, or hereafter shall take out a Writ or Capias, or file any Bill or Declaration in Ejectment against any Person within this Province, in the Supream Court of this Province, he shall, if the Action be already commenced, before he brings the same on Tryal, or if hereafter to be Commenced, before the taking of the said Writ or Capias, or filling the said Bill or Declaration in Ejectment, give Bond unto the Defendant, with Security dwelling in the Province, in the Penalty of *Fifty Pounds,* upon Condition to pay the Costs of Court, if Cast, non-suited, Discontinue or with-draw his Suit, without the Consent of the Defendant; which Bond shall be left with the Clerk of the Court in which the Action is Commenced; and any Clerk neglecting to take such Security, shall pay the Defendants Costs, to be Recovered as aforesaid. *And be it further Enacted,* That so much of the Eighth Enacted Clause, in the Act, entituled, *An Act for shortening Law-suits, and Regulating the practice of the Law,* as relates to that part of it, is hereby Repealed and made void.

An Act for Repealing a Law, entituled, *An Act to Lay a Duty upon Wheat Exported out of the* Eastern Division *of this Province to any of her Majesties Colonies on the Continent of* America.

WHereas there was an Act passed in the Year One Thousand Seven Hundred and Thirteen, Entituled, *An Act to lay a Duty upon Wheat Exported out of the* Eastern Division *of this Province, to any of her Majesties Colonies on the Continent of* America, which Act being found Prejudicial to the Inhabitants of said Division,

Be it therefore Enacted by the Governour, Council and General Assembly, and by the Authority of the same, That the said Act be Repealed, and it is hereby Repealed, to all Intents, Constructions and Purposes whatsoever; any Law, Custom or Usage to the Contrary in any wise notwithstanding.

An Act to Repeal a former Act of General Assembly of this Province, entituled, *An Act for the ascertaining the Place of the sitting of the Representatives to meet in General Assembly.*

WHereas by an Act, entituled, *An Act for the ascertaining the Place of the sitting of the Representatives to meet in General Assembly,* made and Enacted in the Eight Year of the Reign of Our late Soveraign Lady *Anne,*

Anne, Queen of *Great Britain*, &c. Annoq; *Dom*. One Thousand Seven Hundred and Nine. It was enacted, That from thence forward all succeeding Assemblyes should sit at *Burlington*, untill it should be otherways settled by Act of Assembly, which is Contrary to the Royal Instructions, and hath been found to be Highly prejudicial to the *Eastern Division* of this Province, Be it therefore *Enacted by the Governour, Council and General Assembly now met and assembled, and it is hereby Enacted by the Authority of the same*, That the abovesaid Act, entituled, *An Act for the ascertaining the Place of the sitting of the Representatives to meet in General Assembly*, shall be, and is hereby repealed, and declared null, void and of none Effect, to all Intents, Constructions and purposes whatsoever.

These Acts were Published the 25th and 26th Days of January, 1716.

By his Excellency *Robert Hunter*, Esq; Capt. General and Governour in Chief in and over the Provinc s of *New-Jersey*, *New-York*, and all the Territories and Tracts of Land depending thereon in *America*, and Vice-Admiral of the same, &c. in Council.

An Ordinance for altering the Time of sitting of the Courts of Quarter-Sessions and Pleas for the County of Salem.

WHereas by a former Ordinance by his said Excellency, dated the 17th of *April*, in the 13th year of her late Majesty's Reign, *Annoq; Dom.* 1714. it was Ordained, That the General Courts of Sessions of the Peace should be held and kept in the said County, yearly and every year, at the Town of *Salem* on the Fourth Tuesday in *March*, *June*, *September* and *December*, as also, That there should be held a Court of Common-Pleas in the said County immediately after the General Sessions of the Peace ends and terminates.

And whereas it hath been Represented to his said Excellency, That the sitting of the said Courts in the aforesaid time of *June* is very Prejudicial to the Inhabitants, by detaining them from their Harvest, which is commonly at that time, And that it would be a great deal more for their Convenience that the said Courts should be held some reasonable time after.

His said Excellency, by virtue of the Powers and Authority's to him given by his Majesty's Letters Patents under the Great Seal of *Great Britain*, and by and with the Advice and Consent of his Majesty's Council for the said Province of *New-Jersey*, and for the Reasons aforesaid, Hath Ordained, and doth hereby Ordain, That the said Court of General Quarter-Sessions of the Peace, formerly held on the Fourth Tuesday of *July*, shall, from and after the Publication, hereof, be held and kept at the said Town of *Salem*, in the said County of *Salem*, on the second Tuesday in *July*, yearly and every year, and the said Court of Common-Pleas immediately thereafter, and not on the Fourth Tuesday in *June* aforesaid. Given under my Hand and Seal at *Chesterfield*, the 26th day of *January*, in the Third year of his Majesty's Reign, *Annoq; Dom.* 1716.

By His Excellency's Command,
Ja. Alexander. }

Ro. *Hunter.*

An Act for Regulating Stone-Horses or Stallions that run at large in this Province.

Whereas by long Experience it hath been found, that small Stallions runing at large in the Woods, have been, and still are very hurtful to the Breed of Horses in this her Majesties Province of *New-Jersey*, by causing the Breed to be small, and so rendring them less useful to the Inhabitants thereof, *Be it therefore Enacted by the Lieut. Governour, Council and Representatives now met in General Assembly and by the Authority of the same*, That from and after the 15*th* of *May* next, any Person or Persons who shall find any Stone Horse or Horses runing at large in the Woods, of the Age of Eighteen Months, or more, and not of the full height, from the lowest part of the Hoof unto the highest part of the Wither, of Fourteen Hands (Four Inches to each Hand) it shall and may be lawful for any such Person or Persons to take up such Horse or Horses, being under the size aforesaid, and to geld, or cause them to be gelded, who shall receive from the Owner or Owners of every such Horse the Sum of *Twenty Shillings* current Money of this Province, within a Month after gelding, as aforesaid ; and upon neglect or refusal of such Payment, it shall be deemed and esteemed a Due and just Debt to the Person or Persons aforesaid, and to be recovered from the Owner or Owners of such Horse or Horses, as a Debt under *Fourty Shillings Always provided*, That if any Horse so gelded, as aforesaid, happen to dye within one Month, that then and in that case the Owner or Owners shall be free and clear from the payment of *Twenty Shillings,* as aforesaid.

Acts paffed at a General Affembly begun and held at Perth-Amboy, in *New-Jerfey* One Thoufand Seven Hundred and Eighteen.

An Act for the Support of the Government of His Majefties Province of New-Jerfey *for two Years. to commence from the* 23d *of* September *laft paft, and to end the* 23 *of* September *One Thoufand Seven Hundred and Twenty.*

Whereas the Act, entituled, *An Act for the Support of the Government of his Majefties Province of* New-Jerfey *in* America, *for three Years,* Paffed in the Month of *January,* in the Year of our Lord, One Thoufand Seven Hundred and Sixteen, expired by its own Limitation on the Twenty third Day of September, One Thoufand Seven Hundred and Eighteen; and there having fince that Time been no Provifion made for the further Support and defraying the necceff.ry Charges and Sallaries of the refpective Officers of the faid Province. *Be it therefore Enacted by the Governour, Council and General Affembly now met and affembled, and it is hereby Enacted by the Authority of the fame,* That there be Affeffed, Levyed and Raifed in manner here after mentioned within this Collony, for and towards the Support of His Majefties Government in the fame, for two Years, to commence from the Twenty third Day of *September,* laft paft, and to continue until the Twenty third Day of *September* which fhall be in the Year of our Lord One thoufand Seven Hundred and Twenty, the Sum of Sixteen Hundred and Seventy two Pounds, in Money appointed by her late Majefty's Proclamation, and fince enforced by Act of Parliament, in the fixth Year of her late Majefties Reign, entituled, *An Act for Afcertaining the Rates of Forreign Coyns in Her Majefty's Plantations in* America, Which is hereby Given to his Majefty, his Heirs and Succeffors, for and towards the Ufes aforefaid.

And be it further Enacted by the Authority aforefaid, That there be likewife Levyed and Raifed in manner hereafter mentioned, within this Province, the Sum of Eight Hundred and Fourteen Pounds, in Money aforefaid, which is hereby given to his Majefty, his Heirs and Succeffors, for and towards the Defraying the Expences of the Gentlemen of his Majefty's Council, at Five Shillings by the Day to each of them, during the Time of their Attendance, fince the Eighth of *April* laft paft, to the End of this prefent Sitting of Affembly, and to the Reprefentatives of the Province at the Rate of Five Shillings by the Day to each Reprefentative, from the faid Eighth Day of April to to the end of this prefent Sitting of the General Affembly, and for paying, for Printing the Acts, Clerk of the Affembly, Door-keeper of the Affembly and Serjant at Arms, and for the Expreffes,

A

And

Pages 79 to 91, unnumbered in the original, are added here in brackets for the sake of continuity.

[79]

And be it further Enacted by the Authority aforesaid, That in case His Excellency Brigader *Hunter,* our present Governour shall by Death, or otherwise cease to be Governour of this Province, at any time after the Passing this Act, and before the said twenty third Day of *September,* which shall be in the Year of our Lord One Thousand Seven Hundred and Twenty, That then it shall and may be Lawful to and for the Treasurer or Treasurers of this Province, for the Time being, and he or they are hereby directed, authorized, impowered, required and commanded to pay unto his Excellency Brigader *Hunter,* his Executors, Administrators or Assigns, or his or their Order out of the said Sum or Sums of Money hereafter to be assessed levyed and raised for the Support of the Government, as aforesaid, for two Years, all such Sum and Sums of Money as at the time of his ceasing to be Governour, as aforesaid, shall then Remain to be due and unpaid to him for his Sallary, and incidental Charges, in proportion to the Sums of Money he shall have received, or shall be payable to him out of the said Sum or Sums of Money to be assessed and raised by Virtue of this Act, for the Support of the Government from the Twenty third Day of September One Thousand Seven Hundred and nineteen, to the Twenty third Day of September, One Thousand Seven Hundred and Twenty.

And be it further Enacted by the Authority aforesaid, That all other Officers of the Government shall likewise be allowed, and the Treasurer or Treasurers, for the time being, is and are hereby Impowered and directed to pay unto them, respectively, the Sum and Sums of Money which at the time of his said Excellency's ceasing to be Governour, as aforesaid, shall be due and unpaid to them for Sallary, in proportion to the Sums of Money they shall have received, or shall be payable to them, respectively, for those or the like Services, out of the said Sum or Sums of Money to be raised by Virtue of this Act for the support of the Government for two Years, as aforesaid; and that the Treasurer or Treasurers for the time being, shall keep and he or they are hereby required and strictly commanded, under the Penalty of Forfeiting his or their Bonds and Securities given for the true performance of his or their Offices to keep or detain in his or their Hands the Remainder of all such Sum or Sums of Money not disposed of by Virtue of this Act, to be disposed by the Governour Council and Assembly, and not otherwise.

And be it further Enacted by the Authority aforesaid, That there shall be raised, assessed and levyed on the Persons, Real and Personal Estates Goods and Chattles herein after mentioned, the Sum of thirteen Hundred and fifty Pounds, Money aforesaid, for the first Year, being for the Sallaries Incidents and Services for the said Time *viz.* Every single Man that Works for Hire, and is not a Bound Servant, shall pay for each Year, for and towards the Support of Government the Sum of Four Shillings.

The Ferry or Ferries at *Perth-Amboy* shall pay for each Year the Sum of Forty Shillings.

The Ferry above *Delaware Falls,* shall pay for each Year the Sum of Ten shillings.

The Ferry near *Delaware Falls,* shall pay for each Year, the Sum of Ten shillings.   The

The Ferry from *Burlington* to *Bristol*, shall pay for Each Year the Sum of Ten shillings.

The Ferry below *Burlington* at the Ferry Point, shall pay for each Year the Sum of Twenty shillings

The Ferry at *Rancocas*, alias, *Northampton River*, shall pay for each side. by the Year, the Sum of Ten Shillings,

The Ferry from *William Cooper to Philadelphia*, shall pay for each Year the Sum of Ten shillings.

The Ferry from *Gloucester to Philadelphia* shall pay for each Year the Sum of Thirty Shillings.

The Ferry at *Inians* over *Rariton River*, shall pay for each Year the Sum of Ten shillings.

Every Wherry that carries Goods or Passengers for Hire, shall pay for each Year the Sum of Ten shillings.

Every Float that carries Goods or Passengers for Hire, shall pay for each Year the Sum of Six shillings.

Every Wood Boat that carries six Coard, and upwards, shall pay for each Year the Sum of Twelve Shillings.

Every Wood Boat that carries under six to Four Coard shall pay for each Year the Sum of Eight shillings.

Every Wood Boat that carries under four Coards, shall pay for each Year the Sum of Foure Shillings.

All Boats Flats and Wherries comeing from the Neighbouring Provinces into this Province, shall pay at the same Rate as is laid on Boats or Wherries of Persons Inhabiting in this Province.

All Saw-Mills and Grist-Mills shall be assest at the Discretion of the Assessors, of each Town, Divission, Precinct or District wherein they lie, provided they do not exceed the Sum of Three Pounds, not are rated as under the Sum of Five Shillings the Year each.

All Merchant or Shop keepers shall be Rated at the Discretion of the Assessors, not under Fifteen Shillings, nor above four Pounds for each Year.

All Indian Traders shall be Rated at the Discretion of the Assessors, not under Forty Shillings, nor above Ten Pounds for each Year.

Every Person not residing in this Province, that shall bring Goods to Sell by Retail. except in publick Fairs, shall pay for each Year the Sum of Three Pounds.

The owners or Possessors of any Houses or Lots of Land in any of the Towns of this Porvince, the Tax of whose Rateable Estate doth not amount to Eight Shillings, shall pay for the said Houses or Lots at the discretion of the Assessors not under Two nor above Twenty Shillings.

All Cattle, Horses and Mares of one Year Old and upwards, shall be valued at Twenty Shillings.

All Sheep of one Year old and upwerds shall be vallued at Three Shillings.

Every White Male Servant, and every Indian, Negro and Mullatto Slave, from Sixteen Years and upwards, except such Slaves as are not able to Work, shall be rated at Twelve Pence the Head, for each Year.

All Lands and Medows held by Pattents, Deeds or Surveys, belonging to any Person Inhabiting within this Province, settled, improved, or Inclosed Artificially or Naturally, shall be Vallued at Seven Pounds the Hundred Acres. *And*

And Be it Further Enacted by the Authority aforesaid, That the said Sum of Thirteen hundred and Fifty Pounds, Money aforesaid, for the Year One Thousand Seven hundred and Nineteen, and the Sum of Five Hundred and Thirty Six Pounds, Money aforesaid, for the Year One thousand Seven hundred and Twenty shall be assessed, levyed and Raised for the first Year in the proportion following, *viz.* By the County of *Bargen*, the Sum of One Hundred and Eleven Pounds twelve Shillings.

By the County of *Essex*, the Sum of One hundred and Eighty five Pounds five Shillings.

By the County of *Middlesex*, the Sum of One hundred and Fifty Seven Pounds Sixteen Shillings.

By the County of *Summerset*, the Sum of Fifty two Pounds Six Shillings.

By the County of *Monmouth*, the Sum of Two Hundred and Thirty Pounds two Shillings.

By the Counties of *Burlington*, and *Hunterdon*, the Sum of Two Hundred and Seventy Pounds Eighteen Shillings.

By the County of *Gloucester*, the Sum of one Hundred and Sixteen Pounds Nineteen Shillings.

By the County of *Salem*, the Sum of one Hundred and Ninety Four Pounds Fourteen Shillings.

By the County of *Cape-May*, the Sum of Forty two Pounds Eight Shillings, which together with the Sum of Three Hundred Pounds, Money according to Her late Majesty's Proclamation, due and payable by the Farmers of the Excise for the Year One Thousand Seven Hundred and Eighteen, on the Twenty fifth Day of *March* One thousand Seven Hundred and Nineteen, which is hereby directed to be paid, by the Treasurer of the Province, who shall receive the same, towards the Sallaries and Incidents aforesaid, makes up the Sum of Sixteen Hundred and Fifty Pounds, Money aforesaid.

And be it further Enacted by the Authority aforesaid, That the said Sum of Five Hundred and Thirty Six Pounds, Money aforesaid, for the Year One Thousand Seven Hundred and Twenty, be assessed, levyed and raised in the Proportion following, *viz.*

By the County of *Bergin*, the Sum of Forty five Pounds Nine Shilling, and Four Pence.

By the County of *Essex*, the Sum of Seventy Five Pounds Eleven Shillings and Four Pence

By the County of *Middlesex*, the Sum of Sixty four Pounds six Shillings.

B the County of *Summerset*, the Sum of Seventeen Pounds four Shillings,

By the County of *Monmouth*, the Sum of Ninety three Pounds fifteen Shillings.

By the Counties of *Burlington* and *Hunterdon*, the Sum of one Hundred and Ten Pounds Seven Shillings.

By the County of *Gloucester*, the Sum of Forty Seven Pounds eighteen Shillings.

By

By the County of *Salem*, the Sum of Seventy nine Pounds one Shilling.

By the County of *Cape-May*, the Sum of Seventeen Pounds Six Shillings. Which together with the Sum of Three Hundred Pounds, due from the Farmers of the Duty of Excise on the Twenty fifth Day of *March*, which will be in the Year of our Lord One Thousand Seven Hundred and Twenty, and which is hereby directed to be paid by the Treasurer of the Province, who shall receive the same, towards the Sallaries and Incidents aforesaid, making in all the Sum of Eight Hundred Thirty six Pounds Money aforesaid, both which said Sums amounting to Six Hundred Pounds, Money aforesaid, arising from the said Duty of Excise, and payable by the Farmers of the said Excise for the said Years One Thousand Seven Hundred and Eighteen and one Thousand Seven Hundred and Ninteen, are hereby directed to be applyed for and towards the Support of the Government for the said Two Years, and to no other use whatsoever.

And be it further Enacted by the Authority aforesaid; That the Assessors for the Assessing the several and respective Sums aforesaid, shall be, and are, such as are already Chosen, or hereafter shall be Chosen by the several Towns, Divisions, Districts and Precincts, according to the Directions of an Act passed the last Session of this present Assembly, entituled, *An Act for the more Regular Chusing and Electing Assessors and Collectors in the respective Towns and Counties in this Province.*

And be it further Enacted by the Authority aforesaid; That for Collecting and Receiveing the several and respective Sums aforesaid, there shall be appointed for each County within this Province. the Collectors hereafter named, *viz.*

For the County of *Bergin*, Mr. *Richard Edsall.*
For the County of *Essex*, Mr. *Robert Ogden.*
For the County of *Middlesex*, Mr. *William Eirs.*
For the County of *Somerset*, Mr. *Michael Van Veighty.*
For the County of *Monmouth*, Mr. *Henry Leonard.*
For the County of *Hunterdon*, Mr. *Ralph Hunt.*
For the County of *Burlington*, Mr. *Richard Smith.*
For the County of *Gloucester*, Mr. *Thomas Sharp.*
For the County of *Salem*, Major *John Ralph.*
For the County of *Cape-May*, Lieut. Coll. *Jacob Spicer.*

And be it further Enacted by the Authority aforesaid, That all and every the Inhabitants and Housholders of each of the respective Counties within this Province, shall on or before the first Tuesday in *May* next, which shall be in the Year of our Lord One Thousand Seven Hundred and Nineteen, give in a true and perfect List of all their Names and Sir-Names, and an Account in Writing of all their Estate Real and Personal, that are Rated or made Rateable by this Act, to the Assessors chosen or to be chosen and elected by Virtue of An Act *for the more Regular Chusing and Electing Assessors and Collectors in the respective Towns and Counties in this Province;* for the time being, of the Town Division, Precinct or District they shall reside in, and in Case of their Neglect or Refusal, shall be liable to the Penalties and Forfeitures mentioned in the said Act.

B

And

And be it further Enacted by the Authorety aforefaid, That all and every the Inhabitants and Houfholders of each refpective County within this Province, fhall at or before the firft Tuefday in *May*, which fhall be in the Year of our Lord One Thoufand Seven Hundred and Twenty, give a true and perfect Lift of all their Names and Sir-Names, and an Account in Writing of all their Eftates, Real and Perfonal, That are to be Rated or make Rateable by this Act, to the Affeffor chofen and elected by Virtue of an Act, Entituled, *An Act for the more Regular chufing and electing Affeffors and Collectors in the Refpcitive Towns and Counties in this Province*, for the Time being, for the Town, Divifion, Diftrict or Precinct they refide in, which Affeffors of the feveral Towns, Divifions, Precincts or Diftricts of each and every County in this Province, are hereby directed and required, on or before the firft Tuefday in *June*, in the Year One Thoufand Seven Hundred and Nineteen, and on or before the firft Tuefday in *June*, which fhall be in the Year One Thoufand Seven Hundred and Twenty, to meet at the moft Publick and Convenient Place in each refpective County of this Province, (except the Counties of *Burlington* and *Hunterdon*, who are to meet as is in this Act hereafter directed) and fhall then and there Compute what the Sum Total of all the certainties, as laid by this Act in the faid County fhall amount unto, and fhall then and there likewife Compute the Value of all the Eftates Real and Perfonal, given in unto the faid Affeffors, within each of the faid Towns, Divifions, Precincts or Diftricts in each and every County of this Province, at the Value in this Act mentioned and Expreffed, and then Caft up what the Sum Total of the faid Eftates Real and Perfonal amounts unto, and then Affefs what fhall be wanting of the Quoto of their refpective County, the certainties being deducted, together with the Collectors and their own Fees, and the Infolvants for the preceeding three Years, equally on the Pound Value of the Sum Total of the Real and Perfonal Eftates laft mentioned. And the faid Affeffors are alfo hereby Required and Commanded, for the Year One Thoufand Seven Hundred and Twenty, to add to the Quota of their feveral Towns, Divifions, Precinct or Diftricts, all fuch Dificiencies as fhall have hapened in the Year One Thoufand Seven Hundred and Nineteen, by Perfons being Dead, Infolvant or Run away, or otherwife, and fhall likewife do and perform all things required of them according to the Directions and Appointment of the faid Act of Affembly, entituled, *An Act for the more Regular Chufing and Electing Affeffors and Collectors in each refpective Town and County in this Province*, and be Subject to the fame Pains, Penalties and Forfeitures as in the faid Act is mentioned and expreffed.

And be it further Enacted by the Authority aforefaid, That every Perfon Taxed, as aforefaid, fhall on or before the fecond Tuefday of *November*, which fhall be in the Year of our Lord One Thoufand Seven Hundred and Nineteen, for the firft Year, and on or before the fecond Tuefday in *November*, which fhall be in the Year of our Lord One Thoufand Seven Hundred and Twenty, for the fecond Year, pay unto the Collector chofen by Virtue of the aforefaid Act, entituled, *An Act for the more Regular Chufing and Electing Affeffors and Collectors in each refpective Town and County in this Province*, the feveral Sums of Money they

they are Affeffed at on the Pains and Penalties mentioned and Recited in this faid Act.

And be it further Enacted by the Authority aforefaid, That the Collectors of the feveral Towns, Divifions, Diftricts and Precincts, chofen by Virtue of the aforefaid Act, paffed at the laft fitting of this prefent Affembly, Entituled, *An Act for the more Regular Chufing and Electing Aff-ffors and Collectors in each Refpective Town and County in this Province,* fhall pay the Sum or Sums of Money he fhall receive, unto the Collector of the County appointed by this Act, for the Year one Thoufand Seven Hund ed and Nineteen, on or before the fecond Tuefday in *December* next, and for the Year One Thoufand Seven Hundred and Twenty at or before the fecond Tuefday of *December* in that Year, under the Pains and Penalties mentioned in the before-mentioned and Recited Act.

And be it further Enacted by the Authority aforefaid, That the Collectors appointed by Virtue of this Act, fhall and are hereby directed and commanded to do the Duties required of them by Virtue of the before mentioned Act of General Affembly, entituled, *An Act for the more regular Chufing and Electing Affeffors and Collectors in the refpective Towns and Counties in this Province,* and be Subject to the fame Pains, Penalties and Forfeitures, as in the faid Act is mentioned and expreffed.

And be it further Enacted by the Authority aforefaid, That every Non-Refident having brought any Goods. Wares or Merchandizes, by Land or by Water, to fell by Retail, except in Publick Fairs, fhall forthwith repair to the Collector of the County, for the Time being, and give an Account of the Value of the Goods he, fhe or they have brought to fell, and pay the Sum of Three Pounds by the Year, as appointed by this Act, who fhall give a Certificate to the Perfon that hath paid the faid Sum, under his Hand and Seal, which Certificate fhall be a fufficient Permit for that Perfon to Sell Goods by Retail at any Time or Place, within this Province for one Year; and the faid Collector fhall receive for the faid Certificate the Sum of Two Shillings and Six Pence to be paid by the Owners of the faid Goods.

And be it further Enacted by the Authority aforefaid, That if any Perfon or Perfons not refiding within this Province fhall Expofe to Sale any Goods, Wares or Merchandifes contrary to the true Intent and Meaning of this Act, the Collector of the County in which fuch Goods are expofed to Sale fhall forthwith Seize and take into his Cuftody fo much of the Goods, Wares and Merchandizes belonging to any Perfon or Perfons fo Offending, and if the Owner or Owners fhall not Redeem the fame within Twenty four Hours by paying as is by this Act directed, and all the Charges accruing by the faid Seizure, then and in fuch Cafe the faid Collector fhall expofe the faid Goods to publick Sale, by Way of Vendue or Out-cry, to the higheft Bidder and take the Sum or Sums as directed by this Act to be paid, and alfo the Sum of Ten Shillings for all Charges and Trouble for making the faid Diftrefs and Sale, and return the overpluls, if any be, to the Owner.

And be it further Enacted by the Authority aforefaid, That the Treafurer of the Eaftern or Weftern Divifion of this Province fhall give Bond with Sufficient Sureties Dwelling within this Province, to the Value of

B 3　　　　　　　　　　　　　　Two

Two Thoufand Pounds each, for the true performance of his or their Office.

And be it further Enacted by the Authority aforefaid, That the Affeffors within each Refpective Town, Division, District or Precinct in any County of this Province, fhall affefs over and above the Sums herein mentioned, in each County, fo much as will pay themfelves and the Collectors for Affeffing Collecting and Gathering the fame as is allowed by an Act, entituled, *An Act for the more Regular Electing and Chufing Affeffors and Collectors in each refpective Town and County of this Province.*

And be it further Enacted by the Authority aforefaid, That the Collector of each refpective County within this Province, fhall on or before the fecond Tuefday in *February,* for the Year one Thoufand Seven Hundred and Nineteen, and on or before the fecond Tuefday in *February* Which fhall be in the Year of our Lord One Thoufand Seven Hundred and Twenty pay all fuch Sum and Sums of Money, by him received by Virtue of this Act, to the Treafurer of the Division he belongs unto and fhall likewife deliver unto the faid Treafurer an exact Copy of the Duplicate of the Affeffments of each Town, Division, Precinct or District, and an exact Account of all the Deficiencies within each Town Division, Precinct and District within his County, to the Treafurer of the Division to which he belongs, on the Pain and Penalty of Fifty Pounds for each Default therein, to be recovered by Action of Debt, Bill, Plaint or Information, in any Court of Record within this Province, and in which no Effoyn Protection or Wager of Law fhall be allowed, nor any more than one Imparlance one half to the Perfon who fhall profecute the fame to effect, the other half to his Majefty, towards the Support of his Majefties Government in the Province of *New-Jerfey,* with double Cofts of Suit.

And Whereas in an Act paffed the laft fitting of the Affembly of this Province, entituled, *An Act for the Currancy of Bills of Credit for the Sum of Eleven Thoufand Six Hundred and Ninety five Ounces of Plate in the Porvince of* New-Jerfey, it is Enacted, That the Treafurer fhall receive the Duty of Excife in the faid Bills of Credit made Current by the faid Act, and in no other Specie whatfoever, and the Currency of the faid Bills of Credit, being fometime fince Expired by their own Limitation, and not again made Current, excepting for the Payment of the Arrearages of Taxes formerly raifed for the Support of the Government, and other emergent Occafions of this Province, *Be it further Enacted by the Authority aforefaid,* That the Treafurers of the Eaftern or Weftern Division of this Province fhall not receive the faid Duty of Excife from the Farmers of the faid Duty, their Heirs, Executors or Adminiftrators in the faid Bills of Credit formerly made Current in this Province, but in Gold at the Rate of Five Shillings and Six Pence the Penny Weight, or in Silver as the Rate prefcribed in Her late Majefties Proclamation, afcertaining the Rate of Forreign Coyn in Her faid Majefties Plantations, any thing in the faid Act to the Contrary in any wife notwithftanding.

And whereas there remains due and unpaid from the feveral Counties of this Province, for Arrearages of the former Taxes, laid by feveral *Acts of Affembly of this Province,* the following Sums of Money, *viz.*

From the County of *Bergen,* the Sum of Seven Pounds Nineteen Shillings and Four Pence.
From

From the County of *Essex*, the Sum of Fifteen Pounds, Twelve Shillings and five Pence.

From the County of *Middlesex*, the Sum of Ninety Four Pounds, Fifteen Shillings.

From the County of *Summerset*, the Sum of Eleven Pounds Six Shillings and Four Pence.

From the County of *Monmouth*, the Sum of Seventy three Pounds one Shilling and Nine pence.

From the County of *Hunterdon*, the Sum of One Hundred and Eighty Pounds Eight Shillings.

From the County of *Burlington*, the Sum of Two Hundred and Sixty Eight Pounds Four Shillings.

From the County of *Gloucester*, the Sum of one Hundred and five Pounds Nineteen Shillings and Five Pence.

From the County of *Salem*, the Sum of Fourty Nine Pounds Three Shillings.

From the County of *Cape-May*, the Sum of Four Pounds One Shilling, and three Pence, which with Interest for the same, at the Rate of Two Shillings in the Pound, amounts in all to the Sum of Eight Hundred Ninety one Pounds, Nine Shillings and Five Pence.

Be it therefore Enacted by the Authority aforesaid, That there be assessed levyed and raised, for the Payment of the said Arrearages and Interest due from the said Counties the Sums following, *viz.*

From the County of *Bergin*, the Sum of Eight Pounds Fifteen Shillings.

From the County of *Essex*, the Sum of Seventeen Pounds two Shillings and Six Pence.

From the County of *Middlesex*, the Sum of One hundred and four Pounds four Shillings and six Pence.

From the County of *Summerset*, the Sum of Twelve Pounds nine Shillings,

From the County of *Monmouth*, the Sum of Eighty Pounds Seven Shillings and Nine Pence.

From the County of *Burlington* the Sum of Two Hundred and Ninety five Pounds and four Pence.

From the County of *Hunterdon*, the Sum of One Hundred and Ninety eight Pounds, Eight Shillings and Seven Pence.

From the County of *Gloucester*, the Sum of One Hundred and Sixteen Pounds Eleven Shillings and Five Pence.

From the County of *Salem*, the Sum of Fifty four Pounds, One Shilling.

From the County of *Cape-May*, the Sum of Four Pounds Nine Shillings and four Pence.

And be it further Enacted by the Authority aforesaid, That the Assessors for the Assessing the several and respective Sums aforesaid, shall be, and are hereby appointed to be, the same Assessors as are already chosen or hereafter shall be chosen by the several Towns, Divisions, Districts and precincts, according to the Directions of an Act, passed at the last siting of the Assembly, Entituled, *An Act for the more Regular Chusing and Electing Assessors and Collectors in the respective Town and Counties of this Province,* which said Assessors are hereby directed, required and commanded to add above and besides the Quota appointed by this Act to be Rated for and towards the Sup-

C

port

port of the Government of this his Majesties Province of *New-Jersey* for two Years, on their several Towns, Divisions, Precincts or Districts the several and respective Sums due as Arrearages from the said Counties, as before in this Act is mentioned and Expressed, and in Case of Failure therein shall be subject to the same Pains and Penalties, as in the aforesaid Act is mentioned and expressed. And that the said Arrearages may be Speedily Collected, and the Bills of Credit formerly made current in this Province called in and sunk, and the People in whose Hands they are duely paid and satisfied for the same, *Be it further Enacted by the Authority aforesaid*, That the Assessors Chosen or to be Chosen according to an Act past the last Sitting of this present Assembly, entituled, *An Act for the more Regular Chusing and Electing Assessors and Collectors in the respective Towns and Counties in this Province*, are hereby required on or before the first Tuesday in *June* next, to meet at the most Publick and convenient Place in each respective County (except the Counties of *Burlington* and *Hunterdon*, who are ordered to meet as hereafter is directed) and shall then and there Assess the aforesaid Arrearages in the same manner, on the Certainty Real and Personal Estates, as they are given into them to be rated, or are Rated in the former part of this Act, for the raising a Support for this his Majesty's Government of the Province of *New-Jersey*, for two Years Equally and Impartially, according to the Best of their Knowledge and Understanding.

And be it further Enacted by the Authority aforesaid, That the Assessors of the Counties of *Burlington* and *Hunterdon* shall meet together at the House of *Thomas Henlocke* in *Burlington*, on the first Tuesday in *June* next, which will be in the Year of our Lord One Thousand Seven Hundred and Nineteen, and then and there Compute the Value of all the Estates Real and Personal given unto the Assessors of the said Counties, and upon a Computation thereof Settle the Quota of each County and the Arearages.

And be it further Enacted by the Authority aforesaid, That every Person taxed for Arrearages, as aforesaid, shall on or before the first Tuesday in *July*, now next ensuing, pay unto the Collector, chosen by Virtue of the aforesaid Act, Entituled, *An Act for the more Regular Chusing and Electing Assessors and Collectors in each Respective Town and County in this Province*, the several Sums they are Assessed at for the said Arrearages, on the Pains and Penlaties mentioned and recited in the said Act.

And be it further Enacted by the Authority aforesaid, That the Collectors of the several Towns, Divisions, Districts and Precincts, chosen by Virtue of the aforesaid Act, entituled, *An Act for the more Regular Chusing and Electing Assessors and Collectors in each respective Town and County in this Province*, shall pay unto the Collector of the County appointed by this Act, at or before the third Tuesday in *July* next, all such Sum or Sums of Money as he shall recive for the said Arrearages, under the Pains and Penalties mentioned in the before-receited Act.

And be it further Enacted by the Authority aforesaid, That the Collectors of each respective County within this Province, shall on or before the second Tuesday in *August* next pay all such Sum or Sums of Money, by him Received for Arrearages by Virtue of this Act, to the Treasurer or Receiver General of the Division he appertains unto, for and towards the Sinking and Paying all the outstanding Bills of Credit, formerly made Current in in this Province under Pain and Penalty of Fifty Pounds to be sued for and Recovered as is in this Act before directed. *Provided always, and it is the true Intent and Meaning of this Act,* That whereas the Treasurer of the Eastern ro Western Division of this Province, is hereafter in this Act Authorized and Impowered to sue for and recover all such Sum or Sums of Money, that are or may be in the Hands of the Receiver of the Three Thousand and Five Thousand Pound Taxes, in the Western Division of this Province, or in the Hands of any of the Collectors, Constables or any other Persons whatsoever; That what Moneys shall be by them or either of them Recovered and Received, from any Persons in any of the Counties of this Province, that it shall and is hereby directed to be deducted out of the Quota appointed by this Act to be payed by the said County, which Account the Treasurer of the Eastern or Western Division of this Province, is hereby required immediately on the Recovery of any Sum of Money to give to the Assessors of the said County, or some one of them, under his Hand that the same bededucted and allowed accordingly.

And Whereas the Treasurer of this Province, by an Act passed the last Sitting of the Assembly, entituled, *An Act for the Currency of Bills of Credit for Eleven Thousand Six Hundred and Seventy Five Ounces of Plate in the Province of* New-Jersey, was directed to Receive the said Bills of Credit made Current by that Act until the first Day of *April,* now next ensuing, and no longer, at which Time the Arrearages laid on the several Counties in this Proveince, will be unpayed and consequenly the said Bills of Credit will be yet remaining un Sunk in private Hands, *Be it further Enacted by the Authority aforesaid,* That the said Bills of Credit, formerly made Current in this Province shall be received by the Treasurer of the Eastern or Western Division of this Province in Payment for all Taxes Raised for the Payment of Arrearages, until the said Arrearages shall be fully Received and Payed.

And That no Persons who at Present may have any of the said Bills of Credit, formerly made Current, in their Hands may suffer any Loss by the same, *Be it Enacted by the Authority aforesaid,* That the Sum of Two Shillings in the Pound, that is by this Act directed to be Assessed, Collected and Levyed in the several Counties of this Province, from whom Arrearages of the former Taxes are due, be allowed by the Treasurer of the said Province or either of them or any of the Collectors of the Counties, appointed by this Act, besides the Sum specified in the said Bills, unto all and every Person or Persons who shall bring the said Bills of Credit, formerly made Current in this Province, to them to be exchanged, and shall exchange the said Bills at the Rate specified therein, if they have any Money; in Hands without any Fee or Reward or defalcation on any Pretence whatsoever, on Penalty of Forfeiting of Ten Pounds for every Offence, to be recovered by Action of Debt, before any two Justices of the Peace, *Quorum unus,* in the County where the said Treasurer or Collector shall reside.

And whereas there are several Sums of Money of the Arrearages mentioned in this Act, and herein appointed to be raised, remaining in the Hands of Private Persons, or in the Hands of Constables. Collectors of the Counties or of the Tresurer of the Western Division, for the Three

Thousand and Five Thousand Pound Taxes, to the very great Damage of those who have truly and faithfully paid their Proportion of the Taxes Rated by the several Acts of Assembly of this province, in Order to recover the same out of their Hands, *Be it Enacted by the Authority aforesaid,* That the Treasurer of the Eastern or Western Division of this Province, are hereby Impowered, Required and Commanded speedily, in the Division they are Treasurer of, to enquire what Money is due on any of the Taxes formerly raised, for the Support of this His Majesties Government of *New-Jersey,* or for any of the Expeditions against *Canada,* may be remaining either in the Hands of the Treasurer of the Western Division or in the Hands of any Collectors, Constables or Private Persons, in any of the Counties of this Province, and shall on the Obtaining an Account thereof be impowered, and he is hereby Impowered, to Summon the said Treasurer of the Western Division, or the said Collector or Collectors, Constable or Constables, or any other Person or Persons, who have any Publick Money in their Hands before any three Justices of the Peace in the County where such Persons shall reside, one whereof to be one of the Judges of the Court of Common Pleas for the said County, for the time being, which Summons the said Judge of the Court of Common Pleas, on Complaint to them made by the Treasurer, either of the Eastern or Western Division, within their respective Division, is hereby Impowered and required forthwith to grant, under his Hand and Seal, specifying therein the Cause of Complaint and the Time and Place when and where the Person or Persons complained against shall appear and shall at the same Time and Place call to his Assistance other two Justices of the Peace of the said County, at which Time and Place the Treasurer of the Eastern or Western Division of this Province, in their respective Divisions, shall exhibit the Complaint against the said Treasurer of the Western Division, or against any Collector or Collectors, Constable or Constables, or any other Person, in Writing, in his Majesty's Name, in the Nature of an Action of Debt, to which complaint the said Treasurer of the Western Division, Collector or Collectors, Constable or Constables, or any other Persons, are required and commanded forthwith to put in their Answer, before the said Judge and Justices, who are hereby Authorized and Impowered summarily, to hear, try and determine the same, and to give Judgment for the Monies that shall appear to them, or to any two of them, the said Judge of the Court of Common Pleas being one, to be due from the said Treasurer of the Western Division, Collector or Collectors, Constable or Constables, or any other Person or Persons that are so Indebted, and to award Execution for the same against the Goods and Chattles of the said Person or Persons that are so Indebted, and if no Goods or Chattles can be found then to commit the Person or Persons, so Indebted, to the Sheriff of the County, when the said Judgment is given who is hereby required and commanded to receive the said Person or Persons so committed, and them in safe Custody to keep, until the Debt and Charges are payed and satisfyed, and two Shillings in the Pound above the Debt and Charges of the Prosecution, which said two Shillings in the Pound is hereby given to the said Treasurer who shall prosecute the same to Effect, as a Reward for that Service.

And be it further Enacted by the Authority aforesaid, That the Treasurer of the Eastern and Western Division of this Province, and each of them are here by required and commanded to keep a just and fair Account, of what Monies they or either of them shall Receive on Account of the Monies raised for the Support of the Government, and of the Arrearages Received either in Bills of Credit, formerly made current in this Province, or in Gold or Silver, with an Exact Account of the Time when, and the Persons from whom he received, and from what County, and shall take in and carefully preserve the said Bills of Credit he shall receive, to be Exhibited to the Governour, Council and Assembly of this Province, when they are pleased to require the same.

And be it further Enacted by the Authority aforesaid, That the Judge and Justices who are hereby Authorized and Impowered to hear and determine the Complaints before-mentioned, and to adjust the Accounts of Arrearages, brought before them as aforesaid, shall be allowed Six shillings for every Account adjusted, and every Action that is brought before them, and Judgment given on the same. And the Treasurer shall be payed his Costs for prosecuting the said Persons so Indebted in proportion to the Fees already appointed, for such and the like Services in an Ordinance already made, for the Establishing Fees for the respective Offices of this Province.

Provided always, That nothing in this Act shall be construed to oblidge any Persons to pay any Fees or Costs of Suit, if it shall appear on the Auditory of their Accounts, that the Persons are not found to be Indebted on any of the Taxes or Arrearages aforesaid.

An Act for Runing and Afcertaining the Line of Partition or Divifion between the Eaftern and Weftern Divifions of the Province of *New-Jerfey*, and for preventing Difputes for the Future concerning the fame ; and for fecuring to the general Proprietors of the Soil of each of the Divifions, and Perfons claiming under them their feveral and refpective Poffeffions, Rights and juft Claims.

WHereas many Doubts, Debates and Controverfies have arifen concerning the Boundaries or Line of Partition between that part of this Province of *New-Jerfey* now commonly called and known by the Name of the *Weftern-Divifion* of the Province of *New-Jerfey*, and that part of faid Province now commonly called and known by the Name of the *Eaftern-Divifion* of the Province of *New-Jerfey*, which have proved a great Obftruction to the Settlement and Improvement of the faid Province, and will, if they continue, prove a very great hindrance to the further Settling and Improving thereof, and of dangerous Confequence to the Peace and Tranquility of the Government and Inhabitants of the fame. AND whereas nothing can be more effectual to prevent Debates and Controverfies that may otherwife hereafter arife concerning the fame, and for fettling and quieting the Minds of all Perfons concerned, than the Fixing the faid Line of Partition on a juft, follid and lafting Foundation. And whereas a certain Line mentioned in an Indenture *Quinti Partite*, dated the firft Day of *July*, in the year 1676. in the 28*th* year of the Reign of King *Charles* the 2d. made and executed by and between Sir *George Carteret* of *Saltrum* in the County of *Sarum*, Knight and Barronet, of the firft part, *William Penn* of *Rickmanfworth*, in the County of *Hartford*, Efqr. of the fecond part, *Gawen Lowrie* of *London*, Merchant, of the third part, *Nicholas Lucas* of *Hartford*, in the County of *Hartford*, Malfter, of the fourth part, and *Edward Billinge* of *Weftminfter*, in the County of *Middlefex*, Gent. (in whom the Inheritance and Fee fimple of that undivided Part, Share and Moyety of the Province of *New-Jerfey*, which did formerly belong to the Right Honorable *John* Lord *Berckley*, Barron of *Stratton*, was by good and fufficient Conveyances in the Law then vefted) of the Fifth part, was by the Perfons here before mentioned, Parties to the aforefaid Indenture *Quinti Partite*, then fole Owners of the whole Province of *New-Jerfey*, meant, intended and agreed to be the Line of Partition or Divifion of the *Eaftern part* of this Province from the *Weftern part* thereof; Which faid Line was meant, intended and underftood by all the Perfons before mentioned, Parties to the faid Indenture *Quinti Partite*, to be a ftraight and direct Line run from the moft Northerly Point or Boundary of the Province of *New-Jerf.)* on the Northermoft Branch of the River *Delaware*, unto the moft Soutlerly Point of the Eaft-fide of a certain Inlet, Harbour or Bay on the Sea-Coaft of the Province of *New-Jerfey*, commonly called and known by the Name of *Little-Egg-Harbour*,

Be it therefore Enacted by the Governour, Council and General Affembly of this Province, and it is hereby Enacted and Declared by the Authority of the

the same, That the said Line, that is to say, A streight and direct Line from the most Northerly Point or Boundary of this Province of *New-Jersey* on the Northermost Branch on the River *Delaware,* unto the most Southerly Point of a certain Beech or Island of Sand, lying next to and adjoyning to the main Sea, on the North-side of the Mouth or Entrance of a certain Inlet, Bay or Harbour, commonly called and known by the Name of *Little-Egg-Harbour,* Is, and shall forever hereafter remain and be the Line of Partition and Division betwixt the *Eastern* and *Western Division* of this Province: And all the Lands, Islands and Waters within this Province, lying and being to the Eastward of the said Line, is, and shall be, and forever hereafter shall remain and be the *Eastern* Part, Share and Division of this Province: And all the Lands, Islands and Waters within this Province, lying and being to the Westward of the said Line before mentioned and described, is, and shall be, and forever hereafter shall remain and be the *Western* Part, Share and Division of this Province.

AND Whereas the said Line of Partition so agreed on, as aforesaid, has (notwithstanding such Agreement) not been, as yet, really and indeed Run, nor the places through which it ought to pass discovered or made known, although Attempts have been made by Persons appointed by Agreement between some of the Proprietors of the Soil of each of the said Divisions, and Lines have been run for that purpose in some parts of this Province, which Lines have been sometimes supposed to run through such parts of this Province as the said Line, agreed on by the Parties to the *Indenture Quinti Partite* aforesaid, should or ought to have run; and which nevertheless, there is great reason to believe, have been Variant and Different from the true Line of Partition agreed on, as aforesaid, by reason of which several Tracts, Parcels and Quantities of Land have been taken up by the general Proprietors of the Soil of the *Eastern Division* of this Province on the Westerly side of the true *Partition Line* agreed on, as aforesaid; and several Tracts, Parcels and Quantities of Land have been taken up by the general Proprietors of the Soil of the *Western Division* of this Province on the Easterly side of the said Line of Partition, many of which Tracts, Parcels and Quantities of Land have been conveyed away and disposed, as well by the General Proprietors of the Soil of the *Eastern Division* of this Province, as by the said General Proprietors of the Soil of the *Western Division* of this Province, and which are now by sufficient Conveyances in the Law vested in the present Possessors thereof, who have made several Settlements and great Improvements upon the same. In order therefore that the present Possessors may be secured in the Enjoyment of the Fruits of their Labour and Industry, and that equal and impartial Justice may be done to the General Proprietors of each of the said Divisions, as far as the present Circumstances of things will admit, *Be it Enacted by the Authority aforesaid,* That when the Line Enacted and Declared by this Act to be the Line of Partition between the Eastern and Western Divisions of the Province, shall be actually Run streight and direct from any one of the Terms, Limits or Ends of the said Line, unto the other Term, Limit or End of the same, and the several places within this Province, through which it

shall

shall pass, be difcovered and made known, that then there shall be, as near as conveniently may be, a Survey or Computation made of the whole and full Amount of all fuch Tracts, Parcels and Quantities of Land as have been taken up, patented, furveyed, held or poffeffed by the Proprietors of the *Eastern Divifion* of *New-Jerfey,* or in their Right by perfons Claiming under them to the Weftward of the faid Line hereby Enacted and Declared to be the *Line of Partition* aforefaid, fo as the utmoft Limits and Boundaries of all or any the faid Tracts and Parcels of Land do not extend farther to the Weftward of the herein and hereby Enacted and Declared *Line of Divifion* than to a certain Line heretofore Run and Markt out in the year of our Lord 1687. by *George Keith,* then Surveyor General of that part of this Province formerly called and known by the Name of *The Province of Eft-New-Jerfey,* beginning at the moft Southerly Point of a certain Beech or Ifland lying next and adjoyning to the main Sea, to the Northward of a certain Bay, Inlet or Harbour lying on the Sea-Coaft of this Province, commonly called or known by the Name of *Little-Egg-Harbour,* and running thence according to the natural Pofition on a Nor. Nor. Weft Fifty Minutes more Wefterly Courfe to the South Wefterly Corner of a certain Tract of Land lying to the Weftward of the South Branch of *Rariton River,* heretofore granted by the Proprietors of the *Eastern-Divifion* of this Province to *John Dobie,* and commonly called and known by the Name of *Dobies Plantation,* Thence along the Rear of the faid *Dobies Plantation,* and along the Rear of the other Tracts of Land and Plantations, as they were here-to-fore Patented or Surveyed in Right of the Proprietors of the *Eastern-Divifion* of this Province, until it Interfects that part of the North Branch of *Rariton-River* which defcends from a Fall of Water, commonly called and known by the *Indian* Name of *Allamitung;* Then running from that Point of Interfection up the Branch or Stream to the Fall of *Allamitung.* All which faid Tracts, Parcels and Quantities of Land, Plantations and Settlements, fo taken up, patented, furveyed, poffeft, fettled or improved, lying and being to the Weftward of the Line of Partition herein before Enacted and Declared to be the *Line of Partition* and *Divifion* between the *Eastern* and *Weftern Divifions of this Province,* and not extending farther to the Weftward of the faid Line of Partition than is herein before limited and expreffed, shall be and remain to the Patentees, Vendees, Poffeffors or Claimers of the fame, their Heirs and Affigns forever, without any Let, Hinderance, Moleftation or Eviction by any of the General Proprietors of the Weftern-Divifion of this Province, their Heirs or Affigns forever. And the faid Patentees, Vendees, Poffeffors or Claimers of any the faid Tracts, Parcels or Quantities of Land aforefaid, their Heirs and Affigns forever shall have, hold, occupy, poffefs and enjoy all and any the faid Tracts, Parcels and Quantities of Land as fully, to all Intents, Conftructions and Purpofes whatfoever, as if all or any the faid Tracts, Parcels or Quantities of Land had been fo taken up, patented, furveyed, bought, claimed or poffeffed in the *Eastern Divifion* of the Province of *New Jerfey* on the Eaft fide of the faid Line herein before Enacted to be the Line of Partition between the *Eastern* and *Weftern Divifions* of

this

this Province, and not otherwise, any Law, Usage or Custom to the contrary in any wise notwithstanding.

And be it Enacted by the Authority aforesaid, That there shall, as near as conveniently may be done, a Survey or Computation be made of the whole and full Amount of all such Tracts, Parcels and Quantities of Land as have been taken up to the Eastward of the herein and hereby Enacted Line of Partition, by or in Right of the Proprietors of the *Western Division* of this Province, and a Survey or Computation be made of the whole and full Amount of all such Tracts, Parcels and Quantities of Land as have been taken up to the Westward of the herein and hereby Enacted Line of Partition, by or in Right of the Proprietors of the *Eastern-Division* of this Province; and in case such Quantity or Number of Acres of the said Land so Surveyed or taken up by or in Right of the Proprietors of both Divisions, as aforesaid, be Equal, the same is hereby Enacted and Declared to be Vested in the several Possessors, Takers up or Claimers of the same, their Heirs and Assigns forever, as fully and amply, to all Intents and Purposes whatsoever, as if the same had been so taken up, possessed or claimed in the respective Divisions of this Province for which the same was taken up, and not otherwise. But in case it shall so happen that upon the aforesaid Computations, the Total Sum or Amount of all the Tracts, Parcels and Quantities of Land taken up by or in Right of the Proprietors of the *Eastern-Division*, to the Westward of the Line of Partition herein and hereby Established and Declared, shall be found to exceed the Quantity or Number of Acres contained within that Tract herein before described and allowed to have been taken up by or in Right of the Proprietors of the *Western Division*, to the Eastward of the said Line of Partition, Then and in such Case there shall be Cut off from all or any of those Tracts and Parcels of Land which have been surveyed or taken up by or in Right of the Proprietors of the *Eastern Division*, either on the West or East side of the said Line of Partition (Excepting such as have been taken up in Right or on account of a first Dividend, or the proportion of Ten Thousand Acres to one Propriety, or Twenty Fourth Part of said Division and Quit-Rent Lands) or out of any Unsurveyed Lands in the said Eastern Division, in such Tracts as shall be thought fit, the full Quantity of such Exceeding, in the most Just and Equal Manner; Which Lands, so taken, shall be an Equivolent to the Proprietors of the Western Division, and shall be held by them, or such of them as shall take up the same, and by their Heirs and Assigns forever, notwithstanding any Survey formerly made thereon, and notwithstanding the said Lands, or some of them, may prove to be scituate on the Eastern side of the Partition Line herein Enacted and Declared, as fully and amply, to all intents and purposes, as if the same had never before been Surveyed to any other person, or were scituate on the Western side of the Partition Line herein before Enacted, any Law, Usage or Custom to the contrary in any wise notwithstanding. But in case it shall so happen, that, upon the aforesaid Computation, the Total Sum or Amount of all the Tracts, Parcels and Quantities of Land taken up by or in Right of the Proprietors of the *Western Division* to the East-

ward

ward of the Line of Partition herein and hereby eftablifhed and declared, fhall be found to exceed the Quantity or Number of Acres contained within that Tract herein before defcribed and allowed to have been taken up by or in Right of the Proprietors of the *Eaftern Divifion* to the Weftward of their faid Line of Partition, Then and in fuch cafe there fhall be taken and cut off from all or any of thofe Tracts and Parcels of Land which have been furveyed or taken up by or in Right of the Proprietors of the *Weftern* Divifion, either on the Eaft or Weft fide of the faid Line of Partition, in Right or on account of a Fourth Dividend, or a Fourth taking up, the proportion of Five Thoufand Acres for each whole Propriety or Hundredth part of the Weftern Divifion, or out of any Un-furveyed Lands within the faid Weftern Divifion, in fuch Tracts as fhall be thought fit, the full Quantity of fuch Exceeding, in the moft juft and equal manner; which Lands, fo taken, fhall be an Equivalent to the Proprietors of the Eaftern Divifion, and fhall be held by them, or fuch of them as fhall take up the fame, and by their Heirs and Affigns for-ever, notwithftanding any Survey formerly made thereon, and notwith-ftanding the faid Lands, or fome of them, may prove to be fcituate on the Weftern fide of the Partition Line herein Enacted and Declared, as fully and amply, to all Intents and Purpofes, as if the fame had never before been Surveyed to any other Perfon, or were fcituate on the Eaftern fide of the Partition Line herein before Enacted, any Law, Ufage or Cuftom to the contrary thereof in any wife notwithftanding.

Provided always, and be it Enacted by the Authority aforefaid, That no Tract or Tracts of Land on which any Settlement and Improvement hath been made, fhall be taken as aforefaid, or applyed to make good fuch Exceeding, or any part thereof, but that all and every fuch Tract and Tracts, or parcels of Land taken up by any of the Proprietors of the *Weftern-Divifion* on the Eaft fide of the aforefaid Line of Partition, on which Tract or Tracts any Settlement or Improvement is made, fhall be held by the Poffeffors or Owners thereof, their Heirs and Affigns, as fully and amply, to all intents and purpofes whatfoever, as if fuch Tract and Tracts had been taken up on the Weft fide of the faid Line of Par-tition, and not otherwife. And all and every fuch Tract and Tracts or Parcels of Land taken up by any of the Proprietors of the *Eaftern-Divifion* on the Weft fide of the aforefaid Line of Partition, on which Tract or Tracts any Settlement or Improvement is made, fhall be held by the Poffeffors or Owners thereof, their Heirs and Affigns, as fully and amply, to all intents and purpofes whatfoever, as if fuch Tracts had been taken up on the Eaft fide of the faid Line of Partition, and not otherwife.

Provided alfo, That if any Proprietor of the *Eaftern-Divifion,* from whom any Lands are take to make good the Equivalent to the Proprietors of the *Weftern Divifion,* as aforefaid, have, or fhall procure within two years after the fame are taken, to make good the Equivalent aforefaid, a Proprietary Right to any unfurveyed Lands within the *Weftern Divifion* of this Province, fuch Proprietor of the *Eaftern Divifion* may retain and keep to himfelf fuch Lands as otherwife he might by this Act have been obliged to furrender to the Weftern Proprietors, by laying on the fame a good Proprietary Right to the fame Quantity of Land in the *Weftern*

(2) *Divifion*

Division of this *Province,* any thing herein contained to the contrary notwithstanding.

Provided also, That if any Proprietor of the Western Division, from whom any Lands are taken up to make good an Equivalent to the Proprietors of the *Eastern-Division,* as aforesaid, have, or shall procure within two years after the same are taken to make good the Equivalent aforesaid, a Proprietary Right to any unsurveyed Lands within the Eastern Division of this Province, such Proprietor of the Western Division may retain and keep to himself such Lands as otherwise he might by this Act have been obliged to surrender to the Eastern Proprietors, by laying on the same a good Proprietary Right to the same Quantity of Land in the Eastern Division of this Province, any thing herein contained to the contrary notwithstanding.

And be it Enacted by the Authority aforesaid, That upon the Computation made, in case it shall happen that the Quantity of Lands taken up by or in Right of the Proprietors of the Western Division on the East side of the herein and hereby Enacted Line of Partition does exceed the Quantity of Lands taken up by or in Right of the Proprietors of the Eastern-Division, on the West side of the herein and hereby Enacted Line of Partition, the Surveyor General of the Eastern Division, or his Deputy, and Commissioners or Mannagers for the same, herein after appointed, or the major part or Survivor of them, shall forth-with survey, allot, take up and ascertain such Exceeding on the Lands out of which the same is by this Act directed to be taken, and shall cause to be Recorded a Certificate under their hands how and in what manner they have done the same, in the Secretary's Office of this Province, and Surveyor General's Office of the Eastern Division, there to be in publick View, and shall send a true Copy thereof to the Council of Proprietors of the *Western Division* of this Province. And upon the Computation made, in case it shall happen that the Quantity of Lands taken up by or in Right of the Proprietors of the Eastern Division on the West-side of the herein and hereby Enacted Line of Partition, does exceed the Quantity of Lands taken up by or in Right of the Proprietors of the Western Division, on the East side of the herein and hereby Enacted Line of Partition, the Surveyor General of the *Western Division,* or his Deputy, and Commissioners or Mannagers for the same, herein after appointed, or the major part or Survivor of them, shall forth-with survey, allot, take up and ascertain such Exceeding on the Lands out of which the same is by this Act directed to be taken, and shall cause to be Recorded a Certificate, under their hands, how and in what manner they have done the same, in the Secretary's Office of this Province, and in the Surveyor General's Office of the Western Division, there to be in publick View, and shall send a true Copy therof to the Proprietors of the *Eastern Division* of this Province. After which Certificate Recorded and Returned, as aforesaid, the respective Proprietors who had Right to take up such Exceeding, shall be and are hereby forever Barr'd of claiming any other Lands in Right of such Exceeding, any thing herein contained to the Contrary notwithstanding.

And the more Equally to preserve to each Division the same Quantity of Land which falls to it by the Line of Division or Partition between the Eastern and Western Divisions of this Province, *Be it Enacted by the Authority aforesaid*, That all the Tracts of Land which have been formerly Patented or Surveyed to the Proprietors of the *Eastern Division*, & to others claiming under them, to the Westward of the said Line of Partition, as also all such Lands as shall or may fall to them as an Equivolent out of the *Western Division*, and to the Westward of the said *Partition Line*, shall be taken, construed and forever hereafter deemed to be a part, share and portion of the *Eastern Division* of this Province. And all the Tracts and Parcels of Land which the Proprietors of the *Western Division*, or persons claiming under them, shall, in pursuance of this Act, and according to the true intent and meaning thereof, fall on the East side of the said Line of Partition, (excepting any small parcels which shall be Remote, and wholly severed from the Body of the said Division) shall be taken, construed and forever hereafter deemed to be a part, share and portion of the *Western Division* of this Province; Of which all Bodies Corporate and Politick, and all other Persons, are to take Notice, and govern themselves accordingly, any thing herein contained to the contrary notwithstanding.

And for the more Effectual doing of Justice to such Proprietors who shall be entituled to take up any Lands either in the Eastern or Western Divisions of this Province, for or by reason of any Deficiency or Exceeding of the Lands mentioned to be taken up within the Eastern Division of this Province, by or in Right of the Proprietors of the Western Division of the same, *It is further Enacted by the Authority aforesaid*, That from and after the Publication of this Act, until such time as it shall be determined in the manner before in this Act directed, of what Number of Acres such Defect or Exceeding of the Quantities of Land herein before mentioned, does consist, No Land shall be surveyed or taken up (above the Quantity of one hundred Acres in one Tract, and by one Person, and this only among the Inhabitants and Settlements) within either of the Divisions of this Province. And in case any person or persons whatsoever shall survey or take up any Land contrary to the true intent and meaning hereof, All and every such Survey and Surveys, and Taking up, is, and are hereby declared to be so far void, that any of the persons entituled to take up any Lands in either of the Divisions aforesaid, as his part and share of the Equivalent, before mentioned, due to him, may survey and take up any such Land, and shall thereupon be as fully and absolutely entituled to hold the same, to him, his Heirs and Assigns forever, as if no such former Survey had been made thereon.

And Whereas the Surveys of Lands, and the Quantities held thereby, in this Province, have frequently been Uncertain, and difficult to be discovered, by reason of the Office of Surveyor General has not been duly established and regularly kept within the respective Divisions,

Be it therefore Enacted by the Authority aforesaid, That the Surveyor General of the Eastern Division, shall, by himself or his lawful Deputy, hold a publick Office in the City of *Perth-Amboy* for all the Eastern Division of this Province; and the Surveyor General of the Western Division shall, by himself or his lawful Deputy, hold a publick Office in the Town

of

of *Barlington* for the Western Division of this Province, in which Offices, respectively, shall be carefully entered and kept the Surveys of all Lands which shall hereafter be made within this Province; and such Entries shall be of Record, and may be pleaded as Evidence in any of his Majesties Courts of Judicature within this Province. And the said Surveyor and Surveyors General is and are hereby Authorized and Impowered to collect, demand, receive, sue for and recover from all Persons whatsoever within this Province, all Books of Surveys, general Charts, Maps and Draughts of Lands heretofore made by any publick Surveyor or Surveyors for the Lands within his or their District or Districts, which may be of general Use for proving the Rights of the Proprietors, or of persons claiming under them, to any Tracts or Parcels of Land surveyed and taken up within this Province; and the same shall be safely lodged and kept in the said respective Offices within the Division within which the Lands, whereunto such Books, Charts, Maps and Draughts do belong, are respectively scituate (excepting such Books of Surveys as he shall recover belonging to the *Eastern Division*, which upon Recovery he shall forth-with deliver into the Recorders Office of the said Division, there to be kept for publick Use and View) *Providing always*, That he Re-deliver, with all convenient speed, such of them as are the Property of any particular person, to the person whose Property they are, after he or they the Surveyor or Surveyors aforesaid have either taken Authentick Copies thereof, or Recorded them in their Books. And the said Surveyor or Surveyors General shall give Security to his Excellency Brigadeer *Hunter*, our present Governour, or to the Governour or Commander in Chief, for the time being, for the use of the Proprietors of each respective Division, and their Successors, in the Sum of *One Thousand Pounds* of lawful Money of *Great Britain*, for his and their delivering up to his and their respective Successor and Successors therein all Books of Surveys, general Charts, Maps and Draughts, which he shall have received and recovered, as aforesaid, and which have not otherwise been directed to be delivered, as aforesaid, and the Books he or they shall have kept during the Execution of his or their respective Offices.

And Whereas great Inconveniencies have happened by the making and not recording of Surveys, whereby many have not only got Lands Survey'd, which have been formerly surveyed, not knowing of any former Survey, but have settled and made great Improvement of the same, and have been afterwards Ousted thereof. For the Remedying whereof for the Future, *It is hereby Enacted and Declared by the Authority aforesaid*, That all Surveys heretofore made, the Certificates whereof are in the hands of any of the Inhabitants of this Province, or any of the Neighbouring Provinces, which are not within two years; and that all Surveys heretofore made, the Certificates whereof are in the hands of People living beyond Seas, which are not within three years after the Publication hereof, duely Recorded, either in the Recorders Office, or in the Surveyor General's Record of the respective Division in which such Lands are surveyed, be forever hereafter Void and of none Effect; and any succeeding Survey, duely made thereof, and Recorded, shall be as good and sufficient as if no former Survey had been made.

And

And to the end that the good Intention and Defign as well of a certain Act or Law paffed this prefent Seffion of Affembly, entituled, *An Act for Running and Afcertaining the Divifion Line betwixt this Province and the Province of* New-York, may the more fpeedily have the defired effect, *Be it Enacted by the Authority aforefaid,* That there shall be raifed by the General Proprietors of the *Eaftern Divifion* of this Province, or out of their Eftates therein, in proportion to their refpective Shares, fuch Sum or Sums of Money as may be judged neceffary for defraying their part or proportion of the Charges of Runing or procuring to be Run the Divifion Line between the *Eaftern Divifion* of this Province and the Province of *New-York,* and of Runing the feveral Lines and difcovering the feveral Quantities of Land herein before mentioned, as the fame are by this Act directed. And there shall alfo be raifed by the General Proprietors of the *Weftern Divifion* of this Province, or out of their Eftates therein, in proportion to their refpective Shares, fuch Sum or Sums of Money as may be judged neceffary for defraying their part or proportion of the Charge of finding or procuring to be found the *North Point of Partition* upon *Delaware-River,* and of Runing the feveral Lines and difcovering the feveral Quantities of Land herein before mentioned, as the fame are by this Act directed. And for the more fpeedy and effectual Runing of the faid Lines, there shall be Commiffioners and Mannagers appointed, and accordingly *John Hamilton, David Lyell, George Willocks* and *John Harrifon,* Eqrs. all of the faid *Eaftern Divifion,* are hereby appointed to be Commiffioners or Mannagers for raifing, collecting and receiving fuch Sum or Sums of Money as is or are to be raifed out of the Eaftern Divifion, as aforefaid. And *Ifaac Sharp, James Logan, Tho. Lambert* and *John Reading,* Efqrs. all of the faid Weftern Divifion, are hereby appointed to be the Commiffioners or Mannagers for raifing, collecting and receiving fuch Sum or Sums of Money as is or are to be raifed out of the Weftern Divifion, as aforefaid. In order whereunto the faid *John Hamilton, David Lyell, George Willocks* and *John Harrifon,* or the major part of them, shall, on the fecond *Tuefday* of *May* next, meet with the General Proprietors of the *Eaftern Divifion* at *Perth-Amboy,* to advife and confult with them what Sum or Sums of Money may be neceffary to be raifed by the faid General Proprietors for the purpofes aforefaid, not exceeding *Six Hundred and Fifty Pounds,* and in what manner the fame may beft be done. And the faid *Ifaac Sharp, James Logan, Thomas Lambert* and *John Reading,* or the major part of them, shall, in like manner, on the firft *Tuefday* of *May* next, or fuch other Day or Days, (Twenty Days before the faid Day) to be prefixed, meet with the Council of Proprietors of the Weftern Divifion, to advife and confult with them what Sum or Sums of Money may be neceffary to be raifed by the faid General Proprietors of the Weftern Divifion, for the aforefaid purpofes refpectively, not exceeding *Five Hundred Pounds,* and in what manner the fame may beft be done. And the faid *John Hamilton, David Lyell, George Willocks* and *John Harrifon,* Commiffioners or Mannagers for the Eaftern Divifion, or the major part or Survivor of them; and the faid *Ifaac Sharp, James Logan, Thomas Lambert* and *John Reading,* Commiffioners or Mannagers for the Weftern Divifion, or the major part or

Survivor

Survivor of them, after the faid respective Sums, and the manner of raising them are agreed on, may and shall proceed, respectively, to raise, collect and receive every such Sum and Sums of Money, and in such manner as aforesaid. To which end they the said Commissioners or Mannagers, respectively, or the major part or Survivor of them, are declared to be vested with full *Power* and Authority, in their own Names, but in behalf of all the other General Proprietors of each respective Division whom (as there may be Occasion) they shall represent, to appear in Courts, Implead and Profecute, Sell and Convey Lands, and to do every other lawful Act and Thing whatfoever, which shall be found necessary to the raising of such Money, as aforefaid, and Recovering the same out of the Estate or Estates of the General Proprietors, all or any of them respectively, but not otherwife. *Providing always,* That the Mannagers of the Eastern Division aforesaid, do not fell, for the Purpofe aforefaid, above *Four Thousand Acres,* and that to be in one Tract, out of the Unappropriated Lands. And in cafe it be found necessary to make Sale of any of the said General Proprietors Lands in either Division, for raising fuch Sum or Sums respectively, as aforefaid, or any part of the fame, Every fuch Sale and Conveyance made by the said Commissioners or Mannagers, or by the Major part or Survivor of them respectively, in each Division, shall be as absolute, vallid and unquestionable a Title for fuch Lands, to the Vendees or Purchasers thereof, their Heirs and Assigns, as if the fame had been made by all and every one, or any of the General Proprietors of fuch respective Division, any Law, Usage or Custom to the contrary notwithstanding. And the said Commissioners or Mannagers are hereby Required, in the first place, to pay out of fuch Sum and Sums of Money as they shall receive, the respective parts, shares and proportions of Money which are respectively to be advanced for defraying the Charges of Runing, or procuring to be run, the Line of Division between the *Eastern Division* of this Province and the Province of *New-York,* to fuch Person or Persons as are or shall be appointed by virtue of the herein before recited Act or Law passed for that purpose. And the said Commissioners or Mannagers of the *Eastern Division,* or the Major part or Survivor of them, by and with the Consent and Approbation of the other General Proprietors of the Eastern Division, their Agents or Attornies, or the Majority of those that can be advised with; And the said Commissioners and Mannagers of the *Westren Division,* or the Major part or Survivor of them, by and with the Advice and Consent of those called the *Council of Proprietors* in the Western Division, are hereby respectively Authorized and Impowered to appoint the Surveyor General, and fuch other Surveyors and fit able Persons as shall be judged necessary for running the Lines, making the Divisions and Discovering the Quantities of Land herein before mentioned, which are to be done by virtue of this Act, and to do and Transact all other Matters whatfoever necessary for the fame; and out of the said Sum or Sums of Money raised as aforefaid, to defray the Charges thereof; For their Trouble in all which, they shall take to themselves, respectively, after the Rate of *Ten per Cent.* or *Two Shillings in the Pound,* out of all they shall receive. And for the Ballance, if any should remain, they shall be respectively accountable

able to the General Proprietors of that Division out of which the Money left was raised. And for their more effectually being accountable, the Commissioners or Mannagers aforesaid, shall yearly, and every year, fairly state their Accounts, and deliver them in to the Secretary's Office of this Province, upon Oath, or Affirmation, if *Quakers*, there to remain and be seen by the Proprietors of the respective Divisions, each of which Proprietors are hereby entituled to their share of the remainder, in proportion to their Right, after all the Services aforesaid are performed, and their reasonable Charges deducted, over and above the *Ten per Cent.* aforesaid.

Providing always, That in case any of the Commissioners or Mannagers aforesaid, before named, shall dye, or refuse to accept, then and in that case, if he be of the *Eastern Division*, his Excellency the Governour, for the time being, and if of the *Western Division*, those called the Council of Proprietors, are hereby impowered to appoint one in the place of such dying or refusing to accept, who is hereby vested with the same Powers, and subjected to the same Directions as herein is set down to the Mannagers herein named.

An Act for Runing and Ascertaining the Division Line betwixt this Province and the Province of *New-York*.

WHereas many Disputes and Controversies have of late happened betwixt the Proprietors and Owners of Land in this Province of *New-Jersey*, and the Owners of Land in the Province of *New-York*, which lie near to or adjoyning upon the *Division Line*, as well as between the Officers of the Government, and a Number of Lawless Men there, who Elude the Laws of both Provinces, and pay Taxes and Obedience to neither, pretending to be scituate in each of them, to serve their evil purpose of Disobedience to the lawful Commands and Demands of the Officers of the Government. To prevent which for the Future, and in order that such of the Inhabitants of this Colony, whose Estates or Habitations are adjacent to and border on the said Partition Line, may Peaceably, and without Molestation, enjoy the Fruits of their Labour, and the Government may not be defrauded of the publick Taxes that are or may arise and become due from the said Inhabitants, by their pretending that they do not dwell within this Colony,

Be it Enacted by the Governour, Council and General Assembly, and it is hereby Enacted and Declared by the Authority of the same, That there shall be two or more Commissioners, with the Surveyor General, appointed by his Excellency the Governour of this Province, or the Governour or Commander in Chief of this Province, for the time being, by and with the Consent of the Council, who shall be Impowered by a Commission under the Great Seal of this Province, to joyn with such Commissioners and Surveyors as shall be appointed on the part and behalf of the Province of *New-York*. Which said Commissioners and Surveyors, so Appointed and Commissionated, as aforesaid, shall, on the part and behalf

of

of this Province of *New-Jersey*, Run, Survey, Agree and Ascertain the said Line, Limits and Boundaries betwixt this Province of *New-Jersey*, and the said Province of *New-York*, according to the true Limits thereof, as near as conveniently can be done.

And be it further Enacted by the Authority aforesaid, That when such Commissioners as shall be appointed by his Excellency the Governour, or the Governour or Commander in Chief for the time being, by and with the Advice and Consent of the Council, with the Surveyor General of this Province, have joyned with such Commissioners and Surveyors as shall be appointed for and on the behalf of the Province of *New-York*, and have Ascertained, Run and Agreed on the *Line of Partition* or *Division* betwixt this Province and the Province of *New-York*, they shall make Return of the same, under their Hands & Seals, to his Excellency the Governour, or the Governour or Commander in Chief of this Province, for the time being, which Return shall be Filed and Recorded in the Secretary's Office of this Province. Which said Line of Division or Partition betwixt this Province and the Province of New-York, being Ascertained, Run and Agreed on, and Recorded, as aforesaid, shall forever hereafter be Deemed, Taken, Be, Remain and Continue the *Partition Line, Limit* and *Boundary* betwixt this Province and the Province of *New-York*, and all Bodies Politick and Corporate, and all other Persons whatsoever within this Province, or Claiming any Right and Property therein, shall be Concluded by the same, any Law, Usage or Custom or Pretence to the contrary in any wise notwithstanding.

An Act to prevent Clandestine Marriages.

WHereas of late years several Young Persons have been by the Wicked Practices of evil disposed Persons, and their Confederates, inticed, inveigled and deluded, led away and Clandestinely Married, which has often been to the Ruin of the Parties so married, as well as the great Grief of their Parents and Relations. In order therefore to prevent the like, as much as may be, for the future, *Be it Enacted by the Governour, Council and General Assembly of this Province, and it is hereby Enacted by the Authority of the same,* That from and after the Publication of this Act, no Licence shall be given to Marry any Person under the Age of One and Twenty years, until such Person have had the Consent of his or her Parent or Parents, Guardian or Guardians, or Person or Persons under whose Care and Government he or she shall be, signified by a Certificate in Writing, under the hand of the Parent or Parents, Guardian or Guardians of him and her intended to be Married ; or in case any the said Persons intending to be Married have no Parent or Guardian, then by a Certificate in Writing under the Hand of the Person or Persons under whose Care and Government the said person intending to be Married, at that time, shall be; which Certificate shall be filed in the Secretary's Office of this Province, and Registred in a Book to be kept for that purpose, for doing of which is shall be lawful for the Secretary

of

of this Province. or his lawful Deputy, to receive the Sum of three Shillings as a Fee or Reward.

And be it further Enacted by the Authority aforesaid, That any Person or Officer that now is, or hereafter shall be appointed by the Governour or Commander in Chief, ofor the time being, to give out Licence of Marriage within this Province, who shall give or issue the same to any person or persons contrary to the directions, true intent and meaning of this Act, or any part thereof, shall Forfeit the Sum of *Five Hundred Pounds* lawful Money of his Majestys *Plantations* in *America,* to be recovered by Action of Debt. with cost of Suit, by the Parent, Guardian or of (or person under whose care) any person married by virtue of such Licence, shall be, in the supreme Court within this Province, in which there shall be no Essoyn, Protection or Wager of Law, or any more than one Imparlance. And any Minister or pretended Minister of the Gospel, Justice of the Peace or other Person, having or pretending to have, Authority to joyn Persons together in the holy Bands of Matrimony, who shall joyn any Persons together in Marriage, not having a Licence mentioning such Certificate had, as by this Act is directed and Intended, or without having been Published, as in and by this Act is appointed and intended, or contrary to the true Intent and Meaning of this Act, or any Part thereof, every such Minister or pretended Minister of the Gospel, Justice of the Peace or other Person, having, or pretending to have Authority to joyn Persons together in the holy Bands of Matrimony, shall for every such Offence forfeit the Sum of two Hundred Pounds, Lawful Money of his Majesty's Colonies and Plantations in *America,* the one half thereof to His Majesty, His Heirs and Successors, the other half thereof to the Parents or Guardian of such Person who shall be so joyned in Marriage as aforesaid, or to such other Person or Persons who shall prosecute the same to Effect, to be recovered by Action of Debt, Bill, Plaint or Information in any of his Majesties Courts of Record within this Province.

And for the more effectual preventing Frauds in the Obtaining Licences for Marriage, *Be it Enacted by the Authority aforesaid,* That every Person under the Age of Twenty one Years, as aforesaid, praying a Licence to be married, and producing a Certificate as by this Act is directed, shall, before he or she obtaines such Licence, take an Oath upon the Four Holy Evangelists of Almighty God, or if really of tender Conscience, shall make a Solemn Affirmation and Declaration in such Form and Manner, as in and by the Act or Acts of the General Assembly of this Province is or shall be prescribed and directed, That the Certificate by him or her produced is true and genuine, and truly and *bona fide* figned by the Person or Persons said to sign the same ; which Oath, Affirmation or Declaration, the Person or Officer impowered to give out Licences, as aforesaid, is hereby Impowered, Directed and Required to administer. And the Person or Persons, so Praying a Licence as aforesaid, shall also before the Obtaining such Licence, enter into Bond to his Excellency Brigadeer *Robert Hunter,* Esq; now Governour of this

(4) Province

Province, or to the Governour or Commander in Chief of this Province for the time being, with two Sufficient Sureties, dwelling and having Real Estates within this Province, in the Poenal Sum of five Hundred Pounds Lawful Money of His Majesties Colonies and Plantations in *America*, on the Conditions following, *viz.*

THE Condition of this Obligation is such, That whereas there is a mutual Contract of Marriage between *A. B.* of   on the one Party, and *C. D.* of   on the other Party, and Certificates having been produc'd and sworn to, or have taken a Solemn Affirmation, according to one Act of General Assembly of this Province, made in the fifth Year of the Reign of our Sovereign Lord *GEORGE,* by the Grace of God King of *Great Britain, France and Ireland,* and the Territories and Dominions thereunto belonging, entituled, *An Act to prevent Clandestine Marriages.* Now if it shall hereafter appear that the said Certificates, or either of them, have been fraudulent, or that either the aforesaid *A. B.* of   or the aforesaid *C. D.* of   had not the Consent of their Parents, Guardians, or Persons under whose care they were, signing the said Certificates, or that the said *A. B.* and *C. D.* or either of them, had some Lawful Let or Impediment of Pre-contract, Affinity or Consanguinity, to hinder their being joyned in the Holy Bands of Matrimony, and afterwards of Living together as Man and Wife, Then this Obligation to stand and remain in full Force and Virtue, otherwise to be Void and of none Effect.

Which Bond shall be and remain in the Secretaries Office of this Province to be produced as Occasion shall require.

And be it Enacted by the Authority aforesaid, That in Case it shall so happen that any Person under the Age of Twenty one Years aforesaid, shall be deluded and married, contrary to the true Intent and Meaning of this Act, that then, and in such Case, it shall and may be lawful for the Parent or Guardian of such Person, under the Age of Twenty one Years, so married by Virtue of such Licence, as aforesaid, or the Person under whose Care and Government such Person so married as aforesaid, shall have been, to put the Bond, before in this Act mentioned, in Suit, in the superiour Court of this Province, and recover to his, her or their Use the Sum therein mentioned, the said Parent or Parents, Guardian or Guardians or other Person or Persons, by this Act impowered to put the said Bond in Suit, first giving sufficient Security with two sufficient Sureties, dwelling in this Province, in the Sum of Twenty Pounds to pay the Costs of Suit in case they become Non-Suit, Discontinue, or Verdict be given against them, or Judgment be given against them, on Demurrer, any thing in this or in any other Act to the contrary hereof in any wise notwithstanding.

And for the better and more effectually Preventing Private and Clandestine Marriages to be made contrary to, and to defeat and elude the true Intent and Meaning of this Act, or any Part thereof by

fraudulent

fraudulent and deceitful Practices in the Publications of the Intentions of Marriage between any Persons, hereafter to be married within this Province, *Be it Enacted by the Governour, Council and General Assembly, and it is hereby Enacted by the Authority of the same,* That every Person and Persons under the Age before-mentioned, not taking a Licence, but intending to publish their Intentions of Marriage, in Order to their being lawfully joyned together in the holy Bands of Matrimony, shall, before any such Publication be made, repair to the Clerk of the Peace, or County-Clerk of such County within this Province in which the Parent or Parents, Guardian or Guardians, Person or Persons under whose Care or Government each Person, so intending to be married, does usually dwell and reside, and shall produce to such Clerk of the the Peace such Certificate, as is herein before directed, and make Oath or Affirmation, to be administred by the said Clerk, and enter into Bond accordingly, with Sureties, in the Sum and Manner directed, which Bond shall be carefully kept in the Clerks Office of the said County, and the Certificate enregistered in a Book to be kept for that purpose, upon which the said Clerk, within Fourteen Days thereafter, shall affix a Writing in a fair legible Hand, in the *English* Tongue, at Three the most publick Places in the said County, setting forth the Persons Names, Places of abode and Intentions of Marriage, to be between them, for all which Certificate, Bond and Publication the said Clerk shall receive as a Fee or Reward, from the Person desiring such Publication, the Sum of Twelve Shillings, Money aforesaid; And if the said Writing so affixed stand and remain Publick, for and during the Space of One and Twenty Days, from the Time of setting up the same, and no Objections made to it, and signified by Writing to the Clerk aforesaid, by the Parent or Parents, Guardian or Guardians, of either of the said Persons mentioned in the said Publication, or Person or Persons under whose Care and Government the said Persons, or either of them, so intending to be married, shall be, then upon Certificate thereof made by the said Clerk, it shall and may be Lawful for any Person, having Authority so to do, to joyn the said Persons together in the holy Bands of Matrimony, and not otherwise. And in Case it shall so happen that the Parent or Parents, Guardian or Guardians of any such Person under Age and published as aforesaid, or that the Person or Persons under whose Care, Tuition or Government any such Person under Age shall be, at any time, during the Space of One and Twenty Days, after the time of such Publication set up, as before is Directed, signify his, her or their Dislike or Disapprobation of such Marriage so intended to be consumated, by Writing under his, her or their Hands, to the Clerk of the Peace aforesaid, that then and in such case the said Clerk shall not give them the Certificate before-mentioned, of their being lawfully published, nor shall any Person Presume, without such Certificate, to joyn the said Persons together in the holy Bands of Matrimony, unless the said Persons, so Intending to be married and published as beforesaid, produce a Licence legally obtained, as by this Act is directed; and every Clerk of the Peace offending contrary to the Directions, true Intent and Meaning

of

of this Act, or any Part thereof, shall, for every such Offence, forfeit the Sum of Five Hundred Pounds, lawful Money aforesaid, any thing in this or any other Act to the contrary hereof in any wise notwithstanding.

And be it further Enacted by the Authority aforesaid, That if any Persons published as before directed, shall be joyned together in the Bands of Matrimony without first having had the Consent of their Parents or Guardians or Persons under whose Care they at that Time shall be, it shall and may be lawful for the Parent or Parents, Guardian or Guardians or Person or Persons under whose Care such Minor shall at that time be, to put the said Bond in Suit in the Supream Court of this Province, or in any the Inferiour Courts of Common Pleas in any County within the same, where the Cause of Action shall arise, and recover to the use of such Parent, Guardian or other Person before-mentioned, empowered, by this Act, to sue for the same, the Penalties in such Bond contained, such Parent, Guardian or other Person having first given Security for the Paying the Costs of Suit, as in and by this Act is before directed and appointed,

Provided always, And it is hereby further Enacted, That neither this Act, nor any Part thereof, shall be construed to be meant and intended to prohibit the Marrying within any Degrees of Affinity or Consanguinity, but such only as by the Laws and Statutes now in Force, or hereafter to be in Force, within his Majesties Kingdom of *Great Britain,* are or shall be prohibited.

Provided always, That it shall and may be Lawful for all or any Religious Societies in this Province, to joyn together in the Holy Bands of Matrimony, such Persons as are of the said Society, according to the Rules and Customs of the Society they appertain to, provided they have the Consent of Parents, Guardians or of such Person under whose Care and Tuition they are, signified in Writing, under the Hand or Hands of such Parent or Parents, Guardian or Guardians, or such Person or Persons under whose Care and Tuition the said Persons so to be Married are, any thing in this Act to the contrary, in any wise notwithstanding.

An Act for the Building, Rebuilding, Repairing or Amending of Bridges in the respective Towns and Precincts within this Province.

WHereas there are many large Bridges within this Province, which belong to particular Towns and Precincts to amend and repair, which cannot sufficiently be repaired by Day Labour, without the Assistance of particular Handicrafts Men,

Be it therefore Enacted by the Governour, Council and General Assembly, and it is hereby Enacted by the Authority of the same, That where there are any large Bridges in any the Towns, Precincts, Districts or Divisions

of

of this Province, which cannot well be Repaired by Day Labourers, that the Over-feers of the High-ways, from time to time, shall give notice to two Justices of the Peace of the County (one whereof being of the *Quorum*) and the two Free-holders chosen by said Town, Precinct or Division by virtue of an Act, entituled, *An Act for raising of Money for building and repairing of Goals and Court-houses,* &c. in which said Bridge or Bridges do lie, together with the Surveyors of the High-ways of the said Town, Precinct or Division in which said Bridge or Bridges do lie, to assemble and meet together at such time and place as the said Over-feer shall appoint, and then and there shall Contract and agree with such Trades-men, and others, as they, or the major part of them, then and there met, shall think fit, to build, rebuild, amend or repair such Bridge or Bridges as they shall then think necessary to be built, rebuilt, amended or repaired, so as to make them strong and substantial, fit for all Travelers to pass and re-pass the same; which Sum or Sums of Money so agreed for, or otherwise expended in building, re-building or amending said Bridge or Bridges, shall be assessed and collected in the said Town or place to which said Bridge or Bridges doth belong, by the Assessors and Collector chosen according to an Act of Assembly of this Province, entituled, *An Act for the more regular chusing & electing Assessors and Collectors in the respective Towns and Counties of this Province,* and paid by the said Collector to the person or persons so imployed in building, re-building or repairing said bridge or bridges, by virtue of a Note or Notes drawn on said Collector for paying the same, by such Justices, Surveyors and the two Free-holders aforesaid, or the major part of them who contracted or agreed with the person or persons so imployed as aforesaid; which Note or Notes, with the Work-mans Receipt thereon shall be the said Collectors Discharge for the same. And when any such bridge or bridges are to be built, re-built, repaired or amended between two Towns, Divisions or Precincts, which is to be done at the charge of both Towns, the Over-feers of said Towns shall give notice to two of the Justices of the Peace of the County (one whereof being of the *Quorum*) and the two Free-holders, as aforesaid; and if between two Counties, to two of each County, together with the Surveyors of both said Towns, and the two Free-holders chosen by each Town, as aforesaid, to meet together to agree with proper persons to build, rebuild, repair or amend such bridge or bridges, and for assessing and collecting such Sum or Sums of Money as is necessary for defraying the Charge, in manner as is before mentioned in this Act.

And be it further Enacted by the Authority aforesaid, That if there remain any Money in the hands of any Collector or Collectors in any Town, Division or Precinct within this Province, over and above what is expended in building, rebuilding, repairing or amending any such Bridge or Bridges, such Collector or Collectors shall give account thereof, and pay the Over-plus Money to the Collector or Collectors of such Town or Precinct where it was collected, to be applyed to the making good and maintaining the publick high Roads of such Town, Division or Precinct, any Law, Custom or Usage to the contrary in any wise notwithstanding.

An Act for the Preserving of Oysters in the Province of New - Jersey.

WHereas it is found by daily Experience, that the Oyster-beds within this Province are wasted and destroyed by strangers, and others at unseasonable times of the year, the Preservation of which will tend to the great benefit of the poor People, and others inhabiting this Province,

Be it therefore *Enacted by the Governour, Council and General Assembly, of this Province, and it is hereby Enacted by the Authority of the same,* That no person or persons whatsoever shall Rake or gather up any Oysters or Shells from and off any the Beds within the said Province, from the Tenth Day of *May* to the First Day of *September,* yearly and every year, after the Publication hereof.

And be it further Enacted by the Authority aforesaid, That no Person or persons whatsoever, not residing within this Province, from and after the Publication hereof, shall not, directly or indirectly, rake, gather up any Oysters or Shells within this Province, and put them on board any Canow, Periauger, Flat, Scow, Boat, or other Vessel whatsoever, not wholly belonging to and owned by persons who live within the said Province, under the Penalty of Seizing and Forfeiting of all such Canow, Periauger, Flat, Scow, Boat, or other Vessel, as shall be found doing the same, together with all the Oysters, Shells, Oyster-Rakes, Tongs, Tackle, Furniture and Apparel thereto belonging.

And be it further Enacted by the Authority aforesaid, That the Persons hereafter nominated and appointed, shall and are hereby authorized, required and commanded, strictly, to put this Act in Execution, and as they, or either of them shall think fit, at all times and places to enter and go on board of all and every such Canow, Periauger, Flat, Scow, Boat, or other Vessel aforesaid whatsoever, which shall be by him or them suspected to be Transgressing this Act, and all such, so found, the same to seize and secure in such way and manner as he or they shall think fit, for his Majestys Service, together with all and every the Oysters, Shells, Oyster-Rakes, Tongs, Tackle, Furniture and Apparel thereunto belonging.

For the County of *Bergin,* Andries van Buskirck & Minheard Garbrant.
For the County of *Essex,* Joshua Hunlock and Joseph Meaker, jun.
For the County of *Middlesex,* John Stevens, Andrew Redford, John Brown and James Clarkson.
For the County of *Monmouth,* Robert Carhart, Abraham Watson, Tho. Kearney, John Brown and Richard Brittain.
For the County of *Burlington,* Richard Willet and Rudduck Townsend.
For the County of *Gloucester,* Richard Sommers and James Steelman.
For the County of *Cape May,* Jacob Spicer and Aaron Leeman.

And be it further Enacted by the Authority aforesaid, That the abovesaid Persons, and any others whom his Excellency the Governour, or the

Governour

Governour or Commander in Chief, for the time being, shall appoint for the Executing of this Act, shall and may at all such times and places as he or they shall think fit, Require and Command, in his Majestys Name, such and so many persons as he or they shall think necessary to aid and assist him or them in the due Execution of this Act.

And be it further Enacted by the Authority aforesaid, That any of the abovesaid Persons or any others, who shall at any Time hereafter be appointed by Virtue of this Act, who shall Seize and Secure any of the Vessells afore-mentioned, in manner and Form aforesaid, the said Person or Persons shall immediately Inform two of his Majesties Justices of the Peace (one whereof to be of the *Quorum*) of the County where such Seizure shall ibe made, who are hereby required forthwith, on such Notice, to meet together, and upon Oath made by any of the aforesaid Persons, above appointed, or of any other Person, shall give Judgment against, and Condemn the same, one half to His Majesty, for and towards the Support of Government of this Province, and the other half to the Person who shall Seize and Prosecute the same, to his own Costs and Charges.

And be it further Enacted by the Authority aforesaid, That every Vessel so Seized, Tryed and Condemned, as aforesaid, with all thing thereunto belonging, shall, by the said person who seized the same, be Sold at a publick Vendue, and one half part of the Produce thereof paid to the Treasurer, for the time being, for and towards the Support of his Majesties Government of this Province, and the other half Part to his own Use, for his Trouble, Costs and Charges, as aforesaid.

And be it further Enacted by the Authority aforesaid, That if any Master, Seaman or other Person, on Board any Canow, Perreauger Flat Scow, Boat or other Vessel whatsoever, shall refuse and not suffer to enter, or resist before or after Entring, any of the aforesaid Persons, or any other by their or either of their Order, the Person or Persons, so Refusing or Resisting, shall forfeit the Sum of Fifty Pounds, to be recovered by the said Person in an Action of Debt, in any Court of Record within this Province, with Costs; one half Part thereof to His Majesty, for Support of the Government of this Province, the other half Part thereof to the said Person who shall Prosecute the same to Effect, any Law Custom or Usage to the contrary hereof in any wise notwithstanding.

An Act to Restrain Tavern-keepers and Retailers of strong Liquors from Crediting any Person more than Ten Shillings.

WHereas it is evident that many Persons in this Province do spend their time and waste their Substance by frequenting Taverns and Tippeling houses, to the great detriment of themselves and Families; and such are the rather induced thereunto by reason they can be trusted until it amount to a great Sum.

Be it therefore Enacted by the Governour, Council and General Assembly of this Province, and it is hereby Enacted by the Authority of the same, That after the Publication of this Act, if any Tavern-keepers or publick-House-keepers shall trust any person above ten Shillings before payment be made, that then and in such case, he, she or they so Crediting any person, shall loose the same, and forever be debarr'd from suing for or Recovering the said Debt.

And be it further Enacted by the Authority aforesaid, That no Tavern-keepers or Publick-house-keepers shall take any Bill, Bond or other Security for any Liquors by them sold and drank in or at their houses amounting to above ten Shillings.

And be it further Enacted by the Authority aforesaid, That if any Tavern-keeper or Publick-house-keepers shall take Bill, Bond or any other Security for any Liquors sold and drank in or at their houses, contrary to the true intent and meaning of this Act, under pretence of selling Victuals, Pipes Tobacco, or any other thing, whereby to evade the intent of this Act, he, she or they so offending, are hereby rendered uncapable of Recovering any such bill, bond or other security, as above-said, for such Liquors, so sold and drank in or at their houses, and the Defendant may plead this Act in bar.

Provided always, That nothing in this Act shall be construed or taken to debar or hinder any publick house-keeper from taking or receiving any sum or sums of Money that is or may become due and owing to them from all or any such Person or Persons that are or may be Lodgers in his, her their houses, or Travellers not residing in that County, any thing herein contained to the contrary in any wise notwithstanding.

An Act to prevent Mistakes and Irregularities by Assessors and Collectors.

BE It Enacted by the Governour, Council and General Assembly, and it is hereby Enacted by the Authority of the same, That from and after the Publication hereof, all Money to be raised in the several and respective Counties in this Province, for building or repairing Goals and Court-Houses, as well as all other Money to be raised for the publick and necessary Service of all the several Counties, shall be assessed and collected by the Assessors and Collectors elected and chosen by the several Towns, Divisions, Precincts and Districts, according to the directions of an Act of General Assembly of this Province, entituled, *An Act for the more regular chusing and electing Assessors and Collectors in the respective Towns and Counties in this Province,* and no other ways, any thing contained in an Act, entituled, *An Act for raising of Money for building and repairing of Goals and Court-houses in each respective County in this Province,* or in any other Act, to the contrary hereof in any wise notwithstanding.

And be it Enacted by the Authority aforesaid That when Money is raised in any the Counties in this Province for building or repairing of Goals and Court-houses, or for any publick Service of the said County or Counties, and gathered in Manner aforesaid, That it shall be paid by said Collector or Collectors, to the Collector of the County or Counties for which it is gathered, to be disposed of as shall be appointed by the Justices of said County or Counties, with the Free-holders chosen according to the said Act of General Assembly of this Province, entituled, *An Act for Raising of Money for Building and Repairing Goals and Court Houses, within each respective County in this Province.* Which said assessors, and Collector or Collectors shall have for what Money they assess and collect in their several Towns, Divisions, Precincts or Districts, or where Counties are not Divided into Towns, Divisions, Precincts or Districts, for so much as they severally and respectively shall assess and collect, and no more, and the Collectors of the several Counties shall have for what they receive and pay, the same Rewards that are allowed and appointed them by the said Act, entituled, *An Act for the more Regular Chusing and Electing Assessors and Collectors, in the respective Towns and Counties within this Province,* and no more. And if any of the said Officers Refuse or Neglect to perform their Services required by this Act, shall be and are hereby Subjected to the Penalties mentioned in the aforesaid Act.

And be it further Enacted by the Authority aforesaid, That that Part of the aforesaid Act, entituled, *An Act for raising Money for Building and Repairing of Goals and Court-Houses within each respective County in this Province,* which relates to Assessors and Collectors, is hereby Repealed and made Void, any thing contained in the said Act to the contrary notwithstanding.

An Act to Restrain extravagant and excessive Interest.

WHereas the Great and Excessive Usury now commonly taken in this Province, is found to be a very great Discouragement to the Trade and an Obstruction to the Settlement of the same; for Remedying and preventing of which for the future,

Be it therefore Enacted by the Governour, Council and General Assembly, and by the Authority of the same, That no Person whatsoever shall after the Publication of this Act, take, directly or indirectly, any greater Use or Interest than Eight Pounds current Money of this Province, for the Forbearance of one Hundred Pounds for a Year, and so after that Rate for a greater or lesser Sum, or for a longer or shorter Time, for the Loan of any Moneys, Wares, Merchandizes, or any Commodities whatsoever. And that all Bonds, Contracts and Assurances, of what nature and kind soever they be, made after the time aforesaid, for Payment of any Principal, or Money, Goods, Wares, Merchandize or Commodities lent, or covenanted to be performed, upon or for any Usury, whereupon or whereby there shall be Reserved or taken, directly or indirectly, above the Rate of Eight Pounds in the Hundred, as afoesaid, shall be utterly Void; and that all and every Person or Persons whatsoever, which shall after the time aforesaid, upon any Contract to be made

(6)

after

after the Publication of this Act aforesaid, by way or means of any Bargain, Loan, Chevisance, Shift of any Wares, or Merchandizes, or other Thing or Things whatsoever, or by any deceitful Way or Means, or by any Coven, Craft, Invention, Fetch or deceitful Conveyance, or under the Notion of Brokage, Storage, Procurage, Service, or by any other ways or means whatsoever, it be contrary to the true Intent and Meaning of this Act, or to elude and avoid the Ends and Intentions thereof, take, accept or receive, directly or indirectly, for the Forbearing or giving Day of Payment, for one whole Year, of and for their Money or other thing, above the Sum of Eight Pounds for the Forbearing of One Hundred Pounds for a Year, and so after that Rate for a greater or lesser Sum, or for a longer or shorter Term, shall forfeit and loose, for every such Offence, the treble Value of the Monies, Wares, Merchandizes, or other things so lent, bargained, sold, exchanged, shifted, stored or procured.

And be it further Enacted by the Authority aforesaid, That all and every Scrivener or Scriveners, Broker or Brokers, Solicitor or Solicitors, Practitioner of the Law or Practitioners, Driver or Drivers of Bargains or Contracts, who shall after the Time aforesaid, take or receive, directly or indirectly, any Sum or Sums of Money or other Reward or Thing, for Brokage, Soliciting, Driving or Procuring the Loan or Bargain, or the Forbearing of any Sum or Sums of Money over and above the Rate and Value of Two Shillings and Six Pence for the Loan or Forbearing of one Hundred Pounds, for one Year, and so proportionably for a greater or lesser Sum ; or above the Sum of Eighteen Pence for the making or renewing a Bond or Bill for the Loan, or for the Forbearing thereof, or for any Bond, Counter-Bond or Bill, concerning the same, shall forfeit for every such Offence Twenty Pounds, and have Imprisonment for half a Year.   The one Moiety of all which Forfeitures mentioned in this Act, to His Majesty, his Heirs and Successors, and the other Moiety to him or them that will sue for the same, in any Court of Record within this Province, by Action of Debt, Bill, Plaint or Information, in which no Essoin, Wager of Law or Protection to be allowed, any Law, Custom or Usage to the contrary in any wise notwithstanding.

An Act to Establish a Road laid out from the River *Passaick,* in the County of *Bergin,* between the Farmes of *Jacob Walense van Winkle* and *Johannes Walense van Winkle,* through the Land of *Jacobus van Ostrand* to *Passaick* River.

WHEREAS several Controversies and Disputes have happened concerning the Roads laid out, one along the Bank of *Pyssaick* River, by the Farm of *Jacob Walense van Winkle,* to the Farm of *Jacob van Ostrand,* and one other Road laid out between the Farmes
of

of *Johanes Walenſe van Winkle* and *Jacob VValenſe vanVVinkle*, and running up the Lane that is betwixt the ſaid Farmes, and thro' the Woods, on the back of the Improved Lands of the ſaid *Jacob Walenſe van Winkle*, the former of which Roads, running along the Bank of *Paſſaick* River, appearing to be very injurious to the ſaid *Jacob van Winkle*, and on worſe Ground than the other Road.   In order to the putting an end to the ſaid Controverſy, and quieting the Minds of the People by a final Determination of the ſame,

Be it *Enacted by the Governour, Council and General Aſſembly now met and aſſembled, and it is hereby Enacted by the Authority of the ſame,* That the Road laid out to four Rod wide, by the Surveyors of the High-Ways of ſaid County of *Bergn, viz. Paulus van der Beck, Derick Epke Banta, Cornelius van Horn, Thomas France, Jacobus van Gelder,* and *John Ryerſon,* beginning at the Tranſporting-place on *Paſſaick* River, between the Lands of *Johannes Walenſe van Winkle* and *Jacobus Walenſe van Winkle,* and running along the Lane and over the Cauſeway or Bridge, to the North Eaſt Corner of *Jacobus Walenſe van Winkle's* improved Land, and ſo along a Path or Line of marked Trees, till it comes to the Land of *Jacob van Oſtrand,* and ſo through the Land of ſaid *Jacob van Oſtrand,* till it comes to *Paſſaick* River, as it is laid out by the aforeſaid Surveyors, and Recorded by order of the Juſtices of the ſaid County of *Bergin,* and is now cleared and made up, ſhall be and remain the publick Road, and that the other Road pretended to be laid out through the Land of ſaid *Jacobus Walenſe van Winckle,* along the Bank of *Paſſaik* River, ſhall and is hereby declared Null and Void, to all Intents and Purpoſes whatſoever.

And be it *further Enacted by the Authority aforeſaid,* That it ſhall not be in the Power of any Surveyors hereafter to be Choſen in ſaid County, to lay out any other Road through the ſaid Land of ſaid *Jacobus Walenſe van Winkle,* along the ſaid River of *Paſſaick,* any Law, Cuſtom or Uſage to the contrary in any wiſe notwithſtanding.

An Act to Enforce the due Adminiſtration of the Eſtate of Capt. *John Bown*, Deceaſed, late of the County of *Monmouth*, and Province of *New-Jerſey*.

WHereas *Richard Salter,* one of the Executors of the laſt Will and Teſtament of ſaid Capt. *John Bown,* deceaſed, by his humble Petition preſented to this General Aſſembly, now ſitting at *Perth-Amboy,* hath ſet forth, That ſaid *John Bown,* by his laſt Will and Teſtament, made in Writing and duly Executed and Proved, did appoint him the ſaid *Richard Salter,* together with his Brother *Obadiah Bown,* joynt Executors of the ſame, and Reſiduary Legatees of his Eſtate, after Payment of his Debts and Legacies, which Will was legally proved before his Excellency the Governour, as Ordinary of this Province, and they the ſaid *Obadiah* and *Richard* took their Oaths

to

to execute the said Will, and also upon Oath exhibited an Inventory consisting of Deeds of Sale of Lands, Conveyances, Mortgages, Bonds, Bills, Accounts and other Goods and Chattles, amounting to about Seventeen Thousand Pounds, all which Deeds of Sale, Mortgages and other Conveyances, Bonds, Bills, Books of Accounts, and other Goods and Chattles of the said *John Bown,* deceased, came into the Hands and Possession of the said *Obadiah Bown,* who afterwards refused to admit the said *Richard Salter* into the joynt Administration of the said Deceased's Estate with him, but set himself up Heir at Law, nor would he pay the Creditors of the said Deceased, notwithstanding the many Actions at Law that were commenced against them as Executors of the said Estate; and that at the Complaint of the said *Richard* to his Exellency the Governour, as Ordinary in Chief of this Province, That on a full hearing by Council of both Executors, his Excellency the Governour determined, That the said *Richard* should be admitted into the joynt Administration, and that the said Executors respectively, with Sureties, should enter into Bonds unto him in the Sum of Twenty Thousand Pounds, for the due Administration of the said Estate, which Order the said *Richard* performed, and the said *Obadiah* Contemned ; and legal Methods being wanting in this Province to compel him the said *Obadiah* to obey the said Order, the said *Richard* was necessitated to exhibit a Bill of Complaint against him in the High Court of Chancery, and the said *Obadiah,* with a Cross Bill, and otherwise, Postpon'd the Case from Coming to a hearing for near two Years : And then the said *Obadiah* proposed to his Excellency, the Chancellor, when the Case was to be heard, and a Decree to pass, That a Decree should be passed by his Consent, That the said *Richard* might with him be admitted into the joynt Administration ; That all the Deeds, Specialties and Books of Accounts should be put into the Hands of Mr. *Willam Lawrence,* for the ease of both Executors; That neither of them should sue for or pay Debts, but by Mutual Consent. And that for the Performance thereof they should give Bond respectively each to the other, in the Sum of Twenty Thousand Pounds. Which Proposals the said *Richard* assented to, and it was accordingly Decreed, Bonds mutually given and the Conveyances, Writings and Books of Accounts were put into the Hands of the said Mr. *William Lawrence.* But that notwithstanding the repeated Requests, utmost Endeavours, and an Action brought by the said *Richard* against the said *Obadiah,* upon his Bond, hath and doth still refuse to joyn with the said *Richard* either to recover Debts, or to pay any of the numerous Judgments that are obtained against them the said Executors: By means of which the said Creditors and Legatees are like to be defrauded, the Estate wasted, and the said *Richard* Ruined.

Therefore the said *Richard Salter,* by his humble Petition prays, That an Act of General Assembly may be passed to Enforce the due Administration of the Estate of the said Capt. *John Bown,* deceased, according to the true Intent of the said Last Will and Testament. All which being by the said Petition more largely set forth, and the

the Truth thereof fully appearing upon a hearing of the Parties and Examination of the Allegations on both sides.

Be it Therefore Enacted by the Governour, Council and General Affembly and it is hereby Enacted by the Authority of the fame, That in Order to Enforce the due Adminiftration of the faid Eftate, within Twenty Days after the Publication of this Act, they the faid Executors *Obadiah Bown* and *Richard Salter,* fhall each of them enter into Bonds unto his Excellency the Governour and his Succeffors, with fuch fufficient Sureties as his faid Excellency the Governour or Commander in Chief, for the Time being, (or fuch as he fhall appoint) fhall approve of, in the Sum of Ten Thoufand Pounds, feverally, with Condition, That each of them fhall, upon Receipt of the equal Moiety or half Part of the faid Conveyances, Deeds of Sale, Mortgages, Bills, Bonds, Accounts, Goods and Chattles of the faid Eftate, according to the Inventories thereof by them and every of them Exhibited into the Prerogative Office of this Province, fhall forthwith well and truely pay the Equal Moyety or half part of all the Debts due to the Creditors of faid Eftate, and the half part of the Legacies given by faid Teftator by his faid Laft Will and Teftament aforefaid.

And be it further Enacted by the Authority aforefaid, That Mr. *William Lawrance,* upon Notice to him given by his faid Excellency the Governour or Commander in Chief, for the Time being, or fuch as he fhall appoint as aforefaid, of fuch *Bonds* with Securities, as aforefaid, being Executed, he the faid *William* fhall and is hereby required and commanded, upon Penalty of Thirty Thoufand Pounds and Imprifonment until Payment, immediately to Deliver unto the faid Perfons aforefaid, to be by his faid Excellency the Governour or the Commander in Chief, for the time being, for that purpofe appointed, all *Deeds* of Sale, Mortgages, Bonds, Bills, Accompt Books and other Effects of the faid Eftate whatfoever, which are now in the Hands of the faid *William Lawrence,* for which the faid Perfons, fo appointed as aforefaid, fhall give the faid *William* a particular Receipt of what they receive, which Receipt fhall be a fufficient Difcharge thereof, to him, his Executors and Adminiftrators forever.

And be it further Enacted by the Authority aforefaid, That the faid Perfons, fo appointed by his Excellency the Governour of this Province or Commander in Chief, for the time being, fhall and are hereby Required to make a juft and equal Divifion of all fuch Deeds of Sale, Conveyances, Mortgages, Bonds, Bills, Accounts and other Effects of the faid Eftate whatfoever, and deliver one Moyety or half Part thereof unto the faid *Obadiah,* his Executors or Adminiftrators, and the other Moyety or half Part unto the faid *Richard* or his Executors or Adminiftrators, whofe feveral Receipts for the fame fhall be and is hereby declared to be a fufficient Difcharge to the faid Perfons fo appointed, as aforefaid, for the fame refpectively.

Provided always, That all fuch part or parcel of faid Eftate as the faid Executors, or either of them, had in their Hands in the Month of *July* laft, or any time before that Date, or have fince got into their

7

or

or either of their Hands, shall be accounted as Part of his Moyety in whose Hands it is, and the Debt of the said Estate by him paid, shall be accounted as part of his Moyety of said Debt to be by him paid, due by said Estate to the Creditors thereof.

And be it Enacted by the Authority aforesaid, That upon the Executors both or either of them, entring into Bonds, as aforesaid, Then the Bonds mutually given each to the other in the Sum of Twenty Thousand Pounds, in the Month of *July* last, and all Suits and Actions in Law Commenced, and all other Bonds and Obligations, Decrees, Judgments, Penalties, Forfeitures, and all other Proceedings whatsoever, depending thereupon, both in Common Law and Equity, shall be and are hereby declared to be Exonerated, Acquited and discharged, and to be Void, Null and of none Effect.

And be it further Enacted by the same Authority, That the said *Obadiah* and *Richard* shall be and are hereby Authorized and Impowered well and truely to administer, severally and respectively, such Part of the said Estate, as shall be delivered to them, as aforesaid, and no other Part thereof; and each of them shall and may, severally and respectively Sell, Compound, Sue for, Recover, Receive and Discharge all such Deeds of Sale of Lands, Conveyances, Mortgages, Bonds, Bills, Accounts and other Effects whatsoever, which each of them shall so receive, as aforesaid, severally and respectively, in both their Names, but Executed by each of them severally, and respectively, for what shall be in each of their Hands, as aforesaid.

And be it further Enacted by the Authority aforesaid, That all Deeds of Sale, Reconveyances of Mortgages, and Deeds of Land upon Letters of Trust, Receipts, Acquitances and Discharges of all Sums contained in Obligations, Bonds, Bills, Accounts, &c. made and Executed by each of them severally, for such Part in each of their Hands, as aforesaid, shall be a good, sufficient and effectual Title in the Law to all Persons and Grantees of Land, to them their Heirs and Assigns forever, and to such Persons as shall pay such Obligations, Bonds, Bills, Debts and Accounts whatsoever, to them their Executors and Administrators forever.

Provided always, And it is hereby Declared, That all Persons whatsoever, who have made any Mortgages to the said *John Bown* in his Life Time, or to the said Executors since his Decease, and all Deeds of Sale made by any Person or Persons whatsoever, to the said *John Bown,* in his Life time, or to the said Executors since his Decease, where Instruments or Letters of Trust have been given to the Grantors of the said Deeds, Declaring said Deeds of Sale to be in Trust for the payment of such Sum and Sums of Money, as are in the said Letters of Trust mentioned and contained, with the Interest and Costs, *It is hereby Enacted and Declared,* That upon Payment made to each or either of them the said Executors, respectively in whose Hands the Deeds of Sale shall happen to be, or to the Assignees of him the said *John Bown,* deceased, or them the said Executors, or either of them, with Interest, Costs and Charges, they, the said Executors, or they the said Assignees are hereby Required and Commanded to Reconvey the said

Deed

Deeds of Sale of said Lands to the said Grantors, their Heirs and Assigns, in due form of Law. And in Case of Delay or Denyal, the said Grantor or Grantors shall and may, and are hereby Authorized and Impowered to Sue and prosecute the Person or Persons, so Delaying or Refusing, as aforesaid, in an Action of Debt, in any Court of Record in this Province; in which Suit the said Grantor or Grantors shall recover the whole and full Value of the said Lands, so delayed or refused to be reconveyed as aforesaid, with Costs of Suit, any Law, Custom or Usage to the Contrary in any wise notwithstanding.

And be it further Enacted by the *Authority aforesaid,* That the said *Obadiah Bown* and *Richard Salter,* Executors aforesaid, or their Executors and Administrators, shall forthwith proceed to administer such Part of the said Estate as shall be delivered to them, and in their Hands as aforesaid; and with all Expedition recover Payment thereof, by all ways and means in the Law, or otherwise, whatsoever, and forthwith pay the Creditors and Legatees of said Estate. And in Case he the said *Obadiah,* or he the said *Richard* shall Neglect, Delay or Refuse to enter into Bond with sufficient Sureties, within the time appointed as aforesaid, then and in that Case the other Executor, who shall enter into Bond and Administer as aforesaid, he the said Administring Executor shall be and is hereby Authorized, Impowered, Required and Commanded to take upon him the Administration of the other equal Moyety or half Part of said Estate, and shall thereupon enter into another Bond with Sufficient Sureties, to his Excellency the Governour or Commander in Chief, for the time being, in the aforesaid Sum of Ten Thousand Pounds, with Condition for due Administring the other Moyety or half Part of said Estate, as afore-mentioned, and shall immediately proceed to Administer accordingly.

And be it further Enacted by the *Authority aforesaid,* That if the said Executors shall enter into Bonds as aforesaid, and receive each of them the said equal Moyety or half Part of said Estate, into each of their Hands as aforesaid, and yet either of them shall at any time afterwards Delay, Neglect or Refuse to recover Payment of such Part of the said *Estate* as shall be in either of their Hands, and to pay and satisfy the equal Moyety or half part of all the Debts due to the Creditors of the said *Estate,* and of the Legacies given by said last Will and Testament as aforesaid, Then and in that Case, upon Proof made of such Delay, Neglect or Refusal as aforesaid, before his Excellency the Governour or Commander in Chief, for the time being, or such Person or Persons as shall be by him, for that Purpose appointed, the said Administring Executor shall enter into another Bond with Sureties, to his Excellency the Governour or Commander in Chief for the time being, in the aforesaid Sum of Ten Thousand Pounds, with Condition for due Administring the said other Moyety or half Part of said Estate, as aforem-entioned.

And be it further Enacted by the *Authority aforesaid,* That all Deeds of Sale of Lands, Reconveyances of Mortgages, Reconveyances of Lands made for Performance of Instruments or Letters of Trust, made by the Administring Executor for the said other Moyety or half Part of said Estate, shall be a Good Sufficient and Effectual Title in the Law to all

Persons

Perfons and Grantees of fuch Lands, their Heirs and Affigns, and all Receipts, Acquitances and Difcharges of all Sum and Sums of Money mentioned and contained in any Obligations, Bonds, Bills and Accounts, made and granted by faid Adminiftring Executor for faid other Moyety or half Part of faid Eftate, fhall be Good Sufficient and Effectual in the Law to Difcharge, Exonerate and Acquit the faid Obligations, Bonds, Bills, Accounts, Debts, Dues and Demands whatfoever in the Law, notwithftanding the faid Obligations, Bonds, Bills and Accounts are or may be in the Hands or Poffeffion of the other Non-adminiftring Executor, any Law, Cuftom or Ufage to the Contrary notwithftanding.

And be it further Enacted by the Authority aforefaid, That if, after the Creditors of faid Eftate are Paid and Satisfied all their juft Debts, due to them, and all the Legacies paid, either of the faid Adminiftring *Executors* fhall receive Payment of more than his juft and equal Moyety or half part of the refiduary Part of the Eftate of faid *John Bown,* deceafed, and fhall delay or refufe to pay the faid Over-plus to the other *Executor,* or his *Executors* or Adminiftrators, That then and in that Cafe i fhall and may be lawful for the other *Executor,* and he is hereby Impowered and Authorized to profecute and Sue for, Recover and Receive the faid Over-plus due to him, to make up his Refiduary Part, Share and Proportion of the faid *Eftate,* equal to the other *Executors* Refiduary Part Share and Proportion of faid *Eftate,* by an Action of Debt in any Court of Record within this Province, any Law, Cuftom or Ufage to the Contrary in any wife notwithftanding.

Thefe Acts were Publifhed the 27 *and* 28 *Days of* March, 1719.

By his Excellency

Robert Hunter, Efq; Capt. General and Governour
in Chief in and over the Provinces of *New-Jerfey, New-York,* and all the Territories and Tracts of Land depending thereon in *America,* and Vice-Admiral of the fame.

An ORDINANCE

For Eftablifhing the Place for Keeping and Holding the Courts of Judicature for the County of *Hunterdon,* and the Time for Holding or Keeping the Court of Quarter-Seffions for the City of *Perth-Amboy,* in the Province of *Nova-Caefarea* or *New-Jerfey.*

WHereas His faid Excellency, by Virtue of the Power and Authority unto him given, by Letters Patents from Her late Majefty Queen *Anne,* of bleffed Memory, under the Great Seal of *Great Britain,* by and with the Advice and Confent of Her then Council, in the faid Province of *New-Jerfey* did by an Ordinance under his Hand and Seal, bearing Date the 7*th* Day of *April,* in the 13*th* Year of Her faid late Majefty's Reign, Entituled

Entituled, *An Ordinance for Establishing the Courts of Judicatre within Her Majesties Province of* Nova-Caesarea *or* New-Jersey, amongst other things therein contained, Ordain that there should be kept and holden a Court of *Common Pleas* in each respective County within the said Province of *New-Jersey*, at such Places as the General Courts of Sessions are generally held and kept, to begin immediately after or the next Day after the General Sessions of the Peace ends and terminates, and then to hold and continue not exceeding Three Days, which several respective Courts of Pleas should have Power and Jurisdiction to Hear, Try and finally Determine all Causes, Actions or Causes of Actions, and all Matters and Things tryable at Common Law, of what Nature or Kind soever. And it was further in the said Ordinance Ordained, that the Courts of General Sessions for the Peace should be held and kept for the said County of *Hunterdon* at *Maidenhead* the first *Tuesday* of *June* and *December*, and at *Hopewell* the first *Tuesday* of *March* and *September*, until the Court-House and Goal for the said County should be built, as in and by the same may appear.

His said Excellency the Governour taking the same into Consideration, that the keeping and holding of the said Courts of General Sessions of the Peace and Courts of Pleas alternately at *Maidenhead* and *Hopewell* for the said County of *Hunterdon*, hath been Represented to him as very Inconvenient, he therefore by and with the Advice and Consent of His Majesties Council for the said Province of *New-Jersey*, by Virtue of the Power and Authority unto him given by Letters Patents from his Majesty under the Great Seal of *Great Britain*, hath Repealed and doth hereby Repeal that Part of the Ordinance aforesaid, for keeping said Courts of General Sessions of the Peace and Court of *Common-Pleas* for the County of *Hunterdon* alternately at *Maidenhead* and *Hopewell*. And his said *Excellency* by and with the Advice and Consent of His Majestys Council of the said Province doth Ordain, That from and after the next General Sessions of the Peace and Court of *Common-Pleas*, to be holden and kept at *Maidenhead* in the Month of *June*, next ensuing the General Courts of Quarter-Sessions of the Peace, for the said County of *Hunterdon*, shall be held and kept at *Trenton* in the said County, the first *Tuesdays* of *September*, *December*, *March* and *June*, from hence-forth, and that the Court of *Common-Pleas* for the said County begins when the General Court of Sessions Terminates or the next Day following, and then to hold and continue at *Trenton* aforesaid, for any Time not exceeding Three Days, and to have all the Authority, Power and Jurisdiction as was given by the above-mentioned Ordinance.

And be it Ordained by the Authority aforesaid, That the Court of General Sessions for the City and Precincts of the City of *Perth-Amboy* shall be held and kept on the first *Tuesdays* of the Months of *April*, *July*, *October* and *January*, and that the said Courts of General Sessions may hold and continue for any time not exceeding two Days.

Given under my Hand and Seal this 28th *Day of* March *in the* Fifth *Year of the Reign of* George *over* Great Britain, France *and* Ireland, King, &c. *Annoq;* Dommini, 1719

By his Excellency's Command,
Ja. Alexander. D. Cl.   Ro. Hunter.

An Act for the Support of the Government of his Majesty's Province of *New-Jersey* for Five Years, To Commence from the Twenty Third Day of *September*, One Thousand Seven Hundred and Twenty, and to end the Twenty Third Day of *September*, One Thousand Seven Hundred Twenty and Five.

VVHEREAS the Act entituled, *An Act for the Support of the Government of this His Majesty's Province of New-Jersey, for two Years,* Paffed in the Month of *March,* in the Year of our Lord One Thoufand Seven Hundred and Eighteen, expired by its own Limitation on the Twenty Third Day of *September*, One Thoufand Seven Hundred and wenty, and there having fince that Time been no Provifion made, for the Support of the Government, and Defraying the neceffary Charges and Sallaries of the refpective Officers of the fame,

Be it therefore Enacted by the Governour, Council and General Affembly now Met and Affembled, and it is hereby Enacted by the Authority of the fame, That there be Affeffed, Levyed and Raifed in the Manner hereafter mentioned, within this Colony, for and towards the Support of His Majefty's Government within the fame, for five Years, to commence from the Twenty Third Day of *September,* which was in the Year of Our Lord One Thoufand Seven Hundred and Twenty, and to continue until the Twenty third Day of *September,* One Thoufand Seven Hundred Twenty and Five, the Sum of Four Thoufand One Hundred Forty Three Pounds Ten Shillings, in Money of the Value directed and appointed by her late Majefty's Proclamation, and fince enforced by Act of Parliament, entituled, *An Act for afcertaining the Rates of Forreign Coyn in Her Majefty's Plantations in* America. Which is hereby given to His Majefty, His Heirs and Succeffors, for and towards the Support of this His Majefty's Government in and over this Province.

And be it further Enacted by the Authority aforefaid, That in cafe His Excellency *William Burnet*, Efq; our prefent Governour, fhall by Death, or otherwife, ceafe to be Governour of this Province, at any Time after the paffing this Act, and before the faid Twenty Third Day of *September*, which fhall be in the Year of our Lord, One Thoufand Seven Hundred Twenty and Five, that then it fhall and may be lawful for the Treafurers of this Province, for the Time being, and they are hereby Directed, Authorized, Required, Impowered and Commanded to pay unto His Excellency *William Burnet*, Efq. His

¶   8   Executors,

Executors, Administrators or Affigns, or his or their Order, out of the faid Sum or Sums of Money, hereafter to be Affeffed, Levyed and Raifed for the Support of the Government, as aforefaid, for Five Years, all fuch Sum or Sums of Money as at the Time of his ceafing to be Governour, as aforefaid, fhall then remain to be due and unpaid to him for his Sallary, in proportion to the Sums of Money he fhall have received, or fhall be payable to him out of the faid Sum or Sums of Money to be Affeffed and Levyed by Virtue of this Act, for the Support of the Government, from the Twenty Third Day of *September,* Seventeen Hundred and Twenty, to the Twenty Third Day of *September,* Seventeen Hundred Twenty and Five.

And for the more Regular, Juft and Effectual Raifing and Affeffing the Annual Support of the Government, by this Act given and intended to be raifed, *It is hereby further Enacted, by the Authority aforefaid,* That there fhall be Affeffed, Levyed and Raifed on the feveral Inhabitants within this Province, their Goods and Chattles, Lands and Tenements, the Sum of Four Thoufand One Hundred Forty Three Pounds Ten Shillings, in the Manner following, *viz.*

All Publick Houfe-Keepers fhall be rated at the Difcretion of the Affeffors of each Town, Divifion, Precinct or Diftrict wherein they live ; provided they do not exceed the Sum of Fifteen Pounds, nor are rated at lefs than the Sum of Five Pounds, for and towards the Support of Government, for each Year, to commence from the firft Day of *March* laft.

Every Single Man, not a Bound Servant, that works for Hire, fhall pay the Sum of Four Shillings each Year.

For the Ferry above *Delaware* Falls, fhall be paid, the Sum of Twenty Shillings for each Year.

For the Ferry near *Delaware* Falls fhall be paid, for each Year, the Sum of Thirteen Shillings and Four Pence.

For the Ferry from *Burlington* to *Briftol,* fhall be paid, for each Year, the Sum of Fifteen Shillings.

For the Ferry below *Burlington,* at the Ferry Point, fhall be paid, for each Year, the Sum of Fifteen Shillings.

For the Ferry at *Rancocas,* alias *Northampton* River, fhall be paid, for each fide by the Year, the Sum of Ten Shillings.

For the Ferry from *William Cooper's* to *Philadelphia* fhall be paid, for each Year, the Sum of Ten Shillings.

For the Ferry or Ferries from *Gloucefter* to *Philadelphia,* fhall be paid, for each Year, the Sum of Thirty Shillings.

For

For the Ferry at *Injoules*, over *Rariton*, shall be paid for each Year, the Sum of thirteen Shillings and four Pence.

For the Ferry from *Radfords* to *Amboy*, shall be paid, for each side, by the Year, the Sum of twenty Shillings.

For the Ferry over *Weehauck*, shall be paid, for each Year, the Sum of twelve Shillings.

For every Wherry, that carries Goods and Passengers for Hire, shall be paid, for each Year, the Sum of ten Shillings.

For every Flat, that carries Goods and Passengers for Hire, shall be paid, for each Year, the Sum of six Shillings.

For every Flat or Wood Boat, that carries six Cords and upwards, shall be paid for each Year, the Sum of ten shillings.

For every Flat or Wood Boat, that carries four Cords and upwards, shall be paid, for each Year, the Sum of six Shillings and eight Pence.

For every Flat or Wood Boat, that carries under four Cords, shall be paid, for each Year, the Sum of four Shillings.

For all Boats, Flats and Wherries belonging to the Neighbouring Colonies, coming into the Eastern Division of this Province, shall be paid the same Rate as is paid by Persons Inhabiting in this Province.

All Saw-Mills, Grist-Mills and Fulling Mills, shall be Rated at the Discretion of the Assessors of each Town, Division, Precinct or District wherein they lie, provided they do not exceed three Pounds, nor are rated at less than the Sum of ten Shillings each, by the year.

All Merchants and Shop Keepers, shall be rated at the Discretion of the Assessors, not under fourteen Shillings nor exceeding five Pounds by the year.

Every Person not residing in this Province, that shall bring Goods to sell by Retail (except in publick Fairs) shall pay for each year, the Sum of three Pounds.

The Owners and Possessors of Houses or Lots of Land, in any of the Towns or Precincts within this Province, the Tax of whose other rateable Estate does not amount to eight Shillings, shall pay for the said Houses or Lots at the Discretion of the Assessors, not under two Shillings nor above twenty Shillings, by the year.

All Cattle, Horses and Mares, of two years old and upwards, shall be valued at twenty five Shillings each Head.

All Sheep of one year old and upwards, shall be valued at three Shillings each Head.

Every Bound Servant, Indian, Negro and Mullatto Slaves, being Male of sixteen years old and upwards, except such Slaves as are

nor

not able to Work, shall be rated at and pay one Shilling each Head, for each year.

All Tracts of Land, held by Patents, Deeds or Surveys, whereon is any Improvement, shall be valued at five Pounds each Hundred Acres of such profitable Lands.

All Indian Traders shall be rated at the Discretion of the Assessors, not under twenty Shillings, nor above five Pounds by the year.

All the Tax, for the Support of Government, shall be paid in Silver, Gold or Wheat, *viz.* Silver according to her late Majesty's Proclamation, Gold at five Shillings and six Pence the Penny Weight, and Wheat at five Pence *per* Bushel less than the Market Price at *New-York*, for the Eastern Division, and *Philadhlphia* for the Western Division.

And be it further Enacted by the Authority aforesaid, That the Sum of eleven Hundred and eleven Pounds, Money aforesaid, for the first eighteen Months, shall be Assessed, Levyed and Collected in and according to the Proportions following,

By the County of *Bergin*, the Sum of Ninety Pounds.

By the County of *Essex*, the Sum of One Hundred fifty and one Pounds.

By the County of *Middlesex*, the Sum of One Hundred twenty and nine Pounds three Shillings.

By the County of *Somerset*, the Sum of forty three Pounds.

By the Conty of *Monmouth*, the Sum of One Hundred eighty eight Pounds.

By the County of *Hunterdon*, the Sum of Eighty Pounds.

By the County of *Burlington*, the Sum of One Hundred and forty Pounds.

By the County of *Gloucester*, the Sum of Ninety five Pounds.

By the County of *Salem*, the Sum of One Hundred fifty eight Pounds.

By the County of *Cape-May*, the Sum of Thirty six Pounds seventeen Shillings.

Which, together with the Sum of six Hundred Pounds, Money according to Her late Majesty's Proclamation, due and Payable by the Farmers of the Excise, on the Twenty fifth Day of *March* last past, which is hereby directed to be paid to the Treasurer of either of the Divisions of this Province, for the Time being, for the Support of the Government, as aforesaid, makes up the Sum of Seventeen Hundred and eleven Pounds, Money aforesaid, for the first eighteen Months.

By

And be it further Enacted by the Authority aforesaid, That the Sum of One Thousand and forty two Pounds ten Shillings, Money aforesaid, be Assessed, Levyed and Raised, for the second eighteen Months, in Proportion following, *viz.*

By the County of *Bergin*, the Sum of eighty five Pounds one Shilling and seven Pence.

By the County of *Essex*, the Sum of One Hundred and forty Pounds eleven Shillings and nine Pence.

By the County of *Middlesex*, the Sum of One Hundred and twenty Pounds thirteen Shillings and nine Pence.

By the County of *Somerset*, the Sum of Forty one Pounds fourteen shillings and nine Pence.

By the County of *Monmouth*, the Sum of One Hundred seventy six Pounds thirteen shillings and six pence.

By the County of *Hunterdon*, the sum of seventy seven Pounds ten shillings and ten pence.

By the County of *Burlington*, the sum of One Hundred twenty nine pounds four Shillings and nine pence.

By the County of *Goucester*, the Sum of ninety Pounds eight shillings and nine pence.

By the County of *Salem*, the Sum one Hundred Forty six Pounds eighteen shillings and nine pence.

By the County of *Cape-May*, the sum of thirty three pounds Eleven shillings and eight pence.

And be it further Enacted by the Authority aforesaid, That the sum of six Hundred ninety five Pounds, Money aforesaid, be Assessed, Levyed and raised, for the Year of our Lord One Thousand seven Hundred twenty and four, in the Proportions following, *viz.*

By the County of *Bergin*, the sum of fifty six Pounds nineteen shillings.

By the County of *Essex*, the Sum of ninety four Pounds twelve shillings.

By the County of *Middlesex*, the sum of seventy nine Pounds seventeen shillings.

By the County of *Somerset*, the sum of twenty seven Pounds two shillings.

By the County of *Monmouth*, the sum of one Hundred and seventeen Pounds seventeen shillings.

By the County of *Hunterdon*, the sum of fifty one Pounds nine shillings.

By

By the County of *Burlington*, the sum of eighty five Pounds fifteen shillings.

By the County of *Gloucester*, the sum of fifty nine Pounds twelve shillings.

By the County of *Salem*, the sum of one Hundred Pounds three shillings.

By the County of *Cape-May*, the sum of twenty one Pounds fourteen shillings.

And be it Enacted by the Authority aforesaid, That the sum of six Hundred ninety five Pounds, Money aforesaid, be Assessed, Levyed and Raised for the year of our Lord One Thousand seven Hundred twenty and five, in the Proportions following. *viz.*

By the County of *Bergin*, the sum of fifty six pounds nineteen shillings.

By the County of *Essex*, the sum of ninety four Pounds twelve Shillings.

By the County of *Middlesex*, the sum of seventy nine Pounds seventeen shillings.

By the County of *Somerset*, the sum of twenty seven Pounds two shillings.

By the County of *Monmouth*, the sum of one Hundred and seventeen Pounds seventeen shillings,

By the County of *Hunterdon*, the sum of fifty one Pounds nine shillings.

By the County of *Burlington*, the sum of eighty five Pounds fifteen shillings.

By the County of *Gloucester*, the sum of fifty nine Pounds twelve shillings.

By the County of *Salem*, the sum of one Hundred Pounds three shillings.

By the County of *Cape-May*, the sum of twenty one Pounds fourteen shillings.

And whereas it may so happen that the Certainties in this Act mentioned, may in some of the Counties arise to a greater Sum than the Proportions appointed, or to be appointed, for such County to pay,

Be it therefore Enacted, That then and in such Case the over-plus arising by such Certainties, shall be paid unto the Treasurers of this Colony, for the Time being, to be applyed to the Uses aforesaid; and no Tax or Assessment shall be laid within the same County where

such

such Over-plus happens to be, any thing herein contained to the contrary notwithstanding.

And be it further Enacted by the Authority aforesaid, That the Assessors for Assessing the several and respective Sums aforesaid, shall be and are such as are already chosen, or hereafter to be chosen, by the several Towns, Divisions, Districts and Precincts, according to the Directions of an Act of General Assembly of this Province, Entituled, *An Act for the more regular Choosing Assessors and Collectors in the respective Towns and Counties of this Province.*

And be it further Enacted by the Authority aforesaid, That for the Collecting and Receiving the several and respective Sums aforesaid, there shall be appointed, for each County within this Province, the Collectors hereafter named, *viz.*

For the County of *Bergin,* Mr. *William Provoost.*

For the County of *Essex,* Mr. *Nathaniel Bonnel.*

For the County of *Middlesex,* Mr. *Moses Rolph.*

For the County of *Somerset,* Mr. *Michael Van Veighty.*

For the County of *Monmouth,* Mr. *William Lawrence,* jun.

For the County of *Hunterdon,* Mr. *Joseph Peace.*

For the County of *Burlington,* Mr. *Thomas Hunlock.*

For the County of *Gloucester,* Mr. *Joseph Cooper,* jun.

For the County of *Salem,* Mr. *Thomas Hill.*

For the County of *Cape-May,* Mr. *Richard Downs.*

And be it Enacted by the Authority aforesaid, That in Case any of the Collectors, named in this Act, shall dye or depart this Province, before the Expiration of the Time limited in this Act, that then and in such Case the Justices of the Peace, or the greater Number of them, then being of the County, the Collector of which shall so dye or depart, shall, as soon as conveniently may be, meet together and appoint some able and discreet Man to be Collector of the said County, in the Place and Stead of such Collector Dead or Departed, as aforesaid.

And be it further Enacted by the Authority aforesaid, That all and every of the Inhabitants and House-holders of each respective County within this Province, shall at or before the first Tuesday in *June* next, and on or before the first Tuesday in *May,* which shall be in the year of our Lord Seventeen Hundred twenty and three, and on or before the first Tuesday in *May,* which shall be in the year
of

of our Lord, feventeen Hundred twenty and four, and on or before
the firft Tuefday in *May*, which shall be in the year of our Lord,
feventeen Hunderd twenty and five, give a true and perfect Lift, in
Writing, of all the Names and Sir-Names, and an Account, in
Writing, of their Eftates, Real and Perfonal, rated or made rateable by this Act, to the Affeffors chofen and elected, or to be
chofen and elected, by Virtue of an Act of General Affembly of this
Province, Entituled, *An Act for the more regular choofing and electing Affef-*
fors and Collectors in the refpective Towns and Counties within this Province,
for the Time being, for the Town, Division, Diftrict or Precinct
they refide in, which Affeffors of the feveral Towns, Divifions,
Precincts or Diftricts of each and every County within this Province, are hereby directed and required, on or before the fecond
Tuefday in *Auguft*, yearly and every year, during the five years
Support, to meet at the moft publick and convenient Place in each
refpective County of this Province, and shall then and there compute what the Sum total of all the Certainties, as laid by this Act,
in the faid County, shall amount unto, aud shall alfo then and
there likewife compute the value of all the Eftates, Real and Perfonal, given in to the faid Affeffors, within each of the faid Towns,
Divifions, Precincts or Diftricts, in each and every County in this
Province, at the Value in this Act mentioned and expreffed, and
after deducting the Certainties from the Quota by this Act
directed and appointed to be paid by each of their refpective
Counties, the faid Affeffors shall add their own and the Collectors
Fees, together with the Infolvents of the preceding year, to the
Remainder, and affefs fuch Remainder and Addition of Fees and
Infolvents of the preceding year, equally on the Pound value of
all the Real and Perfonal Eftates within each of their refpective
Counties, fo as to make up and pay each of their feveral and re-
fpective Quota's, with the additional Charges of Affeffing and Col-
lecting the fame, and the Deficiencies aud Infolvents of the preceding year; and shall likewife do and perform all Things required
of them, according to the Directions and Apopintment of the faid
Act of General Affembly, entituled, *An Act for the more regular*
Choofing and Electing Affeffors and Collectors in each refpective Town
and County in this Province, and be fubject to the fame Pains,
Penalties and Forfeitures as in the faid Act is mentioned and
expreffed.

And be it further Enacted by the Authority aforefaid, That each
and every Perfon, taxed as aforefaid, shall, on or before the fecond
Tuefday in *October*, yearly and every year, during the Continuance
of this Act, pay unto the Collector of the faid Town, Division,
Precinct or Diftrict, chofen or to be chofen by Virtue of the before recited Act of General Affembly, of this Province, entituled, *An*
Act for the more regular Choofing and Electing Affeffors and Collectors in each
                                                        refpective

respective Town and County in this Province, the several Sums of Money that each and every of them are assessed, on the Pains and Penalties mentioned in the said recited Act.

And be it further Enacted by the Authority aforesaid, That the Collectors of the several Towns, Divisions, Districts and Precincts chosen by Virtue of the aforesaid Act of General Assembly of this Province, entituled, *An Act for the more regular Choosing and Electing Assessors and Collectors in each respective Town and County of this Province*, shall pay the Sum or Sums of Money, he shall receive by Virtue of this Act, unto the Collector of the County, appointed or to be appointed according to the Directions of this Act, on or before the second Tuesday in *November*, yearly and every Year, during the continuance of this Act, under the Pains and Penalties mentioned in the before-mentioned and recited Act.

And be it further Enacted by the Authority aforesaid, That the Collectors, appointed or to be appointed by Virtue of this Act, shall and are hereby required and commanded to do the Duties, required of them by Virtue of the before-mentioned Act of General Assembly, entituled, *An Act for the more regular Choosing and Electing Assessors and Collectors in the respective Towns and Counties of this Province*, and be subject to the same Pains, Penalties and Forfeitures as in the said Act is mentioned and expressed.

And be it further Enacted by the Authority aforesaid, That the Assessors within each respective Town, Division, District or Precinct within any County of this Province, shall and are hereby required and commanded, to assess over and above the Sums herein mentioned in each County, so much as will pay themselves and the Town and County Collectors, for Assessing, Collecting and Gathering the same, and Paying it to the Treasurers of the Province, the same as is allowed by an Act, entituled, *An Act for the more regular Choosing and Electing Assessors and Collectors in each respective County in this Province.*

And be it further Enacted by the Authority aforesaid, That the Collector of each respective County within the Eastern and Western Division of this Province, shall on or before the second Tuesday in *January*, yearly and every year, during the five years Support, pay all such Sum or Sums of Money by him received, by Virtue of this Act, to the Treasurers of this Province, and shall likewise deliver unto the said Treasurer, of the Division he belongs unto, an exact Copy of the Assessment of each Town, Division, Precinct or District, and an exact Account of all the Deficiencies

within

within each Town, Division, District or Precinct within the County for which he is Collector, to the Treasurer aforesaid, on the Pain and Penalty of fifty Pounds for each Default therein; to be recovered by Action of Debt, Plaint or Information, in which no Essoyn, Protection or Wager of Law to be allowed, nor any more than one Imparlance: One Half to the Person who shall prosecute the same to Effect, the other half to His Majesty, His Heirs and Successors, for and towards the Support of Government of this His Majesty's Province of *New-Jersey*, with double Cost of Suit.

And be it further *Enacted by the Authority aforesaid*, That the Treasurers of this Province shall each of them give Bonds, with sufficient Sureties, dwelling in this Province, to the Value of two Thousand Pounds for the true Performance of their Offices.

And be it further *Enacted by the Authority aforesaid*, That every Person that pays their Tax for Support of Government in Wheat, shall pay it to the Collector appointed by this Act, in their respective Counties on or before the second Tuesday in *October*, yearly and every Year during the five Years Support, and the said Collectors Receipt to the Collector of the Town, Division or Precinct chosen by Virtue of an Act, entituled, *An Act for the more regular Choosing and Electing Assessors and Collectors,* &c. shall be his Discharge.

And be it further *Enacted by the Authority aforesaid*, That the Members of this Assembly shall be paid their Wages for their Attendance, as by this Act directed, by the Collectors appointed by this Act, in their respective Counties, so much as shall be certified to them by a Certificate signed by the Speaker, and to the Speaker by a Certificate Signed by two Members, which Certificate with a Receipt thereon, shall be a sufficient Discharge to the Collector for so much.

An Act for the Security of His Majesty's Government of *New-Jersey.*

WHEREAS some Persons in this Province, disaffected to His Majesty's Person and Government, propagate their pernicious Principles, to the great hurt of His Majesty's Faithful and Loyal Subjects inhabiting within the same. And by Reason of their Intermeddling in Publick Affairs, in Contempt of his Majesty's Legal and Just Authority, Obstruct the Publick Administration, and will, if not prevented, prove dangerous to the Government of this Province.

Be it therefore Enacted by the Governour, Council and General Assembly, and it is hereby Enacted by the Authority of the same, That it shall and may be lawful to and for two or more Justices of the Peace, or any other Person or Persons who shall be by the Governour, Commander in Chief, or President of the Council of this Province, for that Purpose specially appointed, by Order in Council, or by Commission under the Seal of this Province, to administer and tender the Oaths and Declaration herein after appointed to be taken and made, to any Person or Persons whatsoever, whom they shall or may suspect to be Dangerous or Disaffected to His Majesty or His Government: And if any Person or Persons, to whom the said Oaths and Declaration shall be so tendred, shall neglect or refuse to take and make the same; such Justices or other Person or Persons, specially to be appointed, as aforesaid, tendring the said Oaths, shall certify the Refusal thereof to the next Supream Court, held in the Division where such Person or Persons shall reside, of this Province of *New-Jersey,* that shall sit after such Neglect or Refusal shall be made, Which Certificate shall be recorded among the Rolls of the said Supream Court, to be provided and kept for that purpose only : And that every Person so neglecting or refusing to take the Oaths and make the Declaration herein after mentioned, shall be, from the time of such Neglect or Refusal, taken, esteemed and adjudged *A Popish Recusant Convict,* and as such to forfeit and be proceeded against.

And to the Intent that no Suspected Person may avoid taking the several Oaths and the Declaration in this Act hereafter particularly mentioned, upon any Pretence whatsoever;
Be it further Enacted by the Authority aforesaid, That it shall and may be lawful unto and for two or more Justices of the Peace, or any other such Person or Persons who shall be by the Governour or Commander in Chief of this Province, for the time being, for that purpose specially appointed, by an Order signed by the said Gover-

nour or Commander in Chief in Council, or by Commission under the Seal of this *Province*, by Writing under their Hands and Seals, to Summon any Person, (except Women and all other Persons under the Age of Eighteen Years) to appear before them at a certain Day and Time therein to be appointed, to take the herein after mentioned Oaths, and make and subscribe the herein after-mentioned Declaration, *viz.*

I A. B. *Do sincerely Profess and Swear, That I will be Faithful, and bear true Allegiance to His* Majesty *King* George. So help me GOD.

I A. B. *Do Swear, That I do from my Heart abhor, detest and abjure, as Impious and Heretical, that Damnable Doctrine and Position,* That Princes excommunicated, or deprived by the *Pope* or any Authority of the See of *Rome*, may be Deposed or Murdered by their Subjects, or any other whatsoever. *And I do declare, That no Foreign Prince, Person, Prelate, State or Potentate hath or ought to have any Jurisdiction, Power, Superiority, Preheminence or Authority, Ecclesiastical or Spiritual, within the Realm of* Great Britain. So help me God.

I *A. B.* Do heartily and sincerely acknowledge, profess, testify and declare, in my Conscience, before God and the World, That our Sovereign Lord King *George* is Lawful and Rightful King of *Great Britain*, and of all other his Majesty's Dominions and Countries thereunto belonging. And I do solemnly and sincerely declare, That I do believe in my Conscience, that the Person pretending to be *Prince of Wales*, during the Life of the late King *James*, and since his Decease, pretending to be, and taking upon himself, the Stile and Title of *King of England*, by the Name of *James the third*, or of *Scotland* by the Name *James the eighth*, or the Stile and Title of *King of Great Britain*, hath not any Right or Title whatsoever to the Crown of *Great Britain*, or any other the Dominions thereunto belonging. And I do renounce, refuse and abjure any Allegiance or Obedience to him. And I do Swear, That I will bear Faith and true Allegiance to His Majesty King *George*, and him will defend to the utmost of

my

my Power, againft all traiterous Confpiracies and Attempts
whatfoever, which fhall be made againft his Perfon, Crown
or Dignity ; and I will do my utmoft Endeavour to dif-
clofe and make known to His Majefty and His Succeffors all Treafons and traiterous Confpiracies which I fhall
know to be againft him or any of them.   And I do
faithfully Promife, to the utmoft of my Power, to Support,
Maintain and Defend the Succeffion of the Crown againft
him the faid *James*, and all other Perfons whatfoever.
Which Succeffion, by an Act, entituled, *An Act for the
further Limitation of the Crown, and better fecuring the Rights
and Liberties of the Subject,* is and ftands limited to the
Princefs *Sophia*, Electorefs and Dutchefs Dowager of *Hanover*,
and the Heirs of her Body, being Proteftants.   And all
thefe Things I do plainly and fincerely acknowledge and
fwear, according to the exprefs Words by me fpoken,
and according to the plain and common Sence and Un-
derftanding of the fame Words, without any Equivocation, mental Evafion or fecret Refervation whatfoever.
And I do make this Recognition, Acknowledgment, Abjuration, Renunciation and Promife, heartily, willingly
and truely, upon the true Faith of a Chriftian. *So help
me* G O D.

I *A. B.* Do folemnly and fincerly, in the Prefence of
God, profefs, teftify and declare, That I do believe,
That in the Sacrament of the Lord's Supper there is not
any Tranfubftantiation of the Elements of Bread and
Wine into the Body and Blood of *CHRIST*, at or after
the Confecration thereof, by any Perfon whatfoever. And
that the Invocation or Adoration of the Virgin *Mary*, or
any other Saint, and the Sacrifices of the Mafs, as they
are now ufed in the Church of *Rome*, are Superftitious
and Idolatrous. And I do folemnly, in the prefence of
God, profefs, teftify and declare, That I do make this Declaration, and every Part thereof, in the plain and Ordinary Sence of the Words read unto me, as they are
commonly underftood by *Englifh* Proteftants, without any
Evafion

Evasion, Equivocation or mental Reservation whatsoever, and without any Dispensation already granted me for this Purpose by the *Pope*, or any other Authority or Person whatsoever, or without any Hope of any such Dispensation from any Person or Authority whatsoever, or without thinking that I am or can be acquitted before *G O D* or Man, or absolved of this Declaration, or any Part thereof, although the Pope, or any other Person or Persons or Power whatsoever, should dispence with or annul the same, or Declare that it was null and void from the Beginning.

Unto which, Oaths so taken, every Person so summoned, appearing and taking the same, shall subscribe his Name, and if he cannot write shall make his Mark, and the Declaration so made by such Persons summoned and appearing, as aforesaid, shall be audibly repeated and subscribed or under-marked by the Person making the same, as aforesaid. Which Summons so made, as aforesaid, shall be served upon such Person, or left at the Dwelling House or usual abode of such Person with one of the Family there, who shall be informed of the Contents of such Summons. And if such Person, who shall be so summon'd, neglect or refuse to appear, according to such Summons, that then, upon due Proof, to be made upon Oath of the Serving the said Summons; which Oath such Justices, or any other Person or Persons specially to be appointed, as aforesaid, are hereby enabled and directed to administer, such Justice, or any other Person or Persons specially to be appointed, as aforesaid, are hereby required to certify the same to the next Supream Court, held in the Division where such Person or Persons shall reside, of the Province of *New-Jersey*, that shall be held after such Neglect or Refusal of any Person, so Summon'd as aforesaid, there to be entred upon the Rolls of the said Court. And if such Person who shall be so summoned to take the said Oaths and make the said Declaration, as aforesaid, shall neglect or refuse to appear and take the said Oaths and make the said Declaration, at the Supream Court aforesaid, the Names of the Persons, so certifyed, being first publickly read, and Proclamation made in the usual Manner, that if the Person or Persons so certifyed shall not appear, during the sitting of that Court, and take the Oaths and make the Declaration, as in and by this Act is directed, he or they shall be judged *Popish Recusants Convict*, that then and in such Case every such Person so neglecting or refusing, as aforesaid, shall be taken, deemed, esteemed and adjudged a *Popish Recusant Convict*, and as such to forfeit and be proceeded against, as a *Popish Recusant* by all or any the

Laws

Laws of *England* should forfeit and be proceeded against, any Usage to the contrary hereof in any wise notwithstanding.

And be it further Enacted by the Authority aforesaid, That any Person or Persons whatsoever, that shall be brought before the Governour, President of the Council or Commander in Chief of this Province, for the Time being, in Council, and shall refuse to take and subscribe the said Oaths, or make and subscribe the said Declaration, as aforesaid, shall enter into Recognizance, with Sufficient Sureties, to appear at the next Supream Court held in the Division where such Person so refusing shall reside, and if the said Person or Persons shall then and there refuse to take the said Oaths, and make and subscribe the said Declaration, as aforesaid, every such Person shall, for such Refusal, be deemed a *Popish Recusant Convict,* and as such be proceeded against.

And whereas the Intermeddling in Publick Affairs by any Person Convict as aforesaid, and forming of Bills to be passed into Laws by the General Assembly of this Province, without Leave and Direction first given by the Governour, the Council or Representatives in General Assembly met and convened, is a high Misdemeanour and Contempt of his Majesty's Authority and Government, and can be done by such Persons on no other View and Design than to obstruct the Administration of His Majesty's Government, and defeat and render ineffectual the good Purposes of the Legislature here.

Be it therefore Enacted by the Authority aforesaid, That if any Person, convict as aforesaid, shall at any time hereafter intermeddle in publick Affairs of this Province, by forming any Bill in order to be passed into a Law, by the General Assembly of this Province, and deliver it to any Member of Council or Assembly for that Purpose, or shall alter any Clause in any Bill under the Consideration of the Council or General Assembly of this Province, without leave from the Governour, or His Majesty's Council, or the General Assembly of this Province, for the time being, first had and obtained, every such Person, who shall so form any such Bill, or alter any Clause, as aforesaid, without leave had and obtained, as aforesaid, shall for every such Offence be forthwith prosecuted to Effect, according to Law, for such his Contempt and Misdemeanour.

Provided always, That this Act, or any Thing therein contained, shall not extend to any Person who hath, since His Majesty's happy Accession to the Throne, taken the Oaths of Allegiance and Supreamacy, and the Abjuration Oath, in any of the Courts of this Province, or as one of His Majesty's Council, or as a Member of the General Assembly of this Province, unless by reason of such Persons having some new Office or Imployment, or his coming

hereafter

hereafter under some of the Qualifications which require the taking the Oaths before-mentioned, by Virtue of this Act, or any other Law now in being.

And be it further Enacted by the Authority aforesaid, That no Person, being out of the Province at the time of such Summons being left at his House, as aforesaid, shall be prosecuted as a *Popish recusant,* if he shall within three Months after his Return into this Province, repair to some Officer appointed for that purpose, and take the Oaths, and make the Declaration, and subscribe, as by this Act directed.

And whereas there are Protestant Dissenters well affected to His Majesty's Person and Government, who for Conscience sake, have and do refuse taking any Oath whatsoever.

Be it therefore Enacted by the Governour, Council and General Assembly, That neither this Act nor any Thing herein contained, shall be construed or taken to extend to such Protestant Dissenter, as aforesaid, who shall take and subscribe the Oaths and Declaration in this Act before mentioned, in such Manner and Form as they have been usually taken here by the People called Quakers, or according to the Laws of *Great Britain,* that now are or shall be made in Relation to those People called Quakers, and their so doing, being Recorded at the next Quarter-Sessions, shall exempt such *Protestant* Dissenters, as aforesaid, from the Penalties of this Act, any thing in this Act to the contrary notwithstanding.

Provided always, and it is hereby further Enacted, That any Person or Persons who shall become *Popish Recusant Convict* by Virtue of any thing in this Act contained, and shall at any Time hereafter take and subscribe the said Oaths before-mentioned, and make and subscribe the said Declaration before the Chief Justice of the Supream Court, for the Time being, in Open Court, or before the Governour or Commander in Chief of this Province, for the Time being, in Council, and shall obtain a Certificate of his so Doing, under the Hand and Seal of the said Governour or Commander in Chief, or under the Hand of the Judge and Seal of the said Court, as the Case shall be, every such *Popish Recusant* by this Act, so Swearing and Declaring, and obtaining a Certificate, as aforesaid, shall be Discharged from all the Penalties and Forfeitures incurred by this Act, and are hereby, from such Time, Discharged from such Conviction, any thing in this Act to the contrary hereof in any Wise notwithstanding.

An Act for the Settling the Militia of this Province.

WHEREAS the Security and *Preservation* of this Province greatly depends upon the Militia being put into such Methods as may make the same most Useful for the Defence thereof and Honour of His Majesty. And whereas the former Act *For settling the Militia of this Province,* is expired by its own Limitation,

Be it therefore Enacted by the Governour, Council and General Assembly, and by the Authority of the same, That every Captain within this Province, already appointed, or that shall hereafter be appointed, shall make a true and perfect List of all the Men that are at present, or that shall hereafter happen to be, within the Districts or Divisions of which they are Captain, between the Age of Sixteen and Fifty Years (except the Gentlemen of His Majesty's Council and the Representatives of General Assembly, Ministers of the Gospel, the Civil Officers of the Government, and all Field Officers and Captains that heretofore bore Commission in the Militia of this *Province,* and all that now do or shall hereafter bear such Commission, Physitians, School-Masters, Millers and Slaves) Every of which, so listed, shall be sufficiently Armed with one good sufficient Musquet or Fuzee, well fixed, a Sword or Bagonet, a Cartouch Box or Powder Horn, Three Charges of Powder and Three Sizeable Bullets, who shall appear in the Field, so armed, twice every Year, the first Monday in *April,* and the second Monday in *October,* (except the County of *Cape-May,* which shall thus appear the third Monday in *April,* and the third Monday in *October,*) yearly, at the Places appointed by their Captains or Superiour Officers, and continue in Arms but one Day at each Time, beside at other Times when they shall be called together by an Order in Writing, under the Hand of the Captain General or Commander in Chief, for the Time being, at such Places as shall be by him appointed, to be taught the Use of their Arms, and then and there shall and are hereby Subjected to the Command of their proper Officers, and upon Disobedience shall and are hereby made lyable to the Penalties and Punishments of the Martial Law, so that the Punishment do not extend to the taking away of Life or Member.

And be it Enacted by the Authority aforesaid, That every person so listed, that doth appear at the Times and Places above, who shall not be Armed and provided with Ammunition, as aforesaid, shall forfeit as followeth, *viz.* For want of a Musquet or Fuzee, Two Shillings; if not well fixed, One Shilling; For want of a Sword or

Bagonet, One Shilling; For want of Three. Charges of *Powder,* and Three fizeable Bullets, one Shilling.   All which Fines to be Levyed by the Serjeant or Corporal of the Company, by a Warrant from the Captain, upon their Goods and Chattles, if they refufe to pay their Forfeitures. Which Forfeitures shall be applyed towards providing the Company with Drums and Colours.

And be it further Enacted by the Authority aforefaid, That it shall and may be Lawful for the Captain General. or Commander in Chief, for the Time being, in Cafe of any Invafion of any Enemy, to call all, or fo many of the Perfons aforefaid together, for the Repelling the Force of any Enemy, or Order fuch Detachments for the Common Defence, as he fhall think fit, to follow and purfue the Enemy into any of the Neighbouring Governments, for expelling the Enemy and Prefervation of his Majefty's Subjects and Government.

And be it further Enacted by the Authority aforefaid, That every Perfon, fo lifted, that doth not appear at the Place appointed, as aforefaid, fhall contribute and pay, towards the Support of His Majefty's Government in this Province, the Sum of Five Shillings for each of the faid Days Abfence, to the Captain or Commanding Officer, for the Time being, of their refpective Companies, (excepting in Cafes of Sicknefs, or any other reafonable excufe, to be allowed of by the Captain) Which Sum, fo raifed by the faid Captain or Commanding Officer, fhall, from Time to Time, be paid unto the Treafurer of the Province. And if any Perfon or Perfons shall refufe or neglect to pay, as aforefaid, the faid Captain or Commanding Officer is hereby required and impowered to make out his Warrant to one of the Serjeants or Corporals, to make Diftrefs upon every Perfons Goods and Chattles fo neglecting or refufing to pay, as aforefaid. *Provided,* That fuch Diftreffes be made but once a Year, for all the Defaults that have been committed within the faid Year before the Time of fuch Diftrefs, and shall expofe the faid Goods to publick Sale, and after Sale thereof, shall return the Over-plus (if any be) to the Owners thereof, after deducting One Shilling for his Trouble, which he is hereby allowed to take.

And be it further Enacted by the Authority aforefaid, That the faid Treafurer shall keep a true and perfect Lift of all the Money collected as aforefaid, and shall have for his, the faid Treafurers Trouble, Ten Pounds for every Hundred Pounds received by Virtue of this Act, and fo in Proportion for a greater or leffer Sum. Which Sum or Sums of Money, fo raifed, fhall be applyed to fuch Ufe or Ufes as the Governour, Council and General Affembly shall appoint.

And

And be it further Enacted by the Authority aforesaid, That if the small Fines, mentioned in this Act, for defraying the Charges of Drums and Colours and other Incidental Charges, are found insufficient, the Captain or other Officer of each Company, who was or shall be at the Charge of furnishing them, shall be allowed by the Treasurer, out of the other Fines, as much as will make up the small Fines, sufficient to Reimburse them, any thing in this Act to the contrary notwithstanding.

And be it further Enacted by the Authority aforesaid, That it shall and may be lawful for such Captains or other Commanding Officers, as live on or near the Sea Side or Indians, on any Descent or Invasion by any Enmey, to call all, or so many of their several and respective Companies together as shall be thought necessary to expel the said Enemy.

And be it further Enacted by the Authority aforesaid, That when the Governour or Commander in Chief, for the Time being, shall think fit to Direct, in Time of War or Danger, any Watch to be kept, in any Place or Places within this Province, the Collonel, Lieutenant Collonel, Major or other Commanding Officer of the Regiment, to whom such Directions is Signified, shall Issue out his Orders to the several Captains under his Command, To appoint such and so many Men to appear with their Arms, at such Time and Places as such Collonel or Commanding Officer shall appoint. Which Watch, so appointed, shall be equally relieved, by Order of the Commanding Officer of said Company; and so equally through all the Companies of the said County. And every Person or Persons neglecting or refusing to appear himself, or send a sufficient Man in his Room, to Watch, during the Time and at the Place appointed, shall forfeit the Sum of Ten Shillings for each Offence: And any Person that shall leave the said Watch, until relieved by some other Person appointed to Watch in his Stead, every such Person so leaving, as aforesaid, shall forfeit the Sum of Forty Shillings, Money of the said Province; to be recovered before any Justice of the Peace of the County where the Offence is committed, one half to the Informer, who shall prosecute the same to Effect, the other half to His Majesty, his Heirs and Successors, to be appropriated to the Use or Uses as is before appointed by this Act. *Provided always,* That no Person shall be obliged to continue longer on the Watch than Twenty Four Hours at one Time.

And be it further Enacted by the Authority aforesaid, That if any Person, appointed by the Captain to be a Serjeant or Corporal, shall refuse the said Office, every such Person, so refusing, shall forfeit the Sum of Twenty Shillings, to be recovered by Warant from any one Justice of the Peace.

Provided

Provided always, That none be appointed Serjeants or Corporals but such as have or shall appear in Arms, as aforesaid; and any Serjeant or Corporal who shall refuse or neglect to distrain, as aforesaid, shall forfeit the Sum of Twenty Shillings for each Default, to be recovered before any one Justice of the Peace, and applyed as it is before directed by this Act.

And be it further Enacted by the Authority aforesaid, That every Person listed within this Province, shall always be provided with one good sufficient Musquet or Fuzee, well fixed, a Cartouch Box or Powder Horn, half a Pound of Powder, and Twelve Sizeable Bullets in his House, and as often as any Person shall be deficient in the Arms and Stores herein mentioned, shall forfeit to the Uses first before-mentioned, and for paying the Serjeants and Corporals for their Pains, the Sum of Three Shillings: And the respective Captains are hereby impowered to appoint their Serjeants and Corporals to examine the same once a Year.

And be it further Enacted by the Authority aforesaid, That this Act shall continue and be in Force for Seven Years, after Publication hereof, and from thence to the end of the first Sessions of Assembly thereafter next ensuing.

An Act for preventing Multiplicity of Law Suits.

WHEREAS many Vexatious Suits have been brought by Troublesom and and Litigious Persons, when upon just Ballance of Accompts, there has been nothing due, or perhaps the Plaintiff over-paid, there being no Law impowering Justices and Juries, in such Cases, to Ballance Accompts, the Defendant can have no Remedy but by a Cross Action. For Preventing whereof,

Be it Enacted by the Governour, Council and General Assembly, and it is hereby Enacted, by the Authority of the same, That if any two or more, dealing together, or having dealt together, be Indebted to each other upon Bonds, Bills, Bargains, Promises, Accompts, or the like, and one of them Commence an Action before a Justice of the Peace, or in any Court of this Province, if the Defendant cannot gain-say the Deed, Bargain or Assumption upon which he is Sued, such Defendant shall plead Payment of all or any Part of the Debt or Sum demanded, giving Notice, in Writing, with the said Plea, of What he will
Insist

Infift upon at the Tryal, for his Difcharge, by any Bond, Bill, Receipt, Accompt or Bargain (fo given Notice of) in Evidence, or elfe forever after be barr'd of bringing any Action for that which he might or ought to have Pleaded, by Virtue of this Act. And if it shall happen that the Defendant hath fully paid or fatisfied the Debt or Sum demanded, the Juftices or Jury before whom the Action is brought, shall find for the Defendant, and Judgment shall be entered, That the Plaintiff shall have nothing for his Writ, and shall pay the Coft. And if it shall appear that any part of the Sum demanded is paid, then fo much as is found shall be Difcounted, and the Plaintiff shall have Judgment for the Refidue only, with Coft of Suit. But if it shall appear to the Juftices or Jury that the Plaintiff is over paid, then they shall give their Judgment or Verdict for the Defendant, and withal Certifie to the Court how much they find the Plaintiff to be indebted or in Arear to the Defendant, more than will anfwer the Debt or Sum demanded; and the Sum or Sums fo Certified shall be Recorded, with the Judgment or Verdict, and shall be deemed as a Debt of Record; and if the Plaintiff refufe to pay the fame, the Defendant, for Recovery thereof, shall have a *Scire Facias* againft the Plaintiff, in the faid Action, and have Execution for the fame, with the Coft of that Action, any Law, Ufage or Cuftom to the contrary in any Wife notwithftanding.

An Act to prevent the Killing of Deer out of Seafon, and againft carrying of Guns and Hunting by Perfons not qualified.

BE it Enacted by the Governour, Council and General Affembly, and it is hereby Enacted, by the Authority of the fame, That if any Perfon or Perfons, after the Publication hereof, shall kill or deftroy any Wild Buck, Doe or Fawn, or any other Sort of Deer whatfoever, at any Time in the Months of *January, February, March, April,* May or *June,* every fuch Perfon shall for every fuch Offence forfeit and pay the Sum of Thirty Shillings, for every fuch Buck, Doe or Fawn, or other Deer, fo killed or deftroyed as aforefaid, contrary to the true Intent and Meaning of this Act; one half thereof to the Poor of the Townfhip or Precinct where the Offence is Committed, and the other half to him who shall Inform or Sue for the fame before any Juftice of the Peace of this Province, who is hereby Impowered and Authorized to hear and determine the fame, and to convict the Offender by the Oath or Affirmation of one or more Witnefs. *Provided,* That fuch Conviction be made within Two Months after fuch Offence committed.

And for the better Convicting of Offenders against this Act, *Be it Enacted by the Authority aforesaid*, That every Person in whose Custody shall be found, or who shall expose to Sale, any Green Deer Skins, Fresh Venison or Deers Flesh, at any Time in any of the Months of *January, February, March, April, May* or *June*, aforementioned, and shall be Convicted thereof, as aforesaid, shall be deemed Guilty of the said Offence.

Provided always, That nothing contained in this Act shall be deemed or construed to hinder any Person from killing any Kind of Deer, within his Field, where Corn is Growing, at any Time in the Month of *January*, nor to extend to any Free Native Indians carrying Guns, Hunting, Killing, or having in their Custody any Skins or Deers Flesh for their own Use, any thing in this Act to the contrary notwithstanding.

And whereas divers Abuses have been committed, and great Damages and Inconveniencies arisen by Persons carrying of Guns, and presuming to Hunt on other Peoples Land; For Remedy whereof, for the Future, *Be It Enacted by the Authority aforesaid*, That if any person or persons shall presume, at any time after the Publication hereof, to carry any Gun, or Hunt on the Improved or Inclosed Lands in any Plantation, and on other than his own, unless he have Lisence or Permission from the Owner of such Lands or Plantation, and shall be thereof Convicted, either upon the View of any Justice of the Peace within this Province, or by the Oath or Affirmation of any one or more Witnesses, before any Justice of the Peace, he shall, for every such Offence, Forfeit the Sum of Fifteen Shillings, with Costs attending such Conviction. And if any person whatsoever, who is not Owner of One Hundred Acres of Land, or otherwise Qualified, in the same manner as persons are, or ought to be, for Electing of Representatives to serve in General Assembly, shall at any time, after the Publication hereof, carry any Gun, or Hunt in the Woods or Uninclosed Lands, without Lisence or Permission obtained from the Owner or Owners of such Lands, and shall be thereof Convicted, in manner aforesaid, such Offender shall forfeit and pay the Sum of Ten Shillings, with Cost, as aforesaid, for every such Offence. All which Penalties and Forfeitures shall go one Moiety to the Informer, and the other to the Poor of the Township or Precinct where such Offence is committed; but if Convicted upon View of a Justice of the Peace, the whole Forfeiture shall be to the Use of the Poor. And if the Offender refuse to pay the same, with Costs, as aforesaid, shall be Levyed on by Distress and Sale of the Offenders Goods, by Warrant under the Hand and Seal of the Justice before whom such Offender shall be Convicted, returning the Over-plus, if any be, the Charge of Distraining being first deducted. And for want of Effects whereon to make such Distress, every person so offending contary to the true intent and meaning of this Act, shall be committed to Prison, when the Forfeiture is Thirty Shillings, for the space of

Fifteen

Fifteen Days; and when the Forfeiture is Fifteen Shillings, for the space of Eight Days; and when the Forfeiture is Ten Shillings, for the space of Five Days, without Bail or Mainprize.

And be it Enacted by the Authority aforesaid, That every Justice of the Peace, before whom any Person or Persons is Convicted of having committed any of the Offences in and by this Act prohibited, is hereby Directed and Required to Issue his Warrants for the bringing such Offender before him, and in case of the want of Effects whereon to make Distress, to make out his Mittimus to commit such Offender to the Goal of the County in which such Conviction is made; and the Sheriff, Under-Sheriff or Goal-keeper is hereby Directed and Required to keep the said Offender in close Goal, according to the Direction of this Act, and tenor of such Mittimus to such Sheriff, Under-Sheriff or Goaler directed. And every Justice of the Peace neglecting or refusing to issue such Warrant or make such Mittimus, and every Sheriff, Under-Sheriff or Goal-keeper who shall not receive such Offender and him keep in close Goal, according to the true intent and meaning of this Act, shall, for every such Neglect or Refusal, or undue Discharge of his Office in the Premises, Forfeit the Sum of Six Pounds, to be Recovered in any Court of Record within this Province, in which there shall be no Essoyn or Protection, the one half to such Person as shall Sue for and prosecute the same to Effect, the other half to the King's Majesty, his Heirs and Successors, for and towards the Support of the Government of this Province.

And it is also further Enacted by the Authority aforesaid, That this Act, nor any part thereof, shall be Construed to extend to Negro, Indian or Mullatto Slaves, so as to Commit them to Prison, during the time in this Act limitted, in case they should be guilty of any the Offences in this Act prohibited, but that then and in such case such Indian, Negro or Mullato Slave killing and destroying any Deer, as aforesaid, or carrying or hunting with any Gun, without Licence from his Master, shall, at the Publick Whipping Post, on the naked Back, be Whipt, not exceeding Twenty Lashes for every such Offence, for which Whipping the Master shall pay to the Whipper the Sum of Three Shillings, and pay no greater or other Cost whatsoever, any Thing in this Act to the contrary hereof in any wise notwithstanding.

The fore-going Five Acts were Published the 5th of May, 1722.